WATCH
AND BE
READY

Preparing for the Second Coming of the Lord

Deseret Book Company
Salt Lake City, Utah

"Enduring to the End" by Stephen E. Robinson © The Church of Jesus Christ of Latter-day Saints. First published in the *Ensign.* Used by permission.

Library of Congress Cataloging-in-Publication Data
Watch and be ready : preparing for the Second Coming of the Lord
    p.   cm.
  Includes bibliographical references and index.
  ISBN 0–87579–911–6
  1. Second Advent. 2. Church of Jesus Christ of Latter-day Saints— Doctrines. 3. Mormon Church—Doctrines.
BX8643.E83W37   1994
236'.9—dc20   94–27762
                                                                    CIP

Printed in the United States of America

10   9   8   7   6   5   4   3   2   1

CONTENTS

1 *AVOIDING DECEPTION IN THE LAST DAYS*
KENT P. JACKSON 1

2 *USING THE BOOK OF MORMON
TO FACE THE TESTS AHEAD*
M. CATHERINE THOMAS 16

3 *FALSE CHRISTS*
JOSEPH FIELDING McCONKIE 39

4 *THE ROLE OF THE HOUSE OF ISRAEL
IN THE LAST DAYS*
ROBERT J. MATTHEWS 63

5 *ESTABLISHING ZION IN PREPARATION
FOR THE SECOND COMING*
RICHARD NEITZEL HOLZAPFEL 105

6 *THE SECOND COMINGS OF THE LORD*
LARRY E. DAHL 134

7 *LIFE IN THE MILLENNIUM*
ROBERT L. MILLET 167

8 *"IF YE ARE PREPARED YE SHALL NOT FEAR"*
GERALD N. LUND 192

9 *ENDURING TO THE END*
STEPHEN E. ROBINSON 220

INDEX 231

CHAPTER ONE

AVOIDING DECEPTION IN THE LAST DAYS

KENT P. JACKSON

Since the time of Joseph Smith, members of the Church have known that these are the last days of the world's history, a fact that we learn through several revelations received in the early days of the Church (e.g., D&C 24:19; 33:3; 43:28). Because we have this knowledge, it is natural for our thoughts to turn to the Second Coming and to the events that will prepare the world for it. In fact, as members of the Church, we are part of that preparatory process and play an important role in it.

Lately this subject has taken on even greater interest than usual. This can be explained in part by the approach of a new century—a time frequently associated with millennial expectations in Christian history, including Latter-day Saint history. That the new century will also introduce a new millennium of our calendar makes it of particular interest to some. End-of-the-world questions have also resulted from current political events and such recent natural disasters as famines, floods, and earthquakes. But in the past few years, interest in this subject among Latter-day Saints has been especially fueled by a surge of rumors, books, tapes, firesides, lectures, and political activities.

Given the sometimes confusing voices that we are hearing, it seems timely and appropriate to step back and take a careful look at what we know and at what we do not know about the last days. To do this we must measure all that we hear and read against the standard that the Lord has provided for us—namely, what has been revealed in the scriptures, especially modern revelation, and the

Kent P. Jackson is professor of ancient scripture at Brigham Young University.

teachings of modern prophets. Frequently what we read or hear from other sources concerning the last days does not square with what God has revealed. In a spirit of deep and genuine concern for those who have been, or might yet be, misled on this subject, may I suggest some fundamental principles to guide our study of the last days.

WISDOM AND CAUTION

There is nothing wrong with being interested in the great events of the last days. The scriptures teach us that these are important events, and we rejoice to see the Lord unfold his plan for our time and for future generations. But some dangers are inherent in this topic, and it should be treated with wisdom and caution. By its very nature, this subject lends itself to sensationalism, speculation, and overzealousness. I have observed that an inordinate interest in any gospel topic usually leads to misunderstanding and a lack of perspective about what is important and what is not. Those conditions seem to increase in proportion to the extent we are misinformed or do not have the influence of the Holy Ghost in our discussions. Usually sensationalism, speculation, and overzealousness lead only to wrong ideas, but from time to time they lead Church members into making unwise decisions, some of which may have eternal consequences.

"LOOSE WRITINGS"

In the early 1970s, President Harold B. Lee spoke out in rather pointed language concerning some misguided ideas about the last days that were then current in the Church. He warned not only about the information that was being conveyed but also about the individuals who were conveying it. In the April 1973 general conference, he said: "We have a rash of writings by certain persons who claim to be of good standing in the Church, going into considerable detail as they recite their past and present Church affiliations and activities in the foreword, interlude, and advertising. There are sensational predictions and observations, and to make their writings appear to have Church sanction, they use quotations and addresses from Church leaders, past and present, taken out of context in such a way as to make it appear as though these quotations were the endorsement of the book they wish to sell to Church members, who may thereby be induced to accept their writings as from unquestioned sources. . . .

"Furthermore, some designing individuals have solicited opportunities to speak at church gatherings, firesides, priesthood quorums, sacrament meetings. Now, brethren, we feel it is of the utmost importance to lift a warning voice so that our people will be safeguarded against such tactics as an all too obvious self-seeking opportunity to spread their own propaganda for their own interests.

"We must urge that priesthood leaders use careful discretion in screening out those whose motives may be subject to serious questions."[1]

At the previous general conference, President Lee taught: "There are among us many loose writings predicting the calamities which are about to overtake us. Some of these have been publicized as though they were necessary to wake up the world to the horrors about to overtake us. Many of these are from sources upon which there cannot be unquestioned reliance.

"Are you . . . aware of the fact that we need no such publications to be forewarned, if we were only conversant with what the scriptures have already spoken to us in plainness?"[2]

We now live in a day when technology has provided a variety of media through which we can communicate. In today's world, perhaps President Lee's term "loose writings" might include such things as videotapes and audiotapes as well as books. And he also mentioned "church gatherings, firesides," and other meetings that might be used to convey questionable information.

As I consider President Lee's statements, two very significant themes stand out: the importance of looking to Church leaders instead of to self-appointed teachers and the importance of looking to the scriptures instead of to the writings of those who have not been called.

LOOK TO THE APOSTLES AND PROPHETS

President Lee warned that those "loose writings" are set forth "as though they were necessary to wake up the world." Church members need to think carefully before they turn to such sources for warnings about the last days. Simply stated, the Lord already has his own system in place for providing us with the warnings that we will need. I am confident that if he wants to wake up the world or the Church, he will do it through his apostles and prophets, who have been called, sustained, and ordained to that purpose.

Shortly after the Church was organized, a member named Hiram Page stated that he had received a revelation concerning the location of the New Jerusalem. It is interesting that the first test of doctrinal authority in the Church had to do with a last-days topic— a pattern that has been repeated many times since then. The Lord reminded the Church that the keys of revelation on such matters are in the hands of him who has been called to preside over the Church (D&C 28:1–7, 11–13). Concerning Hiram Page or anyone else who might feel called to reveal God's thoughts, the Lord said, "Behold, these things have not been appointed unto him" (D&C 28:12).

In a revelation a few months later, the Lord made the principle very clear: "It shall not be given to any one to go forth to preach my gospel, or to build up my church, except he be ordained by some one who has authority, and it is known to the church that he has authority and has been regularly ordained by the heads of the church" (D&C 42:11). This supremely important statement provides a foolproof safeguard against the work of doctrinal adventurers who might come forward claiming the right to teach God's will. If they have not been called, sustained, and ordained by those who have been called, sustained, and ordained by the heads of the Church, they have no authority. "And this shall be a law unto you, that ye receive not the teachings of any that shall come before you as revelations or commandments; and this I give unto you that you may not be deceived, that you may know they are not of me" (D&C 43:5–6).

Those who hold the keys of the kingdom—the First Presidency and the Quorum of the Twelve Apostles—have been called of God. They are his representatives: he knows how to communicate with them, and they know how to make his desires known to us. A little reflection should lead us to the conclusion that anyone else who feels a calling to assume the role that God has assigned to others— in this case to warn the Church—is going beyond the bounds of his or her stewardship. It is the responsibility of apostles and prophets to warn the Church when necessary, and both they and the Lord know how to accomplish the task.

Many Church members have observed that in recent general conferences the General Authorities have said directly very little about the last days. Some individuals view this as a serious problem and feel that it proves something is not right in the Church. They lament that the Brethren do not sound the alarm sufficiently about the coming tribulations nor warn us to the degree that they should about how to avoid those trials. I have heard three reasons proposed to explain why the Brethren do not emphasize these things:

1. "God has silenced the prophets from discussing such things because of our failure to listen to them in the past." This kind of reasoning is a useful tool for those whose personal opinions are at variance with the teachings of the leaders of the Church. It allows them to read God's mind and speak on his behalf. God's silence on the topic is seen as proof of the correctness of their views.

2. "The prophet's counselors have stifled him so that he has never been able to deliver the message that the Lord wanted him to give us." This pernicious, apostate conspiracy theory really means, "The prophet certainly agrees with my point of view, but his failure to teach it surely means that the rest of the Brethren—who disagree with me and the prophet—have prevented him from talking about it." The self-serving motivation behind this mistaken notion is obvious.

3. "The Brethren are asleep at the wheel and cannot read the signs of the times." Because those who believe this notion are convinced of the validity of their opinions, with which the apostles and prophets do not seem to agree, they conclude that the Brethren don't quite know what is going on in the world. And so, believing that Church leaders are not aware of the dangers and the doom that await us, they put forward other interpreters who are not apostles and prophets but who claim to have a better understanding of these things.

Such explanations as these not only are false but, in my opinion, deny the divinity of the Church. Is God incapable of calling the right people? Is he unable to instruct them? Those who are inclined to believe such notions need to assess carefully their testimony that this is the Lord's church and that he has enough wisdom to call leaders who are in tune with his will. The real problem that controls people who entertain these notions is that they are not hearing in general conference the things they want to hear. And because they imagine themselves to be in tune with the Lord's point of view, then obviously, they believe, there is something wrong with what the Brethren are telling us.

Elder Boyd K. Packer addressed this issue in the October 1992 general conference: "There are some among us now who have *not* been regularly ordained by the heads of the Church who tell of impending political and economic chaos, the end of the world. . . .

"Those deceivers say that the Brethren do not know what is going on in the world or that the Brethren approve of their teaching but do not wish to speak of it over the pulpit. Neither is true. The Brethren, by virtue of traveling constantly everywhere on earth, certainly know what is going on, and by virtue of prophetic insight are able to read the signs of the times.

"Do not be deceived by them—those deceivers."[3]

What, then, are the Brethren teaching concerning the last days? The general conference addresses of the First Presidency and the Twelve from the 1980s and 1990s show none of the spirit of doom found in recent sensational teachings and writings. On the contrary, the Brethren have spoken very little about the end of the world. Instead, they have focused positively on living the gospel in our own day, which, if we reflect carefully, is the way to prepare for things to come. Their message to us emphasizes the importance of preaching the gospel of salvation and of living it—through praying, studying the scriptures, strengthening families, making and keeping covenants, observing the ordinances, following Church leaders, and otherwise continuing in faithfulness.

LOOK TO THE SCRIPTURES

As President Lee taught, if we are "conversant with what the scriptures have already spoken to us in plainness," we will not feel a need for the information that comes from "loose writings" about the last days. My experience has been that those who have a firm and broad foundation in the scriptures are generally not attracted to such "loose writings." They find their answers in the standard works, where the Lord has placed them. It has always amazed me that there are people in the Church who never read their scriptures in preparation for their Gospel Doctrine class, and yet they have "itching ears" to the point that they rush to buy questionable books or attend sensational lectures and firesides. Among some Church members, a subculture of discipleship toward learned men, or people who appear to be learned, has developed in recent years. The more exotic their message, the more attractive they are to many. Such behavior is strangely similar to that of those whom Jacob described as "looking beyond the mark" because they "despised the words of plainness, . . . and sought for things that they could not understand" (Jacob 4:14). The esoteric and the sensational always seem to attract more readers or greater audiences than do the simple truths of salvation. Whether it be the Dead-Sea-Scrolls-Prove-the-Church-Is-True excitement of the 1970s or the Keys-to-the-Last-Days phenomenon of the 1990s, some always find the simple, plain gospel of Christ to be dull in comparison.

Some who sincerely desire to learn the truth will become confused or misled by looking for it in the wrong places and by trusting the judgment and interpretations of those who have not been called. That is why priesthood leaders must always safeguard the doctrinal purity of the Lord's church. President Lee warned that these "strange sources" may have "political implications," a caution that may have even more relevance today than it did when he said it. He encouraged the Saints to turn to modern revelation for "the sure word" concerning the last days, "rather than commentaries that may come from those whose information may not be the most reliable and whose motives may be subject to question."[4]

President Lee pointed out that the scriptures speak to us "in plainness." That should come as no surprise, yet some in the Church seem to believe otherwise. It is only reasonable that if the Lord wants us to know and understand something, he will reveal it in such a way that we can know and understand it. With very few exceptions, the Lord's revelations are presented in such a way that they can be comprehended and applied to our lives. And when they are not, it is the prerogative of the prophets to interpret them in behalf of the Church. Elder Packer warned against those who "pretend to have some higher source of inspiration concerning the fulfillment of prophecies than do ward or stake leaders or the General Authorities of the Church."[5] Some individuals with interest in the last days propose to have special methods or even special wisdom or enlightenment for understanding and explaining the scriptures. Such an idea is out of harmony with the Lord's pattern of doing things, and it draws attention to the interpreter rather than to the message. Whatever the motives of such individuals may be, the effect of their work is usually to undermine confidence in the Church and its leaders. The prophets have counseled us to avoid such persons and their teachings.

USE MODERN REVELATION

In 1981, President Ezra Taft Benson, then president of the

Quorum of the Twelve Apostles, gave an important address at Brigham Young University on the topic of the last days. In it he showed both by precept and by example how to teach about this subject. His method, as he explained it, was to "quote liberally from the words of the Lord to our dispensation," so that we will have guidance from the Lord himself.[6] As President Benson taught, the primary source for our study of this and every other gospel topic is the word of the Lord as revealed to Joseph Smith and His other latter-day prophets and apostles. We find the mind and will of the Lord in the Book of Mormon, the Doctrine and Covenants, the Joseph Smith Translation of the Bible, the Pearl of Great Price, and the sermons and writings of the living oracles. I believe that wise students of the scriptures, which we all should be, will follow President Benson's admonition to turn to modern revelation for answers to questions of doctrine.

Sometimes well-meaning Latter-day Saints try to obtain an understanding of the last days by searching ancient prophecies, such as the book of Isaiah or the book of Revelation, rather than modern scripture. Although on the surface this practice may seem harmless and appropriate, there are important reasons why we should focus on what the Lord has revealed in our own time to understand doctrine and to interpret the prophecies of the Bible.

1. Almost all biblical prophecy is written in highly literary poetry, a fact that is not easily observed in the King James Translation. Metaphor, the figurative language that is the primary tool in these writings, is more easily understood when the reader is part of the same cultural, linguistic, historical, geographical, and ideological world as the writer. Perhaps that is what Nephi meant when he spoke of knowing "the manner of prophesying among the Jews" (2 Nephi 25:1). Biblical prophecy is neither mysterious nor mystical. It is simply foreign linguistically, culturally, and literarily. But this all too frequently causes interpretations of it to be subjective and highly susceptible to misunderstanding. In contrast, modern revelation has been revealed for our time, and we can understand it more readily.[7]

2. The Bible has been only imperfectly preserved through the ages to our day. The Prophet Joseph Smith stated that "many important points, touching the salvation of man, had been taken from the Bible, or lost before it was compiled."[8] He said he believed in it "as it ought to be, as it came from the pen of the original writers,"[9] or "as far as it is translated correctly" (Articles of Faith 1:8), with "translated" seemingly referring to the entire process of transmission from original manuscripts to modern-language translations. But "ignorant translators, careless transcribers, or designing and corrupt priests have committed many errors."[10] It is to modern revelation that we must turn for the pure and unadulterated word of the Lord.

3. The Lord proclaimed to Joseph Smith: "This generation shall have my word through you" (D&C 5:10). A careful pondering of this brief statement should tell us that we are to obtain God's word from the revelations of Joseph Smith (and, of course, those who have followed him as prophets, seers, and revelators) and only secondarily turn to the Bible. President Marion G. Romney, in a 1981 First Presidency editorial in the *Ensign,* explained why: "In each dispensation, . . . the Lord has revealed anew the principles of the gospel. So that while the records of past dispensations, insofar as they are uncorrupted, testify to the truths of the gospel, still each dispensation has had revealed in its day sufficient truth to guide the people of the new dispensation, independent of the records of the past.

"I do not wish to discredit in any manner the records we have of the truths revealed by the Lord in past dispensations. What I now desire is to impress upon our minds that the gospel, as revealed to the Prophet Joseph Smith, is complete and is the word direct from heaven to this dispensation. It alone is sufficient to teach us the principles of eternal life. It is the truth revealed, the commandments given in this dispensation through modern prophets by which we are to be governed."[11]

In frank and open terms, though we love the Bible, we get our doctrine from modern revelation. As curious as that principle may seem to some, it is nonetheless an important safeguard against doctrinal misdirection. The words of the biblical prophets can confirm, bear witness to, and illustrate the truths of modern revelation, but our knowledge of the gospel comes through what was revealed to Joseph Smith. Thus as we read the Bible, we interpret it in light of modern revelation.

Unfortunately many popular ideas and discussions about the last days focus on parts of the Bible that are exceptionally obscure. And ironically, it seems that the more obscure the passage or the book, the more readily some Church members are inclined to turn to it to find answers. But that is to be expected. The more obscure the material, the more opportunity for the commentator to project his or her personal views onto it. A plain and clear passage from modern scripture provides very little room for the imaginative interpretations of doctrinal entrepreneurs, but a passage that uses highly figurative language, regardless of the real intent of its ancient author, is an invitation for the creative. That may explain why such books as Isaiah, Daniel, Ezekiel, and Revelation are among the most popular sources for end-of-the-world enthusiasts in the Church. And that also explains the wisdom of the Lord's counsel that this generation is to obtain his word through Joseph Smith (D&C 5:10).

RECEIVE THE SPIRIT

It is sad that so many who are seduced by false doctrine are also seduced into apostate behavior. Very often, the two go hand in hand. There is a real and powerful protection in obedience to the Lord's commandments. In contrast, as Joseph Smith taught, "the moment we revolt at anything which comes from God the Devil takes power."[12] Those who bring themselves into doctrinal opposition against the Church or its leaders make themselves vulnerable to every other variety of sin. Those who live their lives in harmony with the Church and its leaders enjoy the influence of the Holy Ghost.

I find it very interesting that though the prophets, seers, and revelators of the Church seldom speak about the last days, they speak very frequently about obedience to the Lord's commandments. The conclusion that we should draw is clear: our main effort to prepare for the last days—or for tomorrow or for the day after tomorrow—must be to keep ourselves worthy of the Lord's blessings. Too many Church members become confused on this issue and think that our primary emphasis needs to be on the preparation of physical things. Some go so far as to engage in what Elder M. Russell Ballard recently called "extreme preparations."[13] An example might be those who in their zeal for temporal preparation have adopted from the world a survivalist mindset that they equate with gospel living. It is wise to prepare prudently for life's uncertainties, as Church leaders have counseled us, but it is dangerous to equate an overzealous private emphasis about this matter (or anything else) with the gospel. It is most significant that the emphasis in the scriptures is not on temporal but on spiritual preparation—the preparation of righteousness. That preparation invites us to stand with other faithful Saints in holy places (D&C 101:22), which President Benson defined as including "our temples, our chapels, our homes, and the stakes of Zion."[14] This kind of preparation is the preparation of the Spirit—through covenants, service, worship, and worthiness.

I believe firmly in the principle that the Holy Ghost is available to protect us from the deception of false doctrinal ideas. The scriptures promise that if we take the Holy Spirit for our guide, we will be shielded from the things of the world. But we must also be wise, and we must receive the truth (D&C 45:56). If we have the influence of the Holy Ghost in our lives, we will be able to discern the difference between truth and error. Often we cannot explain why we are uncomfortable with an idea, only that it does not feel right and that we want to distance ourselves from it. Those promptings are important, and they must not be ignored, even if we cannot explain them. We need not be great gospel scholars or experts on doctrine who can provide evidence for the basis of all our impressions, but we need to be worthy, so that we can be warned by the Spirit and thus be protected from the efforts of the adversary.

STAY IN THE MAINSTREAM OF THE CHURCH

Motivated by a spirit of dedication and obedience, most Church members have a sincere desire to do what is right in meeting the challenges of living the gospel. Problems arise, however, when our zeal outpaces our wisdom, leaving us unbalanced and vulnerable to the influence of wrong ideas. These dangers exist when one has an inordinate zeal on any gospel topic, but the topic of the last days is one that seems to attract more than its share of sensationalism and extremism.

It may be that individuals who take themselves out of the mainstream of the Church through an excessive zeal about the last days begin with a desire to be obedient. But by placing their focus on one narrow topic, they lose their sense of gospel balance and in due time commit themselves to a point of view that is unscriptural and at variance with what the leaders of the Church have taught. Having done that, and being unwilling to admit that they have gone beyond these, the only legitimate sources of doctrinal authority for the Church, they must reject these sources or modify them to suit their own needs. In doing either, they are really asserting that they have a higher calling or a higher source of information than that of The Church of Jesus Christ of Latter-day Saints. As President Joseph F. Smith and his counselors stated decades ago, the two types of Church members who are most susceptible to being deceived are those who do not keep the commandments and those "who pride themselves on their strict observance of the rules and ordinances and ceremonies of the Church."[15]

These pitfalls are a damning trap, but they can and must be avoided. To do so is not difficult. As Elder Bruce R. McConkie taught, "You don't have to do what Jacob said, 'Go beyond the mark' [Jacob 4:14]. You don't have to live a life that's truer than true. You don't have to have an excessive zeal that becomes fanatical and becomes unbalancing. What you have to do is stay in the mainstream of the Church."[16]

Some, unfortunately, choose not to follow this counsel and enjoy spending their time on the doctrinal fringes, whether out of gospel hobbyism or a lack of maturity and wisdom. But that is a formula for sorrow. Safety is in the mainstream of the Lord's church, where the experience of others who have gone before marks the way to our destination in the presence of God. On that path we can enjoy the company not only of apostles and prophets but also of millions of other faithful Saints who have lived their lives in harmony with the Lord's will and have overcome the world.

NOTES

1. Harold B. Lee, "Follow the Leadership of the Church," *Ensign,* July 1973, 97–98.

2. Harold B. Lee, "Admonitions for the Priesthood of God," *Ensign,* Jan. 1973, 106.

3. Boyd K. Packer, "To Be Learned Is Good, If . . . ," *Ensign,* Nov. 1992, 73; italics in original.

4. Lee, "Admonitions for the Priesthood of God," 106. He recommended the following sources: Joseph Smith–Matthew; D&C 38; 45; 101; 133.

5. Boyd K. Packer, "Reverence Invites Revelation," *Ensign,* Nov. 1991, 21.

6. Ezra Taft Benson, "Prepare Yourselves for the Great Day of the Lord," *Brigham Young University Fireside and Devotional Speeches 1981* (Provo, Utah: Brigham Young University, 1981), 65.

7. Certainly the Doctrine and Covenants, but also the Book of Mormon. See Mormon 8:34–35; Ezra Taft Benson, "The Book of Mormon—Keystone of Our Religion," *Ensign,* Nov. 1986, 4–7, and in *Studies in Scripture, Vol. 7: 1 Nephi to Alma 29,* ed. Kent P. Jackson (Salt Lake City: Deseret Book, 1987), 5–6.

8. 1839 History, in Dean C. Jessee, ed., *The Papers of Joseph Smith,* 3 vols. (Salt Lake City: Deseret Book, 1989–95), 1:372.

9. *The Words of Joseph Smith,* ed. Andrew F. Ehat and Lyndon W. Cook (Provo, Utah: Religious Studies Center, Brigham Young University, 1980), 256.

10. Joseph Smith, *History of The Church of Jesus Christ of Latter-day Saints,* ed. B. H. Roberts, 2d ed. rev., 7 vols. (Salt Lake City: Deseret Book, 1957), 6:57.

11. Marion G. Romney, "A Glorious Promise," *Ensign,* Jan. 1981, 2.

12. *Words of Joseph Smith,* 60.

13. M. Russell Ballard, "The Joy of Hope Fulfilled," *Ensign,* Nov. 1992, 32.

14. Benson, "Prepare Yourselves for the Great Day of the Lord," 68.

15. Joseph F. Smith, Anthon H. Lund, Charles W. Penrose, "A Warning Voice" (1913), in *Messages of the First Presidency of The Church of Jesus Christ of Latter-day Saints,* comp. James R. Clark, 5 vols. (Salt Lake City: Bookcraft, 1965–71), 4:285. See also Harold B. Lee, "To the Defenders of the Faith," *Improvement Era,* June 1970, 63–65.

16. Bruce R. McConkie, "The Probationary Test of Mortality," address delivered at the Salt Lake Institute of Religion, 10 Jan. 1982.

CHAPTER TWO

USING THE BOOK OF MORMON TO FACE THE TESTS AHEAD

M. CATHERINE THOMAS

Our dispensation will embrace the greatest extremes of any: the tares will be of greater virulence than any preceding period. President Ezra Taft Benson has declared: "Wickedness is rapidly expanding in every segment of our society (see D&C 1:14–16; 84:49–53). It is more highly organized, more cleverly disguised, and more powerfully promoted than ever before." But at the same time, the wheat will exhibit greater quality than ever before (D&C 86:1–7), because the Church and kingdom of God are increasing in strength, size, and faithfulness. "It [the church] has never been better organized or equipped to perform its divine mission."[1] Thus, in the midst of the worst trials ever known among the children of men, the Saints will finish up the work of this dispensation under the direction of the Lord Jesus Christ. It is not a defensive position we wish to take but rather a powerful moving forward to establish all of the will of the Lord in preparation for his coming. We need not shrink before the onslaught but prepare to go out to meet the Bridegroom (D&C 133:10).

We will never meet all the challenges of this dispensation unaided. The forces about to be unleashed against the world will be sufficient to decimate the entire population (D&C 5:19). Only those who have learned how to take the Holy Spirit for their guide will be able to read the signs and abide those days (D&C 45:57); only those who have studied how to draw on the grace, on the divine enabling power of the Lord Jesus Christ, will escape through the means the

M. Catherine Thomas is an instructor in ancient scripture at Brigham Young University.

Lord will provide (D&C 63:34). We will have to be a people who understand personal revelation. We will have to live in direct contact with the temporal world, but we will have to know how to be guided by the heavenly, unseen world.

It is possible to make a long list of specific things we would have to do to endure to the end. But the real question is this: What is that quintessential preparation from which all other preparations naturally follow? The Lord has provided the answer, and it lies in the inspired use of the Book of Mormon—in particular, the use of the Book of Mormon as an instrument of personal revelation. Nearly every description of the tests that the Saints will undergo makes it clear that only personal revelation will make faithful endurance possible. Inspired uses of the Book of Mormon lie at the very core of the Saints' preparation so that they, as the children of light, will not be overtaken as by a thief at the Lord's appearance (D&C 106:4–5).

Prophets through the ages have looked at our day and warned us of the trials that lie ahead. President Heber C. Kimball "often used the language, 'A test, a test is coming.'"[2]

"We think we are secure here in the chambers of the everlasting hills, where we can close those few doors of the canyons against mobs and persecutors, the wicked and the vile, who have always beset us with violence and robbery, but I want to say to you, my brethren, the time is coming when we will be mixed up in these now peaceful valleys to that extent that it will be difficult to tell the face of a Saint from the face of an enemy to the people of God. Then, brethren, look out for the great sieve, for there will be a great sifting time, and many will fall; for I say unto you there is a *test,* a TEST, a TEST coming, and who will be able to stand?"[3]

"This Church has before it many close places through which it will have to pass before the work of God is crowned with victory. To meet the difficulties that are coming, it will be necessary for you to have a knowledge of the truth of this work for yourselves. The difficulties will be of such a character that the man or woman who does not possess this personal knowledge or witness will fall. If you have not got the testimony, live right and call upon the Lord and cease not till you obtain it. If you do not you will not stand. . . .

" . . . The time will come when no man nor woman will be able to endure on borrowed light. Each will have to be guided by the light within himself. If you do not have it, how can you stand?"[4]

President Heber C. Kimball was quoted later with respect to the intensity of the tests:

"The judgments of God will be poured out upon the wicked, to the extent that our elders from far and near will be called home; or in other words, the Gospel will be taken from the gentiles, and later on will be carried to the Jews.

"The western boundaries of the State of Missouri will be swept so clean of its inhabitants that as President Young tells us, 'when we return to that place there will not be as much as a yellow dog to wag his tail.'

"Before that day comes, however, the Saints will be put to the test that will try the very best of them.

"The pressure will become so great that the righteous among us will cry unto the Lord day and night until deliverance comes. . . .

"Then is the time to look out for the great sieve, for there will be a great sifting time, and many will fall."[5]

President Ezra Taft Benson expanded on the nature of the tests we will face and confirmed that the process has already begun: "There is a real sifting going on in the Church, and it is going to become more pronounced with the passing of time. It will sift the wheat from the tares, because we face some difficult days, the like of which we have never experienced in our lives. And those days are going to require faith and testimony and family unity, the like of which we have never had."[6]

"The great destructive force which was to be turned loose on the earth and which the prophets for centuries have been calling the 'abomination of desolation' is vividly described by those who saw it in vision (see Matthew 24:15; Joseph Smith–Matthew 1:12, 32). Ours is the first generation to realize how literally these prophecies can be fulfilled now that God, through science, has unlocked the secret to thermonuclear reaction.

"In the light of these prophecies, there should be no doubt in the mind of any priesthood holder that the human family is headed for trouble. There are rugged days ahead. It is time for every man who wishes to do his duty to get himself prepared—physically, spiritually, and psychologically—for the task which may come at any time, as suddenly as the whirlwind."[7]

"We will live in the midst of economic, political, and spiritual instability. When these signs are observed—unmistakable evidences that His coming is nigh—we need not be troubled, but 'stand in holy places, and be not moved, until the day of the Lord come' (D&C 87:8). Holy men and women stand in holy places, and these holy places consist of our temples, our chapels, our homes, and stakes of Zion, which are, as the Lord declares, 'for a defense, and for a refuge from the storm, and from wrath when it shall be poured out without mixture upon the whole earth' (D&C 115:6). We must heed the Lord's counsel to the Saints of this dispensation: 'Prepare yourselves for the great day of the Lord' (D&C 133:10).

"This preparation must consist of more than just casual membership in the Church. *We must be guided by personal revelation and the counsel of the living prophet so we will not be deceived.* Our Lord has indicated who, among Church members, will stand when He appears: 'At that day, when I shall come in my glory, shall the parable be fulfilled which I spake concerning the ten virgins' (D&C 45:56)."[8]

The Lord has given the sobering revelation that in the midst of the latter-day trials, Church members will feel the Lord's refining power as he forges the Saints into a force for fulfilling his divine purposes:

"The kingdom of heaven is like unto a net, that was cast into the sea, and gathered of every kind: which, when it was full, they drew to shore, and sat down, and gathered the good into vessels, but cast the bad away. So shall it be at the end of the world: [and the world is the children of the wicked] the angels shall come forth, and sever the wicked from among the just, and shall cast them into the furnace of fire: [out into the world to be burned] there shall be wailing and gnashing of teeth" (Matthew 13:47–50; JST text in brackets).

"Behold, vengeance cometh speedily upon the inhabitants of the earth, a day of wrath, a day of burning, a day of desolation, of weeping, of mourning, and of lamentation; and as a whirlwind it shall come upon all the face of the earth, saith the Lord. *And upon my house shall it begin, and from my house shall it go forth,* saith the Lord; first among those among you, saith the Lord, who have professed to know my name and have not known me, and have blasphemed against me in the midst of my house, saith the Lord. . . . But purify your hearts before me. . . . Cleanse your hearts and your garments, lest the blood of this generation be required at your hands" (D&C 112:24–33; italics added; see also 88:74).

This refining process will prepare a purified Church membership to meet the Lord Jesus Christ. President Benson warned:

"It is well that our people understand this principle, so they will not be misled by those apostates within the Church who have not yet repented or been cut off. But there is a cleansing coming. The Lord says that his vengeance shall be poured out 'upon the inhabitants of the earth. . . . And upon my house shall it begin, and from my house shall it go forth, saith the Lord; first among those among you, saith the Lord, who have professed to know my name and have not known me. . . .' (D&C 112:24–26). I look forward to that cleansing; its need within the Church is becomingly increasingly apparent."[9]

"Yes, within the Church today there are tares among the wheat and wolves within the flock. As President Clark stated, 'The ravening wolves are amongst us, from our own membership, and they, more than any others, are clothed in sheep's clothing because they wear the habiliments of the priesthood. . . . We should be careful of them.' "[10]

Yet, even as we witness the steady crescendo of sorrows spreading throughout the earth, it is apparent that the Lord has at least a twofold purpose. On the one hand, the wicked will be purged from the Church and from the earth; on the other, the Saints will be purified and refined:

"Behold, the great day of the Lord is at hand; and who can abide the day of his coming, and who can stand when he appeareth? For he is like a refiner's fire, and like fuller's soap; and he shall sit as a refiner and purifier of silver, and *he shall purify the sons of Levi* [the priesthood holders of today; D&C 84:32–34] and purge them as gold and silver, that they may offer unto the Lord an offering in righteousness. Let us, therefore, as a church and a people, and as Latter-day Saints, offer unto the Lord an offering in righteousness" (D&C 128:24; italics added).

The present and the future do not hold so many terrors if we believe the Lord's reassuring words that the refining process is under his benevolent control:

"Fear not thine enemies, for they are in mine hands and I will do my pleasure with them.

"My people must be tried in all things, that they may be prepared to receive the glory that I have for them, even the glory of Zion; and he that will not bear chastisement is not worthy of my kingdom" (D&C 136:30–31).

President John Taylor commented on the necessity of the Saints' being tested but of the insignificance of the pain of the testing process in relation to the great destiny of the Saints:

"It is necessary that we pass through certain ordeals, and that we be tried. But why is it that we should be tried? There is just the same necessity for it now that there was in former times. I heard the prophet Joseph say, in speaking to the Twelve on one occasion: 'You will have all kinds of trials to pass through. And it is quite as necessary for you to be tried as it was for Abraham and other men of God, and (said he) God will feel after you, and He will take hold of you and wrench your very heart strings, and if you cannot stand it you will not be fit for an inheritance in the Celestial Kingdom of God.' . . .

"But all these personal things amount to but very little. It is the crowns, principalities, the powers, the thrones, the dominions, and the associations with the Gods that we are after, and we are here to prepare ourselves for those things. We are after eternal exaltation in the Celestial Kingdom of God."[11]

In fact, Zion will be built by those who are purified by their sufferings and have learned to endure suffering in order to obey the Lord's every command. Zion will have to suffer in order to be redeemed because her citizens have not learned to obey: "Were it not for the transgressions of my people, speaking concerning the church and not individuals, they might have been redeemed even now.

"But behold, they have not learned to be obedient to the things which I required at their hands, but are full of all manner of evil, and do not impart of their substance, as becometh saints, to the poor and afflicted among them;

"And are not united according to the union required by the law of the celestial kingdom;

"And Zion cannot be built up unless it is by the principles of the law of the celestial kingdom; otherwise I cannot receive her unto myself.

"And my people must needs be chastened until they learn obedience, if it must needs be, by the things which they suffer" (D&C 105:2–6).

The sacrificing to obey unlocks the blessings and powers of heaven:

"Verily I say unto you, all among them [the Saints] who know their hearts are honest, and are broken, and their spirits contrite, and are willing to observe their covenants by sacrifice—yea, every sacrifice which I, the Lord, shall command—they are accepted of me. For I, the Lord, will cause them to bring forth as a very fruitful tree which is planted in a goodly land, by a pure stream, that yieldeth much precious fruit" (D&C 97:8–9).

"Let us here observe that a religion that does not require the sacrifice of all things never has power sufficient to produce the faith necessary unto life and salvation. . . . It is through the medium of the sacrifice of all earthly things that men do actually know that they are doing the things that are well pleasing in the sight of God. . . .

" . . . And in the last days, before the Lord comes, he is to gather together his saints who have made a covenant with him by sacrifice."[12]

Elder John Taylor encouraged the Saints to cleave to the Lord as the night darkens: "In relation to events that will yet take place, and the kind of trials, troubles, and sufferings which we shall have to cope with, it is to me a matter of very little moment; these things are in the hands of God, he dictates the affairs of the human family, and directs and controls our affairs; and the great thing that we, as a people, have to do is to seek after and cleave unto our God, to be in close affinity with him and to seek for his guidance, and his blessing and Holy Spirit to lead and guide us in the right path. Then it matters not what it is nor who it is that we have to contend with, God will give us strength according to our day."[13]

Another source of reassurance is the knowledge that our coming to earth at this time in the earth's history was no random event. We were prepared before we came to earth to do the work we would be called to do (see D&C 138:56). President Benson has taught:

"For nearly six thousand years, God has held you in reserve to make your appearance in the final days before the second coming of the Lord. Some individuals will fall away; but the kingdom of God will remain intact to welcome the return of its head—even Jesus Christ. While our generation will be comparable in wickedness to the days of Noah, when the Lord cleansed the earth by flood, there is a major difference this time. It is that God has saved for the final inning some of His strongest children, who will help bear off the kingdom triumphantly. That is where you come in, for you are the generation that must be prepared to meet your God. . . .

"Make no mistake about it—you are a marked generation. There has never been more expected of the faithful in such a short period of time than there is of us. Never before on the face of this earth have the forces of evil and the forces of good been as well organized. Now is the great day of the devil's power. But now is also the great day of the Lord's power, with the greatest number ever of priesthood holders on the earth."[14]

Having faith in our premortal preparation, we can find unique blessings in realizing that the personal tests we face were specially suited to our individual, spiritual needs. Perhaps the greatest insight to come out of this realization is that the Lord orchestrates the details of the lives of his seeking and obedient Saints. With his orchestration of their individual trials comes also deliverance from those trials.

Elder Bruce R. McConkie listed the tasks that lie ahead of these premortally prepared Saints, tasks that will require a greater commitment to spiritual principles than ever before:

"We have yet to gain that full knowledge and understanding of the doctrines of salvation and the mysteries of the kingdom that were possessed by many of the ancient Saints. O that we knew what Enoch and his people knew! Or that we had the sealed portion of the Book of Mormon, as did certain of the Jaredites and Nephites! How can we ever gain these added truths until we believe in full what the Lord has already given us in the Book of Mormon, in the Doctrine and Covenants, and in the inspired changes made by Joseph Smith in the Bible? . . . .

"We have yet to attain that degree of obedience and personal righteousness which will give us faith like the ancients: faith to multiply miracles, move mountains, and put at defiance the armies of nations; faith to quench the violence of fire, divide seas and stop the mouths of lions; faith to break every band and to stand in the presence of God. Faith comes in degrees. Until we gain faith to heal the sick, how can we ever expect to move mountains and divide seas?

"We have yet to receive such an outpouring of the Spirit of the Lord in our lives that we shall all see eye to eye in all things, that every man will esteem his brother as himself, that there will be no poor among us. . . . As long as we disagree as to the simple and easy doctrines of salvation, how can we ever have unity on the complex and endless truths yet to be revealed?

"We have yet to perfect our souls, by obedience to the laws and ordinances of the gospel, and to walk in the light as God is in the light, so that if this were a day of translation we would be prepared to join Enoch and his city in heavenly realms. How many among us are now prepared to entertain angels, to see the face of the Lord, to go where God and Christ are and be like them? . . .

"We have yet to prepare a people for the Second Coming. . . .

"Shall we not now, as a Church and as a people and as the Saints of latter days, build on the foundations of the past and go forward in gospel glory until the great Jehovah shall say: 'The work is done; come ye, enter the joy of your Lord; sit down with me on my throne; thou art now one with me and my Father.'"[15]

On another occasion, Elder McConkie made a sobering statement on the necessity of the development of our faith:

"It may be, for instance, that nothing except the power of faith and the authority of the priesthood can save individuals and congregations from the atomic holocausts that surely shall be."[16]

President Brigham Young also observed that, in general, the Saints are not prepared for the blessings that the Lord anticipates bestowing on them: "Jesus has been upon the earth a great many more times than you are aware of. When Jesus makes his next appearance upon the earth, but few of this Church and kingdom will be prepared to receive him and see him face to face and converse with him; but he will come to his temple. . . .

"When all nations are so subdued to Jesus that every knee shall bow and every tongue shall confess, there will still be millions on the earth who will not believe in him; but they will be obliged to acknowledge his kingly government. You may call that government ecclesiastical, or by whatever term you please; yet there is no true government on earth but the government of God, or the holy Priesthood. Shall I tell you what that is? In short, it is a perfect system of government—a kingdom of Gods and angels and all beings who will submit themselves to that government. There is no other true government in heaven or upon the earth. . . .

"Is man prepared to receive that government? He is not. I can say to these Latter-day Saints, You are not prepared to receive that government. You hear men and women talk about living and abiding a celestial law, when they do not so much as know what it is, and are not prepared to receive it. We have a little here and a little there given to us, to prove whether we will abide that portion of law that will enable us to enjoy a resurrection with the just. . . .

" . . . We have line upon line, precept upon precept, here a little and there a little, and it is something that accords with the capacity of finite beings, and you improve upon this, and the Lord will open your minds to receive more, and let you see the order of the eternal priesthood; *but if you do not live your religion, you cannot receive more.*"[17]

Many of us are not yet living our religion. The Saints can reach for more. In the foregoing statements of the Lord and his prophets and apostles, one common observation is that amidst the latter-day trials, the Saints will need familiarity with the Lord's voice. For example, President Heber C. Kimball said, "Each will have to be guided by the light within himself. If you do not have it, how can you stand?"[18] President Ezra Taft Benson remarked on the current state of the Saints' preparedness to meet the Savior: "Watchmen— what of the night? We must respond by saying that all is not well in Zion. As Moroni counseled, we must *cleanse the inner vessel* (Alma 60:23), beginning first with ourselves, then with our families, and finally with the Church. . . .

" . . . It takes a Zion people to make a Zion society, and *we must prepare for that.*"[19]

Obviously our responses to the Lord's direction have as yet been inadequate to achieve that state of preparation, even though the Lord has made it abundantly clear that the instrument of preparation for the Second Coming is the Book of Mormon. That book is the instrument by which the citizens of Zion will have cleansed the inner vessel.

The Saints, evidently, are still under condemnation for their neglect of the Book of Mormon, the very tool that has the most power to prepare the Church for the advent of the Savior. Upon reflection, we realize that the Saints have not yet adequately made the connection between the comprehensive use of the Book of Mormon and the light that each of them will need to withstand the trials of the latter days. President Benson exclaimed: "Now we not only need to *say* more about the Book of Mormon, but we need to *do* more with it. Why? The Lord answers: 'That they may bring forth fruit meet for their Father's kingdom; otherwise there remaineth a scourge and judgment to be poured out upon the children of Zion' [D&C 84:58]. We have felt that scourge and judgment!"[20]

Perhaps some have thought that a testimony and a general knowledge of the Book of Mormon were sufficient fulfillment of the Lord's injunction. But a testimony of the Book of Mormon is not an end in itself. It is only the most rudimentary beginning. The next step, after learning that the book is true and can be trusted as a source for doctrine and the Spirit, is to learn its multiple uses and virtues. Here is the Lord's fuller text to the Church about using the Book of Mormon:

"Your minds in times past have been darkened because of unbelief, and because you have *treated lightly the things you have received*—

"Which vanity and unbelief have brought the *whole church* under condemnation.

"And this condemnation resteth upon the children of Zion, *even all.*

"And they shall remain under this condemnation until they repent and remember the new covenant, *even the Book of Mormon* and the former commandments which I have given them, *not only to say, but to do according to that which I have written*—

"That they may bring forth fruit meet for their Father's kingdom; otherwise there remaineth a scourge and judgment to pour out upon the children of Zion" (D&C 84:54–58; italics added).

The Church apparently does not yet know all the uses and virtues of the Book of Mormon. It seems that the Lord would like us to use the Book of Mormon in ways it has not been used before and that he is waiting for us to ask his help to that end. President Benson, in urging us to get more deeply into the book, pointed to the relationship between scripture study and the power of the Spirit in our life: "I urge you to recommit yourselves to a study of the scriptures. Immerse yourselves in them daily *so you will have the power of the Spirit to attend you* in your callings. Read them in your families and teach your children to love and treasure them. Then prayerfully and in counsel with others, seek every way possible to encourage the members of the Church to follow your example. If you do so, you will find, as Alma did, that 'the word [has] a great tendency to lead people to do that which [is] just—yea, it [has] more powerful effect upon the minds of the people than the sword, or anything else, which [has] happened unto them' (Alma 31:5)."[21]

In that statement, President Benson has connected immersion in the scripture with the gift and power of the Spirit. Several other Brethren have likewise pointed out the link between personal revelation and a spiritually skilled use of scripture. For example, Elder Bruce McConkie said: "I sometimes think that one of the best-kept secrets of the kingdom is that the scriptures open the door to the receipt of revelation."[22] "However talented men may be in administrative matters; however eloquent they may be in expressing their views; however learned they may be in the worldly things—they will be denied the sweet whisperings of the Spirit that might have been theirs unless they pay the price of studying, pondering, and praying about the scriptures."[23]

Elder Dallin H. Oaks declared: "As a source of knowledge, the scriptures are not the *ultimate* but the penultimate. *The ultimate knowledge comes by revelation. . . .*

" . . . A study of the scriptures enables men and women to receive revelations. . . . because scripture reading puts us in tune with the Spirit of the Lord."[24]

Elder Boyd K. Packer taught: "Buildings and budgets, and reports and programs and procedures are very important. But, by themselves, they do not carry that essential spiritual nourishment and will not accomplish what the Lord has given us to do. . . . The right things, those with true spiritual nourishment, are centered in the scriptures."[25]

One reason that some Church members are not reaping the full reward of scripture study may be that they do not know how vital the reward could be. The Lord promises that we can hear or feel his voice in the scriptures, that we can receive messages in and above what is printed on the page, and that we can repeat that experience over and over again. Scripture reading and feasting on scripture can take on new meaning.

Those who haven't heard the voice may find the scriptures less interesting than other literature. Perhaps some are afraid to hear what the Lord has to say, and so they may read the scripture with a protective veil over their mind and then say they are bored with the scripture. The real problem may be that they are afraid to hear the voice. But the Lord says to us today, "Resist no more my voice" (D&C 108:2).

It appears that the Lord intends an intersection between the daily orbit we move in and the orbit of the Book of Mormon. A power is set in motion when we become deeply involved in what the scriptures are saying to us personally. The Lord has said that "the Book of Mormon and the holy scriptures are given of me for your instruction; and the power of my Spirit quickeneth all things" (D&C 33:16).

Several other scriptures also show that the printed word can yield the living spirit of prophecy to the alert and prepared reader. In the very first chapter of the Book of Mormon, Lehi learned this connection between feasting on the scripture and receiving the power of revelation: "As he read [a book of scripture given him by the Lord] he was filled with the Spirit of the Lord" (1 Nephi 1:12). Nephi said, "And now, when my father saw all these things [scriptures on the plates of brass], he was filled with the Spirit, and began to prophesy" (1 Nephi 5:17). Jacob made the same connection: "Wherefore, we search the prophets, and we have many revelations and the spirit of prophecy; and having all these witnesses we obtain a hope, and our faith becometh unshaken, insomuch that we truly can command in the name of Jesus and the very trees obey us, or the mountains, or the waves of the sea" (Jacob 4:6). The four sons of Mosiah "waxed strong in the knowledge of the truth; for they were men of a sound understanding and they had searched the scriptures diligently, that they might know the word of God. But this is not all; they had given themselves to much prayer, and fasting; therefore they had the spirit of prophecy, and the spirit of revelation, and when they taught, they taught with power and authority of God" (Alma 17:2–3).

The Lord, speaking of scripture, said: "These words are not of men nor of man, but of me; . . . for it is my voice which speaketh them unto you; for they are given by my Spirit unto you . . . ; wherefore, you can testify that you have heard my voice, and know my words" (D&C 18:34–36). To hear the voice of the Lord in the scripture simply means to feel the Spirit of the Lord, because the Lord speaks "by the voice of my Spirit" (D&C 75:1). Furthermore, the Lord's "voice is Spirit" (D&C 88:66).

Thus there is a relationship between the written scripture and the voice of the Lord, or personal revelation. The same Spirit that gave the written word quickens it as one who is prepared reads it. Taking all these insights together, we may conclude that if we wish to guide our life by the Spirit, we cannot do it without also being a spiritual student of the Book of Mormon.

The Book of Mormon itself teaches the progression from feasting on the word of Christ to hearing the voice of Christ through the Holy Ghost: "Feast upon the words of Christ; for behold, the words of Christ will *tell* you all things what ye should do. . . . if ye will enter in by the way, and receive the Holy Ghost, it will *show* unto you all things what ye should do" (2 Nephi 32:3–5).

The stories and principles and doctrines in the Book of Mormon are vitally important to the Latter-day Saints, but we soon discover that an important principle taught by the book is that no collection of writings can tell a person what to do in all circumstances. Many of life's challenges are designed to require divine insight and divine power and divine direction to meet them. Therefore, perhaps no principle is stressed as much as getting the Spirit of the Lord, who "will show you all things what ye should do," as a constant guide.

We can see how the voice of the Lord is a vital component of the gospel plan—not just for prophets but for all of us. Ultimately everyone who hopes to see the face of the Lord and to remain in his presence must learn to discern and obey the voice of the Lord. That skill is essential for the serious candidate for exaltation.

Elder Richard G. Scott explicitly stated that the Book of Mormon is like a personal Liahona or Urim and Thummim: "What does the Book of Mormon mean to you? . . .

"If you have not yet drunk deeply from this fountain of pure truth, with all of my soul I encourage you to do so now. Don't let the consistent study of the Book of Mormon be one of the things that you intend to do but never quite accomplish. Begin today.

"I bear witness that *it can become a personal 'Urim and Thummim' in your life.*"[26]

Indeed, the Book of Mormon describes itself as a Liahona. A primary use of a Liahona or a Urim and Thummim is as a physical symbol to teach the dynamics of revelation. They increase faith until one has learned to get revelation without sole dependence on the physical instrument. How important it is to realize that scripture, as another form of Liahona or Urim and Thummim, instructs our spirits in the processes of revelation.

The link between a tangible object of revelation and the process of receiving revelation without an instrument is illustrated in the

Prophet Joseph's training under the Lord. The Lord started Joseph Smith out with the Urim and Thummim; later, Joseph was able to receive revelation without using it, thus showing that a Liahona and Urim and Thummim, seer stones, and scripture are all variations of the sacred instruments by which a person is taught how to receive increasingly detailed revelation—revelation that is often outside the imagination or experience of the person being so trained. Joseph's experience in translating the Book of Mormon by the Urim and Thummim actually prepared him to be the founding prophet, seer, and revelator of this dispensation.

Alma understood this relationship between instruments of revelation and scripture. In Alma 37, Alma used a succession of words that suggests that relationship: records, plates of brass, holy scriptures, mysteries, holy writ, interpreters, Gazelem, seer stone, counseling with the Lord, and Liahona. When the Nephites used their Liahona, they had miracles every day; whenever they grew lazy and forgot to exercise their faith and diligence, they lost their way and became hungry.

Alma taught that the ball, director, compass, or Liahona was prepared by the Lord as a type of the word of Christ: "For behold, it is as easy to give heed to the word of Christ, which will point to you a straight course to eternal bliss, as it was for our fathers to give heed to this compass, which would point unto them a straight course to the promised land. And now I say, is there not a type in this thing? For just as surely as this director did bring our fathers, by following its course, to the promised land, shall the words of Christ, if we follow their course, carry us beyond this vale of sorrow into a far better land of promise. O my son, do not let us be slothful because of the easiness of the way" (Alma 37:44–46). It is possible that "vale of sorrow" means not only this mortal life as a whole but the individual vales of sorrow that the Saints come upon in their lives. That is, the Lord has given the Saints a Liahona to carry them out of their individual and collective vales of sorrow.

One problem of mortality is the inadequacy of our present

language to provide vocabulary to describe spiritual experience. When missionaries try to teach investigators what the Spirit is, they have to do it by analogy or by metaphor; thus, when they see the Spirit working on an investigator, they will say, "That's it! What you are feeling right now is the Spirit of the Lord!" Elder Boyd K. Packer taught: "We do not have the words (even the scriptures do not have words) which perfectly describe the Spirit. The scriptures generally use the word voice, which does not exactly fit. These delicate, refined spiritual communications are not seen with our eyes, nor heard with our ears. And even though it is described as a voice, it is a voice that one feels, more than one hears."[27]

We identify the Spirit mostly by feeling, and in the scripture the Lord teaches us what the Spirit feels like. If we think we have to feel something extraordinary in hearing the voice of the Lord in the scripture, we might miss the subtle impressions of the Spirit. Many people have experienced the movement of the Spirit in their souls as they read scripture. On some occasions, feelings come, or maybe tears, perhaps heightened appreciation, or a sense of peace on a particular matter, a sense of unexplainable happiness, or a sense of the Lord's love. If we are asked on such an occasion what we heard from the Lord in that experience with the scripture, we might not be able to articulate an answer. Nonetheless, we have felt something sweet, something very tender. That was the spirit of prophecy, the Spirit of the Lord Jesus Christ.

On other occasions, we may be reading along when an issue or problem in our life comes to mind, maybe even a subject unrelated to the scripture being read, and suddenly we just know what to do about it. All these are instances of feeling the voice of the Lord to ourselves. We could develop this skill to a high degree and enjoy a living relationship with the Lord, in which the Lord could teach us many wonderful things. To develop such a skill we must invest time and experience, labor in the Spirit, and make scripture study a part of our daily life, but it is within the capability of any serious seeker.

The Book of Mormon teaches us how to receive revelation from scripture: "I, Nephi, beheld the pointers which were in the ball, that they did work according to the faith and diligence and heed which we did give unto them. And there was also written upon them a new writing, which was plain to be read, which did give us understanding concerning the ways of the Lord; and it was written and changed from time to time, according to the faith and diligence which we gave unto it. And thus we see that by small means the Lord can bring about great things" (1 Nephi 16:28–29).

By studying the spiritual conditions under which the Book of Mormon was translated, we can learn more about the process of receiving the Spirit from the scripture. Joseph Smith showed the way. David Whitmer described what the Prophet had to go through to get the spirit of prophecy so that he could translate:

"At times when brother Joseph would attempt to translate . . . , he found he was spiritually blind and could not translate. He told us that his mind dwelt too much on earthly things, and various causes would make him incapable of proceeding with the translation. When in this condition he would go out and pray, and when he became sufficiently humble before God, he could then proceed with the translation. Now we see how very strict the Lord is, and how he requires the heart of man to be just right in his sight before he can receive revelation from him."[28]

On another occasion David Whitmer recorded: "He [Joseph Smith] was a religious and straightforward man. . . . He had to trust in God. He could not translate unless he was humble and possessed the right feelings towards everyone. To illustrate so you can see: One morning when he was getting ready to continue the translation, something went wrong about the house and he was put out about it. Something that Emma, his wife, had done. Oliver and I went upstairs and Joseph came up soon after to continue the translation but he could not do anything. He could not translate a single syllable. He went downstairs, out into the orchard, and made supplication to the Lord; was gone about an hour—came back to the house, and asked Emma's forgiveness and then came upstairs where we were and then the translation went on all right. He could do nothing save he was humble and faithful."[29]

This account is highly instructive. We must approach the scripture in the same way that the scripture was given to one who was in a state of humility, of desire, of courage, of forgiveness of others.

We can prepare ourselves to hear the word of the Lord by realizing that in opening up the scriptures, we are about to have a conversation with the Lord. Thus we approach such an encounter in a spiritual, prayerful, thoughtful, and solemn way. We read trying to feel, to listen, to hear, and even to make notes. Our heart must be prepared to be written on; we must want to hear what the Lord wants to say to us, what the Lord's counsel is to us. So we approach the scripture with as much humility as we can, with willingness to repent and to grow.

Whenever we feel that movement of the Spirit in our own soul, we are feeling the voice of the Lord to us—the Lord is speaking to us individually. We are connected by the Spirit in that moment to our Savior. In this way, the Book of Mormon can bring us to Christ every time we pick up the book and hear or feel the Spirit. Coming to Christ is the main objective of all scripture. Simply, we feast on the words of Christ and, if we have prepared, he speaks to us through feelings and impressions and happiness and even words, and thus we come to Christ as we study scripture and hear his voice.

This kind of immersion in reading, this knowledge of the Book of Mormon, this learning to discern, to hear or feel, and then to obey the voice of the Lord to us personally may do more to prepare the Saints for the coming of the Lord Jesus Christ than nearly any other activity we could engage in. President Benson urged the priesthood holders of the Church: "One of the most important things you can do as priesthood leaders is to immerse yourselves in the scriptures. Search them diligently. Feast upon the words of Christ. Learn the doctrine. Master the principles that are found therein. There are few other efforts that will bring greater dividends to your calling. There are few other ways to gain greater inspiration as you serve.

"But that alone, as valuable as it is, is not enough. You must also bend your efforts and your activities to stimulating meaningful scripture study among the members of the Church. Often we spend great effort in trying to increase the activity levels in our stakes. We work diligently to raise the percentages of those attending sacrament meetings. We labor to get a higher percentage of our young men on missions. We strive to improve the numbers of those marrying in the temple. All of these are commendable efforts and important to the growth of the kingdom. But when individual members and families immerse themselves in the scriptures regularly and consistently, these other areas of activity will automatically come. Testimonies will increase. Commitment will be strengthened. Families will be fortified. Personal revelation will flow. . . .

"'This book of the law shall not depart out of thy mouth; but thou shalt meditate therein day and night, that thou mayest observe to do according to all that is written therein: for *then thou shalt make thy way prosperous, and then thou shalt have good success*'" (Josh. 1:8; italics added)."[30]

President Benson has also spoken on the centrality of the scriptures to the work that the Saints must do in the winding-up scenes of this dispensation:

"In the Book of Mormon we find a pattern for preparing for the Second Coming. A major portion of the book centers on the few decades just prior to Christ's coming to America. By careful study of that time period we can determine why some were destroyed in the terrible judgments that preceded His coming and what brought others to stand at the temple in the land of Bountiful and thrust their hands into the wounds of His hands and feet."[31]

"My beloved brothers and sisters, I bear my solemn witness that these books [the Book of Mormon and the Doctrine and Covenants] contain the mind and the will of the Lord for us in these days of trial and tribulation. They stand with the Bible to give witness of the Lord and His work. These books contain the voice of the Lord to us in these latter days. *May we turn to them with full purpose of heart and use them in the way the Lord wishes them to be used.*"[32]

It is clear that as wickedness increases, the Saints need a compensatory blessing to carry the Lord's work forward. We have been promised that very blessing. President Benson declared: "I bless you with increased *understanding* of the Book of Mormon. I promise you that from this moment forward, if we will daily sup from its pages and abide by its precepts, God will pour out upon each child of Zion and the Church a blessing hitherto unknown."[33]

Finally, President Benson has spoken on how we will get from where we are now to that day when our Savior appears and the Saints stand before him prepared: "Only a Zion people can bring in a Zion society. And as the Zion people increase, so we will be able to incorporate more of the principles of Zion until we have a people prepared to receive the Lord."[34]

When the Saints have assumed their individual responsibility to possess the Spirit of the Lord in the ways that the Lord has instructed, all other preparations will follow, and we will have a people not only ready to stand in the midst of the trials preceding the Second Coming but able to rejoice under the sanctifying and prospering hand of the Lord Jesus Christ.

NOTES

1. Ezra Taft Benson, in Conference Report, Oct. 1988, 103.

2. Orson F. Whitney, *Life of Heber C. Kimball,* 2d ed. (Salt Lake City: Stevens and Wallis, 1945), 447.

3. Ibid., 446; emphasis in original.

4. Ibid., 449–50.

5. J. Golden Kimball, in Conference Report, Oct. 1930, 59–60.

6. Ezra Taft Benson, Grantsville Utah Stake Conference, 1 Sept. 1974; in Ezra Taft Benson, *The Teachings of Ezra Taft Benson* (Salt Lake City: Bookcraft, 1988), 107.

7. Ezra Taft Benson, *God, Family, Country: Our Three Great Loyalties* (Salt Lake City: Deseret Book, 1974), 345–46; in Benson, *Teachings,* 107–8.

8. Ezra Taft Benson, *Come unto Christ* (Salt Lake City: Deseret Book, 1983), 115–16; in Benson, *Teachings,* 106–8; italics added.

9. Ezra Taft Benson, in Conference Report, Apr. 1969, 10.

10. Benson, in Conference Report, Apr. 1969, 11, citing J. Reuben Clark Jr., in *Improvement Era,* May 1949, 268, or in Conference Report, Apr. 1949, 153.

11. John Taylor, in *Journal of Discourses,* 26 vols. (London: Latter-day Saints' Book Depot, 1854–86), 24:197–98.

12. Joseph Smith, *Lectures on Faith* (Salt Lake City: Deseret Book, 1985), 69–70.

13. John Taylor, in *Journal of Discourses,* 18:281.

14. Ezra Taft Benson, "In His Steps," Church Educational System Devotional, Anaheim, California, 8 Feb. 1987; in Benson, *Teachings,* 104–5.

15. Bruce R. McConkie, *Ensign,* Apr. 1980, 25.

16. Bruce R. McConkie, *Ensign,* May 1979, 93.

17. Brigham Young, in *Journal of Discourses,* 7:142–43; italics added.

18. Whitney, *Heber C. Kimball,* 450.

19. Ezra Taft Benson, *Ensign,* May 1986, 4; italics added.

20. Benson, *Ensign,* May 1986, 5; italics in original.

21. Benson, *Ensign,* May 1986, 82; italics added.

22. Bruce R. McConkie, *Doctrines of the Restoration: Sermons and Writings of Bruce R. McConkie,* ed. Mark L. McConkie (Salt Lake City: Bookcraft, 1989), 243.

23. Bruce R. McConkie, in Benson, *Ensign,* May 1986, 81.

24. Dallin H. Oaks, "Scripture Reading and Revelation," address delivered to BYU Studies Academy, Provo, Utah, 29 Jan. 1993, 3–4; italics in original.

25. Boyd K. Packer, in Benson, *Ensign,* May 1986, 81.

26. Richard G. Scott, *Ensign,* Oct. 1984, 11; italics added.

27. Boyd K. Packer, "The Candle of the Lord," *Ensign,* Jan. 1983, 52.

28. David Whitmer, *Address to All Believers in Christ;* in B. H. Roberts, *A Comprehensive History of The Church of Jesus Christ of Latter-day Saints, Century One,* 6 vols. (Provo, Utah: The Church of Jesus Christ of Latter-day Saints, 1957), 6:130–31.

29. David Whitmer to Wm. H. Kelley and G. A. Blakeslee, 15 Sept. 1882; in Roberts, *Comprehensive History,* 1:131.

30. Benson, *Ensign,* May 1986, 81.

31. Benson, *Teachings,* 59.

32. Ezra Taft Benson, *Ensign,* Nov. 1986, 80; italics added.

33. Benson, *Ensign,* May 1986, 78; italics in original.

34. Ezra Taft Benson, "Jesus Christ—Gifts and Expectations," *Speeches of the Year, 1974* (Provo, Utah: Brigham Young University Press, 1975), 305.

CHAPTER THREE

FALSE CHRISTS

JOSEPH FIELDING McCONKIE

The scriptural warning against false Christs was the first of the signs of the times given by the Savior to his disciples. It, like the other signs, would signal that the time of the destruction of the kingdom of the Jews and their temple was upon them. This same sign, the coming of false Christs, was then repeated by the Lord as the first of the signs by which his disciples in our day are to know the time of his coming and the time of the destruction of the wicked are close at hand (Joseph Smith–Matthew 1:6, 21–22). Indeed, the signs of the times for the meridian dispensation were a foreshadowing of those of the last days. The events that lead to destruction in one era do so in another. This principle makes history marvelously prophetic.

REJECTING THE MESSIAH BROUGHT DESTRUCTION

The Book of Mormon makes it plain that the Jews were destroyed as a nation and scattered throughout the earth because they rejected Christ. That was the cause of their destruction and captivity in the days of Jeremiah and again after the crucifixion of Christ (1 Nephi 1:19–20; 2 Nephi 6:9–12). The Messiah sought by the Jews in the meridian of time was one who would redeem them not from the effects of sin but from the bondage of Rome. They sought a return to the glory of David's kingdom, not a return to the sanctity and purity of the cities of Enoch and Melchizedek, which were taken up into heaven (see JST Genesis 14:33–35). The truth of a Messiah who was God's Son had been lost to them. Diaspora had done nothing for their faith. They wanted a God as erudite as that of the Greek philosophers,

Joseph Fielding McConkie is professor of ancient scripture at Brigham Young University.

one without body, parts, and passions, and they had been busy rewriting the Bible to accommodate those views. What they had not been able to accomplish with a revision of the text, they accomplished with allegory or symbolism. All references to an anthropomorphic God were to be considered metaphorically. A God who is not a personal being can hardly beget a son in anything but a symbolic sense. As their God became more and more impersonal and abstract, so did their feelings toward him. When God becomes a mystery and we cannot know him, then we cannot know what he expects of us. Thus a covenant people become a permissive people. They retain the forms of godliness—ceremony and ritual, along with the profession of loyalty to God—while rejecting, as did King Noah and his priests, the very idea that salvation requires more than outward observance.

The temple was the focal point of Jewish worship in Jesus' day. It was a magnificent edifice, one of the seven wonders of the ancient world. Herod's Temple, like Solomon's Temple before it, evoked awe and reverence. It symbolized the strength of their nation and of the protective hand of the Lord that rested on them. Yet, the Psalmist had prophesied that its builders would reject its chief cornerstone, and so they did (Psalm 118:22). Israel rejected the Christ, lost their birthright, and were dragged off into captivity. In time they returned to rebuild their temple. Yet, when their Savior came to them, they again rejected him (Matthew 21:41–42) and, having done so, were again ripe to lose their birthright and be scattered throughout the earth. Thus, the Savior prophesied, their temple, a type of their nation, would be destroyed and not one stone would be left standing on another, symbolizing their scattering throughout the nations of the earth (D&C 45:16–21).

The story is told with plainness in the Book of Mormon. In some future day when the scattered remnants (the stones) of Israel choose to accept Jesus as the Christ, the Redeemer, and Son of God, they will once again be gathered and their temple restored. Such events await their placing the Chief Cornerstone in its rightful place.

FALSE CHRISTS DESTROYED
THE MERIDIAN CHURCH FROM WITHIN

"Take heed that no man deceive you," Christ told the meridian Twelve, "for many shall come in my name, saying—I am Christ—and shall deceive many; then shall they deliver you up to be afflicted, and shall kill you, and ye shall be hated of all nations, for my name's sake" (Joseph Smith–Matthew 1:5–7). Surely the message was sobering: You will be hated of all nations, and they will both afflict you and kill you. But who in those nations were the disciples being warned against? According to what we have just read, it was false Christs. There seem to be two important implications here: first, the Twelve would be betrayed from within the Church, not by those in the world who opposed their message; and second, the betraying of the faith would spread to all nations. It didn't matter where the Twelve went; they would be opposed and betrayed. That conclusion is sustained by the prophetic dream of Nephi: "Behold the world and the wisdom thereof; yea, behold the house of Israel hath gathered together to fight against the twelve apostles of the Lamb" (1 Nephi 11:35). Thus the Book of Mormon confirms that it was a reverence for the wisdom of the world that caused the house of Israel to betray the apostles.

We can reconstruct the story only in part, but that is sufficient to establish a pattern. The apostles took the message to the various nations. Many were converted but not in full. The Christian convert stood alone, overshadowed by the influence of the Jewish temple on the one hand and the Greek academy on the other. From the temple came the Judaizers, who wouldn't let go of their traditions; while from the academy came those indoctrinated in the monotheism of Plato. As if that were not enough, there were also the Gnostics, who were truer than true, straining everything through the veil of mysticism. And so the newly converted, wanting neither to give offense nor to appear as fools, sought common ground and a spirit of conciliation. In so doing, they modified the Christian message until it passed as it were into a new dialect, one that would have been very strange to the ear of those initially commissioned by Christ.

DECLARING HIS GENERATION

In the Old Testament's great messianic prophecy, Isaiah asked, "Who shall declare his generation?" (Isaiah 53:8), meaning, Who shall declare the genesis, or origin, of Christ? In early Christian history the answer became, Just about anyone, and all the ideas differed. The one idea that no one considered was that Christ was actually the Son of God. The idea that God could actually beget a son was too far-fetched to deserve consideration. Words simply didn't mean what they said where God and the gospel were concerned. The irony of this, if lost on virtually everyone else, was not lost on the editors of *The Shorter Oxford English Dictionary on Historical Principles*. In defining the meaning of *generation* in theology, they cite: "Strange G[eneration] this? Father and Son Co-eval [of the same age], two distinct and yet but one KEN [Kin]."[1]

One of the first departures from the simple story of Christ's birth centers on the account of his baptism. To capture the argument of the Adoptionists, we must pass behind the synoptic Gospels and consult the "Gospel according to the Hebrews," an apocryphal work thought by some to be the original version of Matthew's Gospel. There, as in Justin Martyr and in the Acts of Peter and Paul, the heavenly voice addresses Jesus at the time of his baptism, using the Psalmist's words, "Thou art my Son; this day have I begotten thee" (Psalms 2:7). The Adoptionists reasoned that the investiture of sonship took place on the day of Christ's baptism, that being the occasion on which the divine element entered its human tabernacle and the heavenly adoption was announced by God. This doctrine apparently was first advocated by the Ebionites (Heb., "poor men"), a sect of Jewish Christians that flourished in the early centuries in areas east of Jordan.[2] It seems to have been the "tendency of Jewish Christianity to shrink from the idea" of a God assuming a mortal body and "to be content to regard Jesus as the last and greatest of the prophets." Thus

Ebionism became synonymous with the denial of Christ's divinity and the doctrine of a virgin birth.[3] The Christian ascetics who held to the Mosaic law taught that the humanity of Jesus in no way distinguished him from other men until "the act of divine selection and consecration" that took place on the banks of the Jordan. Thus Christ was said to be of "an earthly lineage and a heavenly investiture."[4]

It has also been held that the apostle Paul was an Adoptionist but that he differed with the Ebionites as to the time of adoption. Paul, that argument goes, believed Jesus to have been adopted at the time of his resurrection, and Romans 1:3–4 is cited as the proof text: "Jesus Christ was born of the seed of David according to the flesh; and declared to be the *Son of God* with power, according to the Spirit of holiness, by his *resurrection from the dead.*"[5]

Providing a complete contrast with the Adoptionist view of Christ's humanity is Docetism. Literally, the name means "to seem," which captures the essence of the idea that Christ's manhood and sufferings were apparent rather than real. Jesus, the Docetists held, came not in the flesh but rather as spirit that exhibited the appearance of the flesh. They believed his body was a "sort of a ghost that miraculously seemed to be a real body." The Docetists denied the birth of Jesus because a mortal birth would have made him subject to the power of the material world.[6]

Christian historians tell us that after such notions developed, the idea of Christ's being divine from birth originated. They argue that the Infancy Gospels, the apocryphal New Testament writings that deal with Christ's childhood, appeared at this point, along with the accounts of the Nativity in Matthew and Luke. "They could not be prefixed, however, to the original baptismal scene without an obvious discordance: if the sonship dated from the nativity, it could not at the baptism be announced as beginning 'this day': and so the phrase from the Messianic Psalm was removed; and in its place the prophetic Spirit supplied the fitter words, 'This is my beloved Son, in whom I am well pleased.'" This concept raised a host of questions for the mind trained in the learning of the Greeks, for to such a mind the difference between that which is divine and that which is not divine is the same as the difference between that which "ever is" and that which "comes and goes." Thus was the notion introduced that the sonship of Christ could not have had a beginning in mortal conditions but must be traceable to the pre-earth estate. The writers of scripture were said to have introduced the idea of his "'glory before the world was'; [in] an eternity 'in the bosom of the Father' [John 1:14, 18]," that is, the doctrine that Christ obtained his divine nature even before the world was and only later became flesh.[7]

The Apologists (Christian writers who, under the guise of defending the faith to the outside world, irreparably compromised it with Greek philosophy, c. 120–220), were all "ardent monotheists" and determined "at all costs" not to betray that principle. "The solution they proposed, reduced to essentials, was that, as preexistent, Christ was the Father's thought or mind, and that, as manifested in creation and revelation, He was its extrapolation or expression. In expounding this doctrine they had recourse to the imagery of the divine Logos, or Word, which had been familiar to later Judaism as well as to Stoicism, and which had become a fashionable cliché through the influence of Philo."[8] Devoid of the Spirit of revelation, that Spirit essential to even the most fundamental understanding of the gospel declared by Christ, the Apologists commenced their "speculations and developed a science about Christ" called Christology, their great labor being "Logos Christology, from the Greek term *logos,* meaning 'the Word.'" The Logos notion was "a prominent concept in the prevailing Neo-Platonic philosophy of the time and so provided the theologians with a means of correlating the Christian revelation not only with the Old Testament but also with the insights of the classical philosophers."[9] That is a kind way of saying they sold out. To cover the treachery of their deed, the argument of traditional Christianity was that the pagan philosophers were "Christians before Christianity" and so their philosophical speculations were more important than the writings of the Old Testament prophets, which those speculations were then used to reinterpret.[10]

Thus with the aid of pagan philosophers, the Christian Apologists were able to discover that Jesus Christ was really just some kind of manifestation of the mind of a Christ in a mortal body. He was Logos, meaning "the intelligence or rational thought" of God. What he was not, in anything other than a metaphorical sense, was God's Son. Such a notion would require God to be a personal being and necessitate our accepting the language of the scriptures to mean what it says. Among other things it would suggest that God actually appeared to the prophets of the Old Testament and conversed with them as one man converses with another. But the Apologists found it "inconceivable that 'the Master and Father of all things should have abandoned all supercelestial affairs and made Himself visible in a minute corner of the world'." "Old Testament theophanies," their argument runs, are "in fact appearances of the Logos. God Himself cannot be contained in space and time, but it was precisely the function of the Word Whom He generated to manifest His mind and will in the created order."[11] Thus Christ, or Logos, meaning some kind of intermediary expression of the mind of Deity, appeared to the Old Testament prophets. Again, how have we come to such an understanding? From Plato and his fellow philosophers, including the Jewish apologist Philo.

These events provided the setting for the famous Arian controversy which divided the Christian world for hundreds of years. "Arius [c. 250–c. 336] was incited to action by the teaching of Alexander the bishop of Alexandria, who taught the eternal generation of the Son," meaning that "'there never was a time when He was not.'" Arius countered with the argument that "as a father must exist before his son, therefore the Son of God did not exist eternally with the Father"; rather, "He was created [by the Father], but before time began. . . . The Council of Nicaea (A.D. 325), convened by the Emperor [Constantine]" to settle the issue, "decided against Arianism, and defined the authoritative doctrine to be that the Son is 'of one substance' *(ousia)* with the Father; that He was 'begotten, not made,' that 'there never was a time when He was not,' that 'He was not created.' The Nicene Creed was established largely by the brilliant advocacy of Athanasius, subsequently bishop of Alexandria,"[12] who argued "that reason must bow to the mystery of the Trinity."[13] Thus a founding principle of Christianity, borrowed from Neoplatonism, became the tendency to make God as transcendent as possible.[14] That is to say, in all things God transcends our ability to understand. "If you can understand it," Augustine explained, "it's not God."[15] Thus in responding to Isaiah's question as it is recorded in the Septuagint, "Who shall explain His generation?" (LXX, Isaiah 53:8), the Christian world has responded: No one, for it is a grand mystery.[16]

Will Durant, in his classic work *Caesar and Christ,* summarizes the early Christian era thus: "*Christianity did not destroy paganism; it adopted it.* The Greek mind, dying, came to a transmigrated life in the theology and liturgy of the Church; the Greek language, having reigned for centuries over philosophy, became the vehicle of Christian literature and ritual; *the Greek mysteries passed down into the impressive mystery of the Mass.* Other pagan cultures contributed to the syncretist result. From Egypt came the idea of a divine trinity, the Last Judgment, and a personal immortality of reward and punishment; from Egypt the adoration of the Mother and Child, and the mystic theosophy that made Neoplatonism and Gnosticism, and obscured the Christian creed; there, too, Christian monasticism would find its exemplars and its source. From Phrygia came the worship of the Great Mother; from Syria the resurrection drama of Adonis; from Thrace, perhaps, the cult of Dionysus, the dying and saving god. From Persia came millenarianism, the 'ages of the world,' the 'final conflagration,' the dualism of Satan and God, of Darkness and Light; already in the Fourth Gospel Christ is the 'Light shining in the darkness, and the darkness has never put it out.' The Mithraic ritual so closely resembled the eucharistic sacrifice of the Mass that Christian fathers charged the Devil with inventing these similarities to mislead frail minds. Christianity was the last great creation of the ancient pagan world."[17]

THE MANY FACES OF JESUS

In a prophetic description of the promised Messiah, Isaiah said "his visage" would be more "marred" than that of any man (Isaiah 52:14). Though no mortal man has endured what Christ did in his matchless labor of atonement, the effect of his suffering was not such that it would distort his appearance in a manner to justify this prophecy. Significantly, the resurrected Christ gave a dual meaning to these words by applying them to another servant of the Lord in the last days (see 3 Nephi 20:44). We understand that to be Joseph Smith, who died a martyr's death, though not in a manner to distort his appearance, either. This evidence suggests that the distortion of image spoken of by Isaiah had reference to the manner in which the promised servant and his labors were to be misinterpreted and misperceived. Surely, the image of no one in earth's history has been as often or as completely distorted as that of Jesus of Nazareth. In like manner, it will be remembered that Joseph Smith was promised that his name (image or visage) would be had for both good and evil among all nations and peoples of the earth (see Joseph Smith–History 1:33).

Recent years have witnessed a remarkable variety of portraits of Jesus. In fact, more has been written about him in the past two decades than in the previous two millennia. In such sources Christ has been "portrayed as a Marxist who provides the blueprints for an economic and social reform; as a Black Messiah who stood against an exploitative white nation, Rome; as a liberator who proclaimed that God's Kingdom belongs to the poor; and as the Prince of Peace who shows the way for nuclear disarmament."[18] Along with being a revolutionary or a social reformer, he has been depicted as a magician, a charismatic teacher, a foreteller of the end of the world, a "marginal" Jew who challenged the teachings and practices of the religious leaders of his day, and as a spiritual master who overcame the humblest of origins to proclaim a gospel of love and forgiveness.

Clearly the prophetic warnings against false Christs embrace more than the strange assortment of souls who periodically come on the scene professing to be the hope of the world. In most instances the false Christs we face will take the form of false systems of salvation which inevitably embrace false notions about the true nature of the Son of God. The preface to the Doctrine and Covenants, given in 1831, describes an apostate world in which people walk after the image of gods of their own making. The authors of these gods, we are told, do not seek the Lord nor do they care to establish his righteousness (D&C 1:16). They have their own agendas. Theirs is a well-worn path, and the mirage they see in the distance is inevitably in their own image and likeness. This may be the first-century desert ascetic who tells us that Christ never owned anything and out of shame of his physical body refused marriage and family, or the twentieth-century radical feminist who emasculated Christ and then enlisted him as a social reformer. Everybody, it appears, wants to assimilate Jesus into the spirit of one's own ambitions. Thus he becomes the model for peasants and kings, celibates and fathers, pacifists and soldiers, hermits and gentlemen, feudal lords and revolutionaries. For some he is the gentle shepherd-teacher; for others he is the rod of iron with which they seek to beat their opponents into submission.

Generally, those who have chronicled the life of Christ have revealed more of themselves than they have of the Master. Albert Schweitzer observed that "there is no historical task which so reveals a man's true self as the writing of a life of Jesus. No vital force comes into the figure unless a man breathes into it all the hate or all the love of which he is capable. The stronger the love, the stronger the hate, the more life-like is the figure which is produced."[19] "George Bernard Shaw, in his Preface to *Androcles and the Lion* . . . described Jesus as a 'highly-civilized, cultivated person,' a Bohemian socialist. William Blake, in *The Everlasting Gospel* . . . portrayed Jesus as proud, independent and mocking. Tolstoy, in his later writings, saw Jesus as the same relentless moralist of altruistic love that he was himself. . . . Nietzsche, in *The*

Antichrist . . . saw Jesus as something between an immature adolescent and a hypersensitive psychopath—Dostoyevsky's Idiot. The poet A. C. Swinburne in his *Hymn to Proserpine* . . . sees Jesus as a morbid ascetic who immolated himself before a cruel dying Father-God." In each instance the writer is projecting his own traits upon Jesus.[20]

History records a bewildering number of contrasting types of Christianity and an equally bewildering variety of Christs. So much is this the case that it has been suggested that we ought to refer to them as Christianities rather than as Christianity, which latter term portrays the idea that there is some sense of unity in it all. "The 1000 pages of the *World Christian Encyclopedia* published in 1982 are mind-boggling in their complexity and variety, with the 20,800 Christian *denominations* which are listed." That, however, is but the beginning of the problem, for within the various denominations are often to be found considerable division. Within the ranks of the Church of England, for example, are "liberals, radicals and conservatives, high and low, Tractarian, Evangelical and Erastian, married clergy and homosexual clergy."[21] If we could somehow discount such differences, we would still be left with the fact that the historical roots of this host of denominations demonstrate that they themselves have changed their doctrines over the course of years. Each succeeding generation has often held a very different image of Christ.

"The inquisition which could once be regarded as the organ of divine providence now seems to most Christians a monstrous institution. Today few Christian sensibilities could endorse crusades. Many would be squeamish even about Christian judgments that other religions are false which would have been axiomatic in most earlier times. Ethical standards have shifted. No Christian now would accept slavery as a legitimate social option, whereas many would welcome sexual freedoms deplored by earlier periods. Some Christian groups have been firmly pacifist, while some bishops have blessed battleships and prayed for the destruction of enemies. At

times Christianity has manifested itself through Communist practices with regard to property, while Protestant Christendom has been
identified as a main pillar of capitalism."[22]

THE CHRIST OF CHRISTIAN LORE

In point of fact, there is little resemblance between the Christ of
Christian lore and the accepted dogmas of orthodox Christianity.
The abstract and incomprehensible Christ of Christian creeds, the
fog of mystery they are expected to reverence, generally finds little
or no place in the hearts of people. The experience of generations
of missionaries sustains an overwhelming propensity on the part of
those who profess faith in Christ to view him as a personal being.
Many do so unaware that this conflicts with their creeds, while others choose to compartmentalize the two conflicting notions in the
hope that somehow both will prove themselves true. Significant
shifts are evident in common perceptions of Christ. From the time
of Constantine, the mother church has sought to establish her sovereignty by teaching the fear of God. The Reformation brought with
it a renewed emphasis on the Fatherhood of God, replacing (after its
first generations) fear with love. With the coming of political freedom came religious freedom and with it the enhanced notion that
God was a God of love rather than a God of wrath. When times of
prosperity came and our lifestyles afforded greater personal expression and leisure, a kinder perception of God was entertained. The
shift has been almost as dramatic as that often supposed to exist
between the Gods of the Old and the New Testaments. The Old
Testament God is seen as jealous and demanding whereas the New
Testament God is perceived as nonjudgmental, warm, and loving. A
permissive society obviously prefers a permissive God, one who is
not concerned with outward ritual, the keeping of commandments,
or denominational preferences. Thus in recent years God has been
viewed as being marvelously tolerant. The basic doctrine is that
everything is fine as long as we profess a love for God and are kind
to one to another. The exception here is the God of evangelicalism,

who introduced a new (or perhaps very old) severity into the religious world. The evangelical God is permissive as far as believers are concerned while being extremely harsh and uncompromising with those outside that circle. While serving as a mission president I was frequently damned to the lowest depths of hell by evangelicals. I pointed out to a leading evangelical that in his lifetime (he was approximately forty-five) more than a billion people have lived and died on this earth without hearing the Christian message and asked what was to become of them, given that they had not professed Christ and were thus ineligible for his brand of salvation. His response was direct and uncompromising. He simply said, "Well, that's their tough luck, isn't it!"

FALSE CHRISTS WITHIN THE CHURCH

I asked a neighbor who is a police detective what kind of crime there is in Orem, Utah. He said, "The same kind that they have everywhere else, just not as much of it." Just as a community of our size cannot avoid the corrupting influences of the world and must constantly fight against them, so must the community of the Saints. We must properly understand our doctrines and carefully protect ourselves from notions that rob them of their purity. Even when the Church was in its infancy the Lord warned, "There are many spirits which are false spirits, which have gone forth in the earth, deceiving the world. And also Satan hath sought to deceive you, that he might overthrow you." This revelation then notes that there were abominations in the Church that professed the name of the Lord and warned that everyone must beware lest they "do that which is not in truth and righteousness" before God (D&C 50:3–9). We too have our false Christs, and in some instances because we are too believing they have become well entrenched. Let us consider a few of the more popular ones.

One very dangerous notion popular on the campuses of our Church schools is the idea that we work out our salvation by obtaining knowledge and that at some future time, when we have gained a mastery of all subjects (laws), we will have obtained our exaltation and can rule and reign as God. This notion holds that God is an eternal copartner with law and that should he violate the same he would cease to be God. Students who have been indoctrinated in this notion are quick to point out that the only way we can become as God is by obedience to law. This is where the sleight of hand takes place. It is true that we must be obedient to law to be saved but not to laws or a body of laws that stand independent of God. The laws to which we must be obedient are those which God ordained. The counter argument here is that if God is the author of law, then he is really an Omnipotent Bully demanding that everyone do things his way or be damned. The flaw in this argument is that God is also the author of agency. His is an "unchanging scepter of righteousness and truth" (D&C 121:46).

The matter is easily resolved by taking Christ as our illustration. He did not work out his salvation by making mathematical calculations to assure that when he performed miracles he was properly reordering the laws of nature. Rather, Christ told us that he did nothing but the will of the Father. That is, the law which he obeyed was the Father's law, not Nature's. All who seek the same salvation must do likewise.

The great danger here is that if we suppose that salvation is found in obedience to the laws of nature, and thus make nature our God, or at least a copartner with God, we are supposing that knowledge rather than Christ saves us. We thus make intelligence the condition of salvation rather than righteousness, diligence, and obedience (see D&C 130:19). Salvation becomes the province of those who are intellectually gifted rather than a gift promised to all of God's children—and of course the higher exaltation would go to the honors students, those most gifted in the realm of intellectual things. Thus professors and teachers become the voice of the Lord rather than apostles and prophets, and the knowledge of men replaces the revelations of heaven.

It is with considerable plainness that the revelations teach us that God is the author, not the servant, of law. "I am the law," he declared (3 Nephi 15:9). Those who inherit the celestial kingdom must be "sanctified through the law which I [God] have given unto you, even the law of Christ" (D&C 88:21). Further, God explains that he gave the law to "all kingdoms" and that there is no kingdom or even space that is not subject to his laws (D&C 88:36; see also vv. 37–38). "He comprehendeth all things, and all things are before him, and all things are round about him; and he is above all things, and in all things, and is through all things, and is round about all things; and all things are by him, and of him, even God, forever and ever. And again, verily I say unto you, he hath given a law unto all things, by which they move in their times and their seasons" (D&C 88:41–42).

The first article of faith among those who hold to the notion that God is the junior partner of the heavenly firm of Law and God is that the gospel embraces all truth. The common expression among them is that all truth can be circumscribed into one great whole. That is simply an extension of the argument that law is greater than God. Again this notion makes the teachers of the laws of the universe our prophets instead of those who come like John the Baptist demanding that we be baptized for the remission of sins. Repentance is not the great issue in such a gospel; rather, intelligence is.

All truths are not of equal worth. To suppose that the gospel embraces all truth would be to create an impossible burden for both the teacher and the student of the gospel. No one could have sufficient knowledge to teach the "fulness of the gospel," nor could anyone have the time or energy to learn it. We could hardly argue that the Book of Mormon contained the "fulness of the gospel" as scripture declares (D&C 20:9; 42:12; Joseph Smith–History 1:40), for no book could contain that much information. We could hardly send out nineteen-year-old young men to teach it or baptize eight-year-old children with the idea that they somehow comprehended it. The fulness of the gospel consists of specific truths essential to salvation, truths that can be understood by all who have an honest heart (3 Nephi 27:13–21).

Another form of false Christ popular for more than a generation among Latter-day Saints is the notion of the quick fix or easy grace that we borrowed, albeit without realizing it, from the Fundamentalists. The idea is to sow your wild oats and then quickly put everything right with the bishop so you can go on a mission or marry in the temple (after a short waiting period). The doctrine of repentance is taught with the "R" formula (recognition, remorse, refraining, and restitution), so we can check things off and get on with life with as little inconvenience as possible. This is justification without sanctification or repentance without pain. The Protestant notion "that Christ died for my sins two thousand years ago and there is nothing that I can do about it" has been refashioned so that it is supposed that confession and a brief verbal scolding by a bishop pretty well take care of things. It is a bit like suggesting that there are some sins that are worth it or that accountability begins at the age of twenty-one.

The problem here is that none of it works. The kingdom of heaven can hardly be made up of a collection of people who have been pronounced clean from sin but who have not been required to conquer the appetite for sin. To be told you are forgiven for a particular transgression doesn't have a thing in the world to do with giving you the strength to overcome it when the craving returns. Our repentance must be of such a nature that no sin is worth it. It must be a process in which the muscles of the soul have been strengthened by pushing against resistance to the point that they constitute a mighty defense, and the sanctification of the soul such that the very thought of transgression is abhorrent.

The false Christ in all of this is the supposition that his suffering was all that was necessary to cleanse and save. Without question, his sacrifice and suffering make all things possible to us, but they do not set at naught the application of all other laws and principles. All actions have their natural consequences, even for the repentant soul. I first learned this lesson as a young missionary. We were on a train returning to our area of labor after a baptism. A young woman we had baptized asked me if her baptism washed away all her sins. I told her it did. She asked, "What if the seed has already been planted?" I responded that if she was truly repentant, all was washed away. In a few weeks it became visibly apparent what she had in mind. She was going to be a mother out of wedlock. The transgression, properly repented of, could be forgiven. The consequence of that transgression remained. All actions have their consequences, and notwithstanding the atonement of Christ, we too must pay to mend the laws that we have broken. Again, no sin can be worth it. No true repentance can be accomplished without suffering. We cannot embrace the cheap grace of a corrupt Christianity in any form.

Closely associated with the Mormon version of cheap grace is the now popular notion among those called to labor with our youth that it is their obligation to "make the gospel fun." We can only assume that they are a little embarrassed by the way God has represented himself in scripture and by his prophets and thus it becomes their lot to rewrite the system of salvation to assure that it is palatable to the youth of the Church. "If we don't entertain them, they will go somewhere else," we are told. The dangers here are real enough to be numbered among the false Christs of our day.

John, the beloved disciple of Christ, stated the matter well: "For he whom God hath sent speaketh the words of God" (John 3:34). I would understand this statement to mean that Christ has been true to the message he was given. Surely it is not within our province to add to or take from the message that God has given. Alma, at the conclusion of a marvelous discourse on the manner in which the gospel is to be preached, said, "This is the order after which I am called, yea, to preach unto my beloved brethren, yea, and every one that dwelleth in the land; yea, to preach unto all, both old and young, both bond and free; yea, I say unto you the aged, and also the middle aged, and the rising generation; yea, to cry unto them that they must repent and be born again" (Alma 5:49).

There are two matters of considerable concern here. First, there are those who dare not let the Lord speak for himself for fear of giving offense. They cause something of a spiritual eclipse as they attempt to stand between the light of heaven and those they have been called to teach or lead. They can be likened to mail carriers who arrogate to themselves the role of editors of the mail entrusted to them to deliver intact. Some act as if Jesus had said, "Blessed are you when all men speak well of you." But the real Jesus said, "Woe unto you, when all men shall speak well of you! for so did their fathers to the false prophets" (Luke 6:26). It just may be that if we never offend anyone, we are not leaving witness of the true Jesus.

The second concern, and this is an even greater one, is those who have no intention of delivering the message they were commissioned to carry. In its stead they advocate sugarcoated activities and a constant diet of fun. Their argument, as previously noted, is, We must make the gospel fun, or we are going to lose our youth. To this we must ask, Will this fun save them, or is it just another way to lose them? The word *fun* is nowhere found in holy writ. The word *joy* is found abundantly. Perhaps we ought to learn the distinction.

Another of the false Christs that many Latter-day Saints sympathetically sustain is the "light" and "love" Christ depicted in the out-of-body experiences of popular literature. Inevitably these chosen souls are carried through a tunnel of light to divine realms where they become the honored guest and are taken on a tour before being sent, usually against their will, back to earth. The message is always the same: God's love is unconditional. He approves of everyone without distinction to race, creed, color, or behavior. We must do the same. Salvation is found in love. Distinctly missing from such accounts is any suggestion that obedience to the laws and ordinances of the gospel is of any moment. There is never any notion that we will be held accountable for our works, nor is it necessary for us to embrace any particular truths. The idea seems to be that we can love properly without necessarily thinking properly. By contrast, although all messengers of God of whom we read in scriptural accounts come declaring repentance, strangely that word is not to be found in popular lore. According to such messengers the gospel has been streamlined to nonjudgmental love.

These accounts don't square very well with their scriptural counterparts. When virtues are overdone, they become vices. When truths are exaggerated, they cease to be truths. By isolating the love or mercy of God from the other attributes of godliness, their true meaning is lost and they come to represent a false Christ or a false doctrine about Christ. That is what is happening in most spiritual fads within the Church. For example, a few years ago we had the then-popular "special relationship with Jesus" movement. In it people made exaggerated efforts to be spiritual and thus able to claim some kind of special relationship with the heavens unknown to others. For reasons that are not entirely clear, they also sought to isolate the Savior from the other two members of the Godhead for special veneration. Such imbalance is always a dangerous thing.

THE FRUITLESS SEARCH FOR JESUS

In medieval times crusaders sought to find Christ in the ruins of ancient shrines. They did not find him. Today our modern crusaders, in the guise of scholarship, seek to find him with scholarly tools. The sword and crossbow have been replaced by textual research, archaeology, and social science. Yet, like their predecessors, they too have been unable to find the Savior. It is, of course, to be expected that as long as people are careful to look in the wrong places, they are not going to find what they are looking for, but that would misjudge their efforts. The fact is, many have found exactly what they were looking for, a non-Savior. If, for instance, you start with the premise that there is no such thing as revelation and then examine the revelations to determine their reliability, rejecting as unreliable everything that purports to be revelation, it would be hard not to find what you sought to find—evidence that the revelations do not contain revelation. Such has been the quest of many in the scholarly world, and such has been their success.

The quest for the historical Jesus was first popularized by Albert

Schweitzer at the turn of the century. His studies led him to the conclusion that the man Jesus was not the Son of God, and that the historical Jesus was not the Christ of faith. Our most current successor to such efforts is the "What Did Jesus Really Say" movement. The idea is to determine what Jesus was saying about himself. At issue is the reliability of our scriptural texts. The most notable recent offering is the creation of a work titled *The Five Gospels*.[23] It is the result of a "Jesus Seminar" that began in the mid-1980s. The seminar's scholars represent a cross section of mainly liberal Bible academics, most coming from seminaries and universities—believers and nonbelievers, clergy and laity, Catholic and Protestant, and even Jewish scholars. They voted with different colored beads on the validity of each statement in the New Testament purportedly made by Christ. Their creation is a color-coded Bible—red, pink, gray, and black. Red ink means that there is enough historical, literary, sociological, and textual evidence to assure that Jesus definitely made the statement. Pink means the scholars think Jesus probably said it; gray means that it is something attributed to Jesus by his followers but not said by him; and black means he definitely didn't say it.

The conclusion of this six-year study is that eight of ten things attributed to Christ in the New Testament were not spoken by him. All statements by Christ that speak of his divine nature or his messianic role have been printed in black ink! The certainty among some scholars is that Jesus is not divine, he is not God's Son, he is not our Messiah, and he is not the Savior. With their help we now know, for instance, that the Gospel of John contains no reliable statements about Christ.

CONCLUSION

We live in a world that has been deluged with false images of Christ, one in which many have despaired of ever obtaining any sure knowledge of God or his plan for the salvation of his children. That is simply to say, Apostasy is alive and well. The doctrines and image of Christ have been sufficiently changed from Bible times that the Bishop of Salisbury observed that the churches of Christendom have retained the name "Jesus" only for the same reason that "one might retain the name of an old-established firm after a takeover. It attracts a certain amount of goodwill, and looks well on the notepaper."[24] But should that Christ known to the peoples of the New Testament come in our day, he would be sufficiently different from the expectation of the greater part of those who profess to preach and believe in his name that precious few could recognize him or would have any real interest in following him.

There is no salvation in ignorance or falsehood. To worship a false Christ is to embrace a false religion, one without the power of salvation in it. We must, as Helaman taught, build on "a sure foundation," and that foundation must embrace the knowledge that Jesus is our Redeemer, the Christ, and the Son of God (Helaman 5:12). To suppose, as much of modern scholarship does, that Christ was simply a great teacher in the community is not only to embrace a false Christ but is to forfeit the hope of salvation. C. S. Lewis stated it well when he said: "A man who was merely a man and said the sort of things Jesus said . . . would not be a great moral teacher. He would either be a lunatic—on a level with the man who says he is a poached egg—or else he would be the Devil of Hell. You must make your choice. . . . You can shut him up for a fool, . . . you can spit at him and kill him as a demon; or you can fall at his feet and call him Lord and God. But let us not come with any patronizing nonsense about his being a great human teacher. He has not left that open to us. He did not intend to."[25]

It is argued by many scholars that the Gospels did not take shape until after various dogmatic propositions had been added to the message of Christ and that as source material for who and what he is, the books of Matthew, Mark, Luke, and John are not reliable. At best the Gospels are seen as a reminiscence, including sayings that have been altered to suit the time and the circumstances of the audience to which they were directed. This, it is held, required some things to be added, others to be radically altered, and still others to be selectively erased or softened.[26] In so saying, scholars are simply projecting the events of known Christian history onto that which is unknown. The doctrine of the Holy Trinity constitutes the classic example. It is a doctrine wholly unknown to those of Bible times and generally admitted to be beyond their comprehension. The doctrine was devised as a protection against polytheism and to secure the notion of God's transcendence, a notion vital to the Greek philosophical conceptions of God that the Christian world sought to adopt to gain respectability.

The cost of this addition to the Christian message was the forfeiture of the doctrine of the Fatherhood of God, for now it was declared that the three persons of the Godhead were absolutely equal. Thus, we are told, it was the Holy Trinity that created all things, not the Father. It was the Trinity that gave birth to Christ, not the Father. Thus Christ was not actually the Son of God who came into the world in the likeness of his Father but rather *Logos,* meaning a representation of the image or mind of God. The doctrine of the Trinity robs Christ of the claim to being the literal Son of God and in so doing also robs us of our claim to being part of the family of God. An invisible God, one without body, parts, or passions, does not father children, either as spirits or as mortals. By this redefinition of the nature of God and Christ, the whole plan of salvation is not merely distorted but entirely lost.

How then does one keep from being deceived by false Christs or false representations of who and what Christ is? The answer must always rest in the principle of revelation. John the Revelator declared that "the testimony of Jesus is the spirit of prophecy" (Revelation 19:10). A classic illustration of this truth is the account of the damsel possessed of an evil spirit who followed Paul, Silas, and Luke, bearing testimony that they were servants of God who would show the people the way of salvation. Though what she said was entirely true, Paul was uneasy with it and eventually realized that demonic testimony was not acceptable to God. He then cast the evil spirit out of the woman (Acts 16:16–18). Why, we ask, would a woman possessed with an evil spirit bear a positive testimony of the gospel message and the servants commissioned to bear it? Because that testimony would eventually give her credibility among believers, thus placing her in a position to do much harm. Her testimony was not rooted in the revelations of heaven, and no other source for the testimony of Christ is acceptable.

Speaking to the Nephites, and prophesying the coming forth of the Book of Mormon, Christ said that anyone who rejected his words as found in the Nephite record "shall be cut off" from "among his people who are of the covenant" (3 Nephi 21:11). In scriptural language, that is to say they will be left without "root" or "branch," meaning they will lose their inheritance as Abraham's seed and will have no claim on the sealing powers of the temple and will not enjoy the society of spouse and family in the eternities to come. The testimony of Christ as found in the Book of Mormon stands at the heart of the message of the Restoration. "Those who receive it in faith, and work righteousness, shall receive a crown of eternal life; but those who harden their hearts in unbelief, and reject it, it shall turn to their own condemnation" (D&C 20:14–15).

All true religion is and ever will be revealed religion. No historical quest, no scholarly search, no philosophical speculation, no portrayal of Christ that stands independent of an immediate and personal revelation, no testimony that does not embrace the reality that Christ is the literal Son of God has the power of salvation in it. Such has been the testimony of the Lord's prophets in all ages of the earth's history. Such is our witness.

NOTES

1. William Little, H. W. Fowler, J. Coulson, *The Shorter Oxford English Dictionary on Historical Principles,* rev. and ed. C. T. Onions (Oxford: Clarendon Press, 1933), s.v. "generation," 1:784.
2. F. L. Cross and E. A. Livingstone, ed., *The Oxford Dictionary of the Christian Church* (Oxford: Oxford University Press, 1990), 626, 438.

3. James Hastings, John A. Selbie, and John C. Lambert, ed., *A Dictionary of Christ and the Gospels,* 2 vols. (Edinburgh: T. & T. Clark Publishers, 1906), 1:506.

4. James Martineau, *The Seat of Authority in Religion* (London: Longmans, Green, 1898), 238.

5. Ibid., 239.

6. Justo L. Gonzaléz, *The Story of Christianity,* 2 vols. (San Francisco: Harper & Row, 1984), 1:60.

7. Martineau, *Seat of Authority,* 240–41.

8. J. N. D. Kelly, *Early Christian Doctrines* (San Francisco: Harper & Row, 1978), 95–96.

9. Thomas Bokenkotter, *A Concise History of the Catholic Church* (New York: Doubleday, Image Books, 1990), 46.

10. Kelly, *Early Christian Doctrines,* 96.

11. Ibid., 97, 99.

12. Hastings, et al., *Dictionary of Christ and the Gospels,* 1:481.

13. Will Durant, *Caesar and Christ* (New York: Simon and Schuster, 1944), 660.

14. Kelly, *Early Christian Doctrines,* 20.

15. Alister McGrath, *Understanding the Trinity* (Eastbourne, E. Sussex: Kingsway Publications, 1990), 111.

16. Kelly, *Early Christian Doctrines,* 105.

17. Durant, *Caesar and Christ,* 595; italics in original.

18. James H. Charlesworth, *Jesus within Judaism* (New York: Doubleday, 1988), 26.

19. Albert Schweitzer, *The Quest of the Historical Jesus* (New York: Macmillan, 1968), 4.

20. Don Cupitt, "One Jesus, Many Christs?" in *Christ, Faith and History,* ed. S. W. Sykes and J. P. Clayton (Cambridge: University Press, 1972), 132–33.

21. John Bowden, *Jesus: The Unanswered Questions* (London: SCM Press, 1988), 53; see also *World Christian Encyclopaedia,* ed. David B. Barrett (Oxford: Oxford University Press, 1982), v.

22. Elizabeth Maclaren, as cited in Bowden, *Jesus,* 66–67.

23. Robert W. Funk, Roy W. Hoover, and the Jesus Seminar, *The Five Gospels: The Search for the Authentic Words of Jesus* (New York: Macmillan, 1993).

24. John Austin Baker, *The Foolishness of God* (London: Darton, Longman and Todd, 1990), 157.

25. C. S. Lewis, as cited by Malcolm Muggeridge in *Jesus the Man Who Lives* (New York: Harper and Row, 1975), 61–62.

26. R. Joseph Hoffmann, *Jesus outside the Gospels* (Buffalo, N.Y.: Prometheus Books, 1984), 68.

CHAPTER FOUR

THE ROLE OF THE HOUSE OF ISRAEL IN THE LAST DAYS

ROBERT J. MATTHEWS

In a discussion of the role of the house of Israel in the last days, three distinct elements require some clarification. First, we must consider what is meant by *the last days;* second, who and what is *Israel;* and third, what is meant by the word *role.* As I define these terms, it should be understood that I alone am responsible for the views presented in this chapter; however, I believe what I have written to be true and consistent with the scriptures and with the teachings of the Brethren. I lay claim to no insight or knowledge beyond what anyone could have who reads the scriptures and the words of the latter-day prophets with prayer, reverence, and a believing heart. It is my hope and desire that whoever reads this discussion will be edified spiritually and will have an increased appreciation for the latter-day work of the Lord and his purposes as they are presented in the scriptures and as they are unfolding daily among the nations of the earth.

THE LAST DAYS

The term *last days,* or the *latter days,* refers to a time preceding the second coming of the Lord Jesus Christ. How many years make up the last days? We don't know, but for the convenience of a working definition, we will say that the last days began with the First Vision of Joseph Smith in the spring of 1820. Even with that beginning date, we must understand that momentous changes had already begun taking place among the nations of the earth in preparation for the last days. The Renaissance, the Protestant Reformation, the

---

Robert J. Matthews is professor emeritus of ancient scripture at Brigham Young University.

Catholic Counter-Reformation, the invention of printing, the colonization of America, the American Revolution, and the establishment of the Constitution of the United States were all preparatory to fulfilling the purposes of the Lord in the last days.

In a sense, the last days can be called the ending period of mortality upon the earth, for when the Savior comes a change will come over the earth, upon mankind, and also upon animal life. Many things typical of mortal life will cease: men shall not learn war any more; the wolf shall dwell peacefully with the lamb; instead of meat, the lion shall eat straw like the ox; the earth shall eventually be full of the knowledge of the Lord as the waters cover the sea; and there shall not be death as we now experience it (see Isaiah 2:4; 11:6–9; D&C 101:23–29).

The last days are a time of fulfillment, enlargement, and intensity. Not only are they a period of restoration and of building the kingdom of God on the earth but they are also a time of increased wickedness and tribulation. The Prophet Joseph Smith explained that whenever the Lord sets up his kingdom on the earth, the devil sets up his kingdom at the very same time in opposition to it.[1] In the last days there is an increase of revelation and gospel knowledge, but at the same time, the devil rages in the hearts of mankind and seeks to destroy the kingdom of God. The devil has increased his efforts to oppose all righteousness and to deceive mankind "because he knoweth that he hath but a short time" left (Revelation 12:12; see also 13:1–18). Thus the purposes of the Lord will be accomplished in the midst of war, turmoil, persecution, distress of nations, and the false philosophies of men because of the devil's determined opposition to the Lord's prophets, apostles, and Church members. The Lord has promised that in the end, righteousness will triumph over wickedness, the Saints over their persecutors, and Christ over the devil. That is the message of all scripture and especially of such writings as the book of Isaiah, the book of Revelation, and the Book of Mormon.

WHO AND WHAT IS ISRAEL?

The word *Israel* is of Hebrew origin, first occurring in Genesis 32:28 and 35:10 as a change of name for Jacob. The meaning is not completely clear to linguists, but the context indicates that *Israel* connotes one who prevails with God, or has power with God. It may mean being a soldier for God. The descendants of Jacob are literally the house of Israel and are primarily the posterity of Jacob's twelve sons. This posterity came to be known as the covenant people of the Lord because Jacob was a prophet and received every aspect of the covenant that had been given to his grandfather Abraham.

A few scriptures will quickly give an account of how the covenant that God made with Abraham was continued through his generations. The Abrahamic covenant is introduced in Genesis 17:1–17 and includes, among other things, a promise of a numerous posterity, a land inheritance, and a declaration that all the nations of the earth were to be blessed through Abraham's posterity. A more precise account of the provisions and stipulations of the covenant is given in Abraham 2:8–11 and shows that it also included obtaining the holy priesthood and a promise that the literal (biological) seed of Abraham's body would be natural heirs of that priesthood, having a right to bear the priesthood by virtue of their lineage, if they are worthy. Furthermore, persons who are not biologically descended from Abraham but who obey the gospel of Jesus Christ could be adopted into the family. It was also declared that it would be Abraham's seed who would carry the priesthood, and the gospel of Christ, and the name of the Lord throughout the whole world from that time forth.

"My name is Jehovah, and I know the end from the beginning; therefore my hand shall be over thee.

"And I will make of thee a great nation, and I will bless thee above measure, and make thy name great among all nations, and thou shalt be a blessing unto thy seed after thee, that in their hands they shall bear this ministry and Priesthood unto all nations;

"And I will bless them through thy name; for as many as receive this Gospel shall be called after thy name, and shall be accounted thy seed, and shall rise up and bless thee, as their father;

"And I will bless them that bless thee, and curse them that curse thee; and in thee (that is, in thy Priesthood) and in thy seed (that is, thy Priesthood), for I give unto thee a promise that this right shall continue in thee, and in thy seed after thee (that is to say, the literal seed, or the seed of the body) shall all the families of the earth be blessed, even with the blessings of the gospel, which are the blessings of salvation, even of life eternal" (Abraham 2:8–11).

The significance of the Abrahamic covenant is that it is centered in Jesus Christ, the Messiah, the Holy One of Israel. The identical covenant made with Abraham, with all of its provisions, was passed on to Isaac (Genesis 17:19–21; 26:1–5) and later to Jacob (Genesis 28:10–17). Although the Bible does not say it, we know that all of the ancient patriarchs were baptized, received the Holy Ghost, and were ordained to the priesthood.[2] Thus, all who receive the covenant at any time must obey the same ordinances. In every instance it was stated that through the seed of Abraham, Isaac, and Jacob, all families of the earth would be blessed. Something about that covenant was desirable and would benefit all peoples, even those outside the biological family.

THE ROLE OF ISRAEL

ALL FAMILIES OF THE EARTH WILL BE BLESSED THROUGH ABRAHAM

The promise that all the people of the earth shall be blessed through Abraham's posterity is fulfilled in at least three ways. The ultimate expression of the promise is in Jesus Christ, the Savior of the whole world. The work of the Messiah is the reason the covenant was given. He conquered death for all mankind, so that every man, woman, and child shall rise from the grave with everlasting life. That is a free gift from the Redeemer. In addition, every person who repents and obeys the gospel of Jesus Christ, including the ordinances of baptism, the laying on of hands, and so on, will be ransomed from the spiritual consequences of his or her own sins and be saved in the kingdom of God. All of that is possible only because Jesus Christ, the Son of God, the Holy One of Israel, the Messiah, was by divine decree a descendant of Abraham, and he made the Atonement for all the world and brought about the Resurrection. Every human being has been and will be greatly blessed by Jesus Christ, who was a child of Mary, who was a descendant of King David, who was of the tribe of Judah, who was the son of Jacob, who was the grandson of Abraham. Paul, in his letter to the Galatian members of the Church, uses the foregoing application to show that it was directly through Christ that all the families of the earth would be blessed, even benefiting the Galatians, who were not biologically of Israel but were Gentiles (see Galatians 3:14–16).

A second aspect of the promise is specified in Abraham 2:8–11, showing that Abraham's biological seed has a natural inherited right to the priesthood, the gospel, and the Abrahamic covenant, and this particular lineage also has the serious responsibility and privilege of taking the gospel of Jesus Christ to all nations of the earth. Thus through Abraham's ministry and the ministry of his descendants the name of the true God shall "be known in the earth forever" (Abraham 1:19).

A third aspect of the promise is that Abraham's seed, that is, the house of Israel, has been scattered throughout the world and has mixed itself through marriage with the other nations. This process has been going on for thousands of years, since the ten tribes were taken captive about 700 B.C. and the Jews were taken to Babylon about 600 B.C. Hence, in the last days, almost all peoples of the earth have the blood of Israel, in greater or lesser amounts, in their veins and are thereby heirs of the covenant.

THE GENTILES

Because it is impossible to read about Israel in the scriptures without encountering the word *Gentile,* a brief explanation of this term is necessary. *Gentile* first appears in the Bible at Genesis 10:5 to designate the descendants of Japheth the son of Noah. *Gentile* is a Hebrew word meaning "the nations," or more precisely, "the *other* people," they who are not of Abraham's lineage. Biblically speaking, to an Israelite, a Gentile was someone not biologically of Israel. To a Jew, a Gentile is someone not a Jew.

These two words, *Israel* and *Gentile,* began as biological identifications but have acquired cultural and political connotations as well. Therefore, a person with some Israelite blood could live in a nation that is politically non-Israelite and thus be considered a Gentile politically or culturally. Such is the thought expressed in Doctrine and Covenants 109:60, wherein the early Brethren (although actually having Israelite blood) are "identified with the gentiles." It has also become traditional in modern Christianity and in Judaism to call anyone a Gentile who is not Jewish. In a unique manner the Book of Mormon uses *Gentile* to identify those nations who are neither Jewish nor descendants of Lehi. Thus in the Book of Mormon the European and North American peoples are identified as Gentiles—meaning "the other people." We know from patriarchal blessings and other revelations that Church members from Europe and North America have much of the blood of Israel in their veins (see, for example, D&C 86:8–10), but their Israelite connection and identity is not evident except by revelation. Thus in the twentieth century the identification of Israel and of Gentile is not as easy nor as simple as it was in the earlier stages of the world, because both terms, which began as biological distinctions, have acquired cultural, political, geographical, and racial meanings. These terms have to be identified in the context wherein each is used.

SPECIAL BLESSINGS FOR ISRAEL

A discussion of the house of Israel would not be adequate without attention to the question: "Are there special blessings for Israel that others do not have?" The answer can best be found in the scriptures. Peter discovered by revelation and by experience with Cornelius that "God is no respecter of persons: but in every nation he that feareth him, and worketh righteousness is accepted with him" (Acts 10:34–35). And Nephi wrote, "Behold, the Lord esteemeth all flesh in one; he that is righteous is favored of God" (1 Nephi 17:35). Nephi also said that the Lord God "doeth that which is good among the children of men; . . . and he inviteth them all to come unto him and partake of his goodness; and he denieth none that come unto him, black and white, bond and free, male and female; and he remembereth the heathen; and all are alike unto God, both Jew and Gentile" (2 Nephi 26:33). And Paul told the Athenians on Mars Hill that God "hath made of one blood all nations of men" (Acts 17:26).

If we were to consider only the foregoing passages, it would indeed seem that there is no difference whatever between Israel and all other peoples. But to stop at this point would be to stop short of recognizing other things that have been revealed concerning the role of Israel in bringing about the Lord's purposes in the earth.

We noted earlier that the Lord promised Abraham that all who were not of his biological seed but who accepted the gospel of Christ would be counted as his seed and rise up and bless Abraham as their father. They would also become heirs of the promises given in the Abrahamic covenant (Abraham 2:10; see also Galatians 3:27, 29). The very nature of such a promise indicates that there must be some kind of favored status in being of Abraham's family; otherwise, why would others (and especially the righteous) be adopted in? Moreover, when Paul spoke of "one blood" for all nations, he knew that the matter was not so simple and one-dimensional and that there were other factors to be considered: again, for emphasis and for convenience, the "God that made the world and all things therein, seeing that he is Lord of heaven and earth, dwelleth not in temples made with hands; neither is worshipped with men's hands, as though he needed any thing, seeing he giveth to all life, and breath, and all things; and hath made of one blood all nations of men for to dwell on all the face of the earth, and hath determined the times before appointed, and the bounds of their habitation" (Acts 17:24–26).

There must be some reason why Paul pointed out that God, who made all men, also "determined the times before appointed" and "set the bounds of their habitation." This passage points toward a premortal appointment, or at least a premortal decision, for mankind and is the basis for the doctrine of election. It also is a reminder of Moses' declaration that the arrangement of the nations of mankind on the earth was done by the Lord himself with consideration for the number there would be of the children of Israel: "When the most High divided to the nations their inheritance, when he separated the sons of Adam, he set the bounds of the people according to the number of the children of Israel. For the Lord's portion is his people; Jacob is the lot of his inheritance" (Deuteronomy 32:8–9).

The message of these passages from Paul and Moses is that the particular construct of the nations as to time, place, and race is the Lord's doing, based upon a premortal knowledge and determination of how many persons there would be of each race, and so on. An acceptance of this truth gives the Lord a role in the developments of history and leads one to believe that life is not left to mere chance.

We further note Paul's words in Romans 3:1–2, as recorded in the Joseph Smith Translation: "What advantage then hath the Jew over the Gentile? or what profit of circumcision, who is not a Jew from the heart? But he who is a Jew from the heart, I say hath much every way; chiefly, because that unto them were committed the oracles of God." Unbelieving Jews had no particular advantage for salvation, but the Jews who did believe had an advantage because to them had been given the "oracles of God" (priesthood, gospel ordinances, covenants, etc.). The Gentiles could have those same blessings and were invited to join in, but they had to get them from the Jews, because the Jews, being of Israel, were literal descendants of Abraham and natural heirs to the covenant and so had the blessings first. It is a matter of the Lord's timetable. As Paul also said, "To the Jew first, and also to the Greek [Gentile]" (Romans 1:16; see also 2:9–10). Whenever Gentiles did come into the gospel by baptism, confirmation, and so forth, they were not to remain Gentiles but were to become Israel.

An interesting working demonstration of this principle as it concerns Israel and the Gentiles is seen in the ministry of Jesus in the Holy Land, a land of varied racial backgrounds. While Jesus was in the vicinity of Tyre and Sidon (which are in Phoenicia) a non-Israelite woman (Mark 7:26 says she was Greek) approached him, desiring a blessing for her afflicted daughter. The account in Matthew 15:22–28 is as follows:

"And, behold, a woman of Canaan came out of the same coasts, and cried unto him, saying, Have mercy on me, O Lord, thou Son of David; my daughter is grievously vexed with a devil.

"But he answered her not a word. And his disciples came and besought him, saying, Send her away; for she crieth after us.

"But he answered and said, I am not sent but unto the lost sheep of the house of Israel.

"Then came she and worshipped him, saying, Lord, help me. "But he answered and said, It is not meet to take the children's bread, and to cast it to dogs.

"And she said, Truth, Lord: yet the dogs eat of the crumbs which fall from their masters' table.

"Then Jesus answered and said unto her, O woman, great is thy faith: be it unto thee even as thou wilt. And her daughter was made whole from that very hour."

Jesus did not at first respond to the woman except to ignore her, and when his disciples pressed him to do something about the situation, he told them that he was sent only to the house of Israel, of which she was not (vv. 23–24). Then, when she approached Jesus the second time, he said, in effect, it is not your time; now is the time for the "bread" to be given to the children of Israel. (Bread in this instance represents the blessings of the gospel which Jesus was able to give.) When the woman acknowledged the fact and was willing to eat only the crumbs, he gave her the blessing because of her faith. This event could not have taken place in the way that it did, and most likely this account of it would never have been entered into the record, had it not demonstrated that Jesus' personal ministry on earth was limited to those of biological Israel. We know that the long-term effects of Jesus' atonement are given to all mankind of all races, but we cannot overlook the fact that his personal contact was by his own choice almost exclusively with those of Israelite blood.

There is, moreover, much additional evidence bearing on this matter from latter-day revelation. Readers of the Book of Mormon know that the "other sheep" of whom Jesus spoke (John 10:16) were the Nephites and Lamanites in the Western Hemisphere. Jesus explained that truth in 3 Nephi 15:12–21 and then announced a significant doctrinal concept that sheds much light upon the subject of Israelite/Gentile privileges. We read in 3 Nephi 15 that the Jews in Palestine did not understand who the "other sheep" were because they did not know the rules and procedures that governed the Lord's ministry. As a consequence of their ignorance, the Jews incorrectly thought that the "other sheep" were the Gentiles. Let us now read carefully Jesus' precise words recorded in 3 Nephi 15:21–24:

"And verily I say unto you, that ye [Nephites] are they of whom I said: Other sheep I have which are not of this fold; them also I must bring, and they shall hear my voice; and there shall be one fold, and one shepherd.

"And they [the Jews] understood me not, for they supposed it had been the Gentiles; for they understood not that the Gentiles should be converted through their preaching.

"And they [the Jews] understood me not that I said they shall hear my voice; and they understood me not that the Gentiles should not at any time hear my voice—that I should not manifest myself unto them save it were by the Holy Ghost.

"But behold, ye [Nephites] have both heard my voice, and seen me; and ye are my sheep, and ye are numbered among those whom the Father hath given me."

This explanation by the Savior is tantamount to saying that the wonderful experience of the Lord's personal ministering, speaking audibly, showing his resurrected body, and doing all else that was recorded in 3 Nephi 11 through 28 could not and would not occur to a Gentile nation. When we accept this principle, we are given a key that unlocks a door of understanding to several other passages of scripture. For example, Jesus told the Nephites that after he left them he would go personally to the lost tribes of Israel, show them his body, and let them see him and hear his voice (3 Nephi 16:1–3; 17:4). The lost tribes, being Israelites, would be granted the same type of glorious experience as were the Nephites. Still further, we learn from Matthew 28:10, 16–18 and 1 Corinthians 15:6 that Jesus, after his resurrection, appeared in Galilee to more than five hundred persons in a group, and they saw him and heard his voice. Of course, they were Israelites. To the three major branches of scattered Israel—the Jews, the Nephites, and the lost tribes—Jesus appeared publicly after his resurrection, showed them his body, and spoke with them. He will also appear personally to the Jews on the Mount of Olives in the future (D&C 45:48–53; Zechariah 12:10; 13:6). According to the Lord's own explanation such events are not available to Gentile nations. If we believe the scriptures, we see that both before and after his resurrection, Jesus regarded his personal ministry to be primarily among those who were biological Israel.

The ancient Jews are not the only ones who have misunderstood Jesus' statement about the "other sheep." One who does not know the principles that govern such things is likely to make the same mistake of interpretation. For example, present-day biblical scholars who do not have the key of interpretation provided by Jesus in the Book of Mormon have thought that the "other sheep" were the

Gentiles. That was the conclusion of the great British theologian F. F. Bruce[3] and the well-known and often-quoted J. R. Dummelow.[4]

Further evidence of the principles that govern the Lord's ministry is seen in the story of Cornelius, a Roman and thus a Gentile, to whom an angel appeared and told him to send for Peter, who would teach him the gospel (Acts 10:1–6). In the ensuing meeting the Holy Ghost came upon Cornelius and his family of Gentiles, and they were baptized forthwith. In contrast, the Lord himself appeared to Paul, a Jew, on the road to Damascus (Acts 9:1–6). These two incidents illustrate the Israelite/Gentile privileges that we have examined from the scriptures.

The principle that Jesus manifests himself to Gentile nations only through the Holy Ghost is alluded to in 1 Nephi 10:11, which states that after Jesus was risen from the dead, he would "make himself manifest, by the Holy Ghost, unto the Gentiles." Nothing is said in this passage about a personal visit to the Gentiles. When we apply Jesus' explanation of 3 Nephi 15, we can see why: there isn't going to be any such visit. If we as Latter-day Saints do not accept the information on this matter that is available to us from both the Bible and the Book of Mormon, then we are like the Jews and the non-LDS scholars who also have not understood this principle.

Perhaps another illustration is Joseph Smith's vision in the grove when the Lord appeared personally to the Prophet. Joseph Smith both saw him and heard his voice. Even if we did not know it from other scriptures, we could confidently conclude that Joseph Smith is therefore a biological Israelite, for otherwise the First Vision could not have happened as it did.

The question that introduced this discussion is whether an Israelite has any advantages or blessing over one not of Israel. It seems to be so, for the scriptures speak of blessings and privileges and responsibilities in the Lord's timetable that favor those who are of Israel. So the answer is yes. In the ultimate sense, however, in the final judgment, those of all nations will be saved precisely by how well they obeyed the gospel of Jesus Christ, and in this way all are equal. But the way by which the gospel is brought to earth, to whom it is first revealed, and the timetable and sequence by which it is disseminated and administered among the nations shows a priority for those of Israelite lineage. The Gentiles will hear the gospel and receive the ordinances and the Abrahamic covenant from the preaching of Israelite prophets. That is a consequence no doubt determined by the Lord in our premortal state.

We must not overlook the important fact that when a Gentile joins the Church, he or she is adopted into the house of Israel by baptism and by the workings of the Holy Ghost and so becomes an Israelite. Such individuals may then receive a personal visit (the Second Comforter) from the Lord as would any natural Israelite. The Prophet Joseph Smith spoke of the adoptive process thus:

"[The Holy Ghost] is more powerful in expanding the mind, enlightening the understanding, and storing the intellect with present knowledge, of a man who is of the literal seed of Abraham, than one that is a Gentile, though it may not have half as much visible effect upon the body; for as the Holy Ghost falls upon one of the literal seed of Abraham, it is calm and serene; and his whole soul and body are only exercised by the pure spirit of intelligence; while the effect of the Holy Ghost upon a Gentile, is to purge out the old blood, and make him actually of the seed of Abraham. That man that has none of the blood of Abraham (naturally) must have a new creation by the Holy Ghost. In such a case, there may be more of a powerful effect upon the body, and visible to the eye, than upon an Israelite, while the Israelite at first might be far before the Gentile in pure intelligence."[5]

Whatever else this explanation by the Prophet may mean, it clearly distinguishes between the natural inheritance of an Israelite and that of a Gentile, while at the same time it does not prohibit the non-Israelite from receiving the promised blessing.

LITERAL OR FIGURATIVE INTERPRETATION?

The most compact and yet detailed treatment in scripture of the scattering, gathering, and restoration of Israel is the allegory of Zenos (Jacob 5) in which Israel is a tame olive tree and the Gentiles a wild olive tree. The scattering, gathering, and adoption are accomplished by cutting off branches of the natural tree and replanting them in distant lands. The wild branches are adopted through being grafted into the "mother" tree. Even the tame branches are grafted back into the original trunk of Israel, signifying its centrality. All this activity indicates a long-term, worldwide project. Although exact historical dates and geographic places are not always definable in the allegory, the overall plan and method of operation are clear: the house of Israel is to be preserved as a people and blessed as they become fruitful in righteousness, and other lineages are able to partake by being grafted in, thus becoming Israelites themselves.

Although the process described in the allegory could be interpreted figuratively rather than literally, such would be out of synchronization with the rest of the Book of Mormon, which uses very definite language to convey a literal, down-to-earth meaning. Following are a few examples:

1. The allegory of Zenos uses different trees to represent Israel and the Gentiles, thus showing a uniqueness to Israel as the "tame" tree (Jacob 5:3–7).

2. Nephi said that in the last days the descendants of Lehi will learn that they are "natural branches" of the house of Israel (1 Nephi 15:12–16).

3. Nephi repeatedly emphasized that the scattering, gathering, and restoration of Israel were all literal, real, and tangible. He said those events would be "according to the flesh" (1 Nephi 22:2); "behold these things are temporal; for thus are the covenants of the Lord with our fathers; and it meaneth us in the days to come, and also all our brethren who are of the house of Israel" (1 Nephi 22:6). "It must needs be upon the face of this earth; and it cometh unto men according to the flesh" (1 Nephi 22:18; see also v. 27).

4. Jacob insisted that the promises of the Lord about the restoration of Israel were literal, that they were "according to the flesh"

(2 Nephi 10:2), and that Israel "shall be restored in the flesh, upon the earth, unto the lands of their inheritance" (2 Nephi 10:7). Jacob quoted the Lord as saying that He will fulfill the covenants He has made "that I will do unto them while they are in the flesh" (2 Nephi 10:15; see also v. 17).

5. The prophet Mormon, speaking to Lehi's descendants who would read the Book of Mormon in the last days, listed several things they ought to know for the salvation of their souls. The first thing he listed was "Know ye that ye are of the house of Israel" (Mormon 7:2). Mormon must have thought that being of Israel was important, for he wrote to the Gentiles that they needed to repent and believe in Jesus Christ, so that they could be "numbered with my people who are of the house of Israel" (3 Nephi 30:2).

6. The Book of Mormon often repeats the statement that by accepting Christ the Gentiles can be "numbered among the house of Israel" (1 Nephi 14:2; see also 15:13–15; 2 Nephi 10:18; 3 Nephi 16:13; 21:6).

Surely such statements from the Book of Mormon are persuasive that the prophecies of a restoration of Israel in the latter days are literal and real, not merely symbolic and figurative. If the membership of the Church today is not biological Israel, then a *restoration* has not occurred, because *restoration* means "bringing something back which once was in place." The meaning of *restoration* should serve as a guide and a control in our accepting the literal meaning of the scriptures.

THE RESTORATION OF ALL THINGS

It is a cardinal doctrine of the Church that the God of heaven has established the dispensation of the fulness of times through the Prophet Joseph Smith and his successors. It is a time in which everything will be restored and accomplished that was spoken of by all the holy prophets since the world began (Acts 3:21). The fulness of times is the dispensation of all dispensations; it is a time of restoration, a time of fruition, accomplishment, completion, and fulfillment of the Lord's purposes for the redemption of mankind and the earth. The fulness of times began with the First Vision of Joseph Smith and shall continue through the Millennium and on to the time when the earth is made celestial. The fact of its being the last dispensation may mean it will never end. As rivers flow into the sea, all dispensations flow into the dispensation of the fulness of times.

The concept of the restoration of all things is far more extensive than one might at first suppose. It includes a restoration of priesthood power, of the true Church organization, of ancient ordinances and covenants, and of much more. All of these are necessary to bring about the other things that are to be restored. The plan of God which the ancient prophets knew is the same plan that is to bring about the final conditions of redemption. The concept of restoration as taught in the Book of Mormon is holistic and worldwide and includes, among other things, the resurrection of the body, the Judgment, and the redemption of the earth and everything that pertains to the earth (see Alma 40:22–26; 41:1–15). This restoration includes the gathering together and bringing home of the scattered tribes of Israel.

The scriptures compare the gathering of Israel and the resurrection of the body. Through the process of death the elements of the physical body are scattered in the dust, yet these elements shall come together again and the body shall be restored to the spirit in the Resurrection. Even so will the scattered remnants of Israel be restored to the "true church and fold of God" and be "gathered home" to the lands the Lord has given them. We see this parallel spoken by Jacob in 2 Nephi 9:1–4:

"And now, my beloved brethren, I have read these things that ye might know concerning the covenants of the Lord that he has covenanted with all the house of Israel—

"That he has spoken unto the Jews, by the mouth of his holy prophets, even from the beginning down, from generation to generation, until the time comes that they shall be restored to the true church and fold of God; when they shall be gathered home to the lands of their inheritance, and shall be established in all their lands of promise. . . .

"For I know that ye have searched much, many of you, to know of things to come; wherefore I know that ye know that our flesh must waste away and die; nevertheless, in our bodies we shall see God."

The comparison of reclaiming the body in the Resurrection with reclaiming the scattered remnants of Israel and gathering them to their homeland is quite clear in the foregoing passage. The resurrection of the body and its restoration to the spirit—each body to its own spirit, the same spirit that inhabited the body in mortality—is real, authentic, individual, and literal. The literal and authentic gathering and restoration of Israel to their own lands is just as real. Such a comparison can hardly be missed in Ezekiel 37:12: "I will open your graves, and cause you to come up out of your graves, and bring you into the land of Israel."

In describing what was necessary to establish the dispensation of the fulness of times, the Prophet Joseph Smith wrote: "It is necessary in the ushering in of the dispensation of the fulness of times, which dispensation is now beginning to usher in, that a whole and complete and perfect union, and welding together of dispensations, and keys, and powers, and glories should take place, and be revealed from the days of Adam even to the present time. And not only this, but those things which never have been revealed from the foundation of the world, but have been kept hid from the wise and prudent, shall be revealed unto babes and sucklings in this, the dispensation of the fulness of times" (D&C 128:18).

To further delineate what actually took place in the founding of this last dispensation, the Prophet told of "divers angels, from Michael or Adam down to the present time, all declaring their dispensation, their rights, their keys, their honors, their majesty and glory, and the power of their priesthood; giving line upon line, precept upon precept;

here a little, and there a little; giving us consolation by holding forth that which is to come, confirming our hope!" (D&C 128:21).

Among the great angels who came to the Prophet Joseph and Oliver Cowdery to bestow the necessary keys and to inaugurate the special work of the last days were Moses and Elias, who conferred the keys for the gathering of Israel and the gospel (covenant) of Abraham. That was done on 3 April 1836, in the Kirtland Temple, and the report reads as follows: "Moses appeared before us, and committed unto us the keys of the gathering of Israel from the four parts of the earth, and the leading of the ten tribes from the land of the north. After this, Elias appeared, and committed the dispensation of the gospel of Abraham, saying that in us and our seed all generations after us should be blessed" (D&C 110:11–12).

Thus to the Prophet Joseph were given the keys, and therefore today in the hands of the First Presidency and the Twelve rest those same keys and the authority and the commission for gathering and restoring the house of Israel. The restoration would not be complete if the keys for gathering Israel and the keys for Abraham's covenant had not been given along with the keys of sealing and all other keys of the fulness of times. That these keys were restored so dramatically by the personal ministration of Moses himself and Elias shows that there is something eternally significant and very necessary about them.

The gathering and restoration of Israel are the work of Jesus Christ. It was for this very purpose that the covenant was given to Abraham in the first place. That was certainly the understanding of Nephi and Jacob. It is eye-opening to note Nephi's explanation of why he quoted so much of Isaiah: "I did read many things unto them which were written in the books of Moses; but that I might more fully persuade them to believe in the Lord their Redeemer I did read unto them that which was written by the prophet Isaiah" (1 Nephi 19:23). The passages of Isaiah cited by Nephi all have to do with the restoration and future glory of Israel (Isaiah 48–49; 2–14). Does not this fact inform us that Nephi believed the redemption of Israel to be the work of Jesus Christ?

For exactly the same reason we must realize that scattered Israel will be restored to its ancient homeland and live in peace and security only when Israel accepts and obeys the gospel of Jesus Christ, including the ordinances of baptism, the laying on of hands, and so forth. Anything less would contradict the purpose and nature of the Abrahamic covenant.

GATHERING AND RESTORATION ARE NOT INTERCHANGEABLE TERMS

Although we customarily speak of the gathering of Israel in an all-inclusive way, it is clear, with a little thought, that gathering alone is not adequate. A group of Israelites could be gathered into a geographic area and yet not be restored in a gospel sense. *Restoration* is more comprehensive than *gathering*. A complete restoration would activate every aspect of the Abrahamic covenant: a gathering to a promised land, the priesthood, the gospel, the ordinances, temples, consecration, stewardship, and the rest of the entire plan of the Lord, including security in the land.

The present-day nation of Israel is a case of gathering without restoration. Upwards of three million people of Jewish descent are situated in the ancient homeland of their ancestors, but they are without the kingdom of God, the priesthood, the ancient covenant, and all that those entail; consequently, they are also without physical security. All that is necessary will come in its time, but the conditions for a peaceful occupation of the land have been established by the Lord and require that the inhabitants must "hearken to my voice" (Abraham 2:6), which means to accept and live by the gospel of Jesus Christ. That day has not yet arrived in the Holy Land, but a "gathering" of a preliminary sort has been going on there for many years.

ISRAEL IN LATTER-DAY SAINT HYMNS

The hopes, aspirations, and religious beliefs of a people are generally found in their music. What people sing about reflects what they feel. In *Hymns of The Church of Jesus Christ of Latter-day Saints,* I discovered four hymns with the word *Israel* in the title: "Redeemer of Israel" (no. 6); "Israel, Israel, God Is Calling" (no. 7); "Hope of Israel" (no. 259); and "Ye Elders of Israel" (no. 319).[6] Furthermore, at least thirty-nine hymns contain expressions about the gathering of Israel, the mission of Israel, the role of Israel in building Zion in the latter days, and other related topics. Frequently, the hymns call for Israel to believe the gospel of Jesus Christ and come "home" from her long dispersion.

The hymns also speak of the descendants of Judah, and of Joseph, and of Ephraim, and of the "remnant" of Israel. Likewise the Lord Jesus Christ is often identified as the "God of Israel." The concept of the restoration of Israel and Israel's glorious future permeates the message of those thirty-nine hymns. The word *Gentile* also occurs a number of times, sometimes in a less favorable context, although several hymns speak of the Gentiles bringing their silver and gold to assist in building Zion and of the Gentiles finding peace through accepting the gospel of Christ.

"The Morning Breaks" (no. 1) speaks of "The dawning of a brighter day" which now has arrived and says that "Zion's light is bursting forth." "The Gentile fulness now comes in, / And Israel's blessings are at hand. / Lo, Judah's remnant . . . / Shall in their promised Canaan stand."

The Gentiles, too, can "turn and live" if they obey Jehovah, who is making bare his mighty arm to receive "His covenant people."

"Now Let Us Rejoice" (no. 3) expresses the belief that now is the day of salvation. The last days are characterized by "trouble and gloom" but the gospel brings hope and joy. All God's promises will be fulfilled, and "Jesus will say to all Israel, 'Come home.'"

"Israel, Israel, God Is Calling" (no. 7) declares, "Israel, Israel, God is speaking / Hear your great Deliverer's voice! / Now a glorious morn is breaking / For the people of his choice. / Come to Zion, . . . / And within her walls rejoice."

"An Angel from on High" (no. 13) refers to the Book of

Mormon, which "speaks of Joseph's seed / And makes the remnant known / Of nations long since dead, / Who once had dwelt alone. / . . . / Lo! Israel filled with joy / Shall now be gathered home."

"Now We'll Sing with One Accord" (no. 25) testifies that the Lord has raised up the Prophet Joseph Smith and brought forth the Book of Mormon, the priesthood, and the covenant so that the righteous can "gather home." It specifically mentions that the covenant and the gathering are offered to both Jew and Gentile.

"Like Ten Thousand Legions Marching" (no. 253) emphasizes the missionary effort of the last days, which is conducted by many youthful persons who are "sons of Joseph, Israel's band." They are the "seed of Abraham and Jacob."

"Ye Elders of Israel" (no. 319) tells of preaching the gospel in all the world, gathering the wheat at the harvest, and bringing it to Zion, the place of rest. The chorus, which is sung after each stanza, declares: "O Babylon, O Babylon, we bid thee farewell; / We're going to the mountains of Ephraim to dwell."

"Come, All Ye Sons of God" (no. 322) addresses "all ye sons of God who have received the priesthood; / Go spread the gospel wide and gather in his people. / The latter-day work has begun, / To gather scattered Israel in, / And bring them back to Zion to praise the Lamb." Later verses speak of the gathering of Israel as the fulfillment of the words of the prophets, with great joy and blessings to follow.

"Go, Ye Messengers of Heaven" (no. 327) speaks of the divinely chosen messengers of the Lord who will go to "island, vale, and mountain" to "gather out the sons of Jacob / To possess the promised land."

Many other hymns refer directly or allude to Abraham, Israel, the noble birthright, David's seed, the Jews, the Lamanites, the Gentiles, Old Jerusalem, New Jerusalem, the promised land, and so on (including nos. 2, 5, 8, 16, 17, 32, 34, 35, 38, 39, 40, 41, 42, 50, 54, 59, 63, 64, 71, 74, 112, 211, 255, 259, 262, 265, 299).

Another hymn of the Restoration that is not in the 1985 hymnbook is "The Seer, Joseph, the Seer," written by Elder John Taylor in memory of Joseph Smith, whom it designates as being of "noble seed."[7] That designation evidently refers to his lineal descent through Ephraim.

Isaiah, the great prophet whose writings we are commanded to search and who "spake as touching all things concerning . . . the house of Israel" and the Gentiles (3 Nephi 23:2), said that the redeemed of the Lord shall come to Zion with songs of everlasting joy (Isaiah 35:10; 51:11). With the realization that the Latter-day Saints are of Israel comes the recognition that the very hymns we have discussed may be among those to which Isaiah referred.

QUESTIONS FREQUENTLY ASKED
ABOUT LATTER-DAY ISRAEL

The scriptures and numerous statements of the Brethren bear upon aspects of the role of the house of Israel in the last days. Those sources help to answer many frequently asked questions about latter-day Israel.

Are Latter-day Saints literally descended from ancient Israel or are they members of the house of Israel only by adoption and "assignment" to a tribe?

As a teacher in the Church Educational System for forty years, I have heard this question asked many times. Some passages of scripture pertaining to the subject of lineage are as follows:

Doctrine and Covenants 86:8–11. The Lord said to the leaders of the Church in 1832 that they had the priesthood because of "the lineage of your fathers" and because "ye are lawful heirs, according to the flesh"; furthermore, the priesthood must "remain through you and your lineage."

Doctrine and Covenants 96:7. John Johnson "is a descendant of Joseph and a partaker of the blessings of the promise made unto his fathers."

Doctrine and Covenants 132:30–31. The Lord told Joseph Smith that the promises made to Abraham were also his because he, Joseph, was of Abraham, and in this manner the promise is continued.

Doctrine and Covenants 113:6–8. Israel has a right to the priesthood because of lineage.

Abraham 2:11. Abraham's descendants (seed) have the right to have the priesthood.

Elder Bruce R. McConkie vigorously answered the question this way: "We are literally of the seed of Abraham. Let's just drill it into ourselves! We are literally of the seed of Abraham. We are natural heirs according to the flesh. We are not adopted nor anything else. I don't know how there could be language more express than these revelations, 'natural heirs according to the flesh,' 'the literal seed of the body.' You see he [the Lord] just goes out of his way to make it literal. The literal seed of your body has the right to the priesthood and the gospel, and that is us. Now, granted that somebody can be adopted in but they are so few and far between up to now, that we can just about forget about them."[8]

Considering that the title page of the Book of Mormon says it will come forth "by way of the Gentile" and that Joseph Smith brought it forth, doesn't that mean that he and the other Church members are actually Gentiles?

Because *Gentile* means "the other people," a Gentile in the Book of Mormon sense can be someone who is not of Lehi's lineage and who is not a Jew. In that sense the United States is called a mighty Gentile nation in the land of promise (1 Nephi 22:7), even though we know there is a lot of Israelite blood in the veins of the people. This distinction is clarified in Doctrine and Covenants 109:60, which says that the Church is "identified with the Gentiles." Thus the title page of the Book of Mormon, which says that the Book of Mormon will "come forth by way of the Gentile," means that neither the Nephites nor the Lamanites nor the Jews will bring it to light.

We know from scripture that Joseph Smith was a descendant of

Joseph who was sold into Egypt (2 Nephi 3:6–16). Joseph Smith was a Gentile of Israelite blood lineage, and so are a lot of other people: the Smiths, the Cowderys, the Youngs, the Kimballs, the Richardses, the Woodruffs, the Goddards, the Taylors, the Snows, the Whitneys, the Pratts, and other early families in the Church were descended from common ancestors and thus were genealogically related. In other words, Joseph Smith was of the same bloodlines as Brigham Young, Heber C. Kimball, John Taylor, Wilford Woodruff, Lorenzo Snow, Heber J. Grant, Harold B. Lee and many others. Moreover, Joseph Smith is linked genealogically with Grover Cleveland, Ulysses S. Grant, Patrick Henry, Winston Churchill, and other prominent persons. Because Joseph Smith was biologically of Ephraim, so are they.

Leaders of the Church have had something to say about Joseph Smith's lineage. President Brigham Young said: "It was decreed in the counsels of eternity, long before the foundations of the earth were laid, that he [Joseph Smith] should be the man, in the last dispensation of this world, to bring forth the word of God to the people, and receive the fulness of the keys and power of the Priesthood of the Son of God. The Lord had his eye upon him, and upon his father, and upon his father's father, and upon their progenitors clear back to Abraham, and from Abraham to the flood, and from the flood to Enoch, and from Enoch to Adam. He has watched that family and that blood as it has circulated from its fountain to the birth of that man."[9]

President Young also said: "Joseph Smith, junior, was foreordained to come through the loins of Abraham, Isaac, Jacob, Joseph, and so on down through the Prophets and Apostles; and thus he came forth in the last days to be a minister of salvation, and to hold the keys of the last dispensation of the fulness of times."[10]

And President Young further declared: "You have heard Joseph say that the people did not know him; he had his eyes on the subject of blood relation. Some have supposed that he meant Spirit, but it was the blood relation. This is it that he referred to. . . . He had the right and the power and was the legal heir to the blood that has been on the earth and has come down through lineage. The union of various ancestors kept the blood pure. . . . That blood has been preserved and has been brought down from father to son, and our Heavenly Father has been watching it all the time."[11]

Even if Joseph Smith and the early Saints were of Joseph, does that mean that the Church membership today is still primarily of that lineage?

President Brigham Young spoke a great deal about the lineage of the Latter-day Saints. In 1855 he said: "Ephraim has become mixed with all the nations of the earth, and it is Ephraim that is gathering together.

"It is Ephraim that I have been searching for all the days of my preaching, and that is the blood which ran in my veins when I embraced the Gospel. If there are any of the other tribes of Israel mixed with the Gentiles we are also searching for them. Though the Gentiles are cut off, do not suppose that we are not going to preach the Gospel among the Gentile nations, for they are mingled with the house of Israel, and when we send to the nations we do not seek for the Gentiles, because they are disobedient and rebellious. We want the blood of Jacob, and that of this father Isaac and Abraham, which runs in the veins of the people. There is a particle of it here, and another there, blessing the nations as predicted. . . .

" . . . It is the house of Israel we are after, and we care not whether they come from the east, the west, the north or the south; from China, Russia, England, California, North or South America, or some other locality; and it is the very lad on whom father Jacob laid his hands, that will save the house of Israel. The Book of Mormon came to Ephraim, for Joseph Smith was a pure Ephraimite, and the Book of Mormon was revealed to him, and while he lived he made it his business to search for those who believed the Gospel."[12]

The years since President Young's statement have shown that it is indeed among people from China, England, North and South America, and many other countries where Israel has been found.

President Young told the Latter-day Saints in 1859 that they had a mission similar to that of Joseph of old because they were Joseph's seed: "[God] foreknew what Joseph, who was sold into Egypt, would do. Joseph was foreordained to be the temporal saviour of his father's house, and the seed of Joseph are ordained to be the spiritual and temporal saviours of all the house of Israel in the latter days. Joseph's seed has mixed itself with all the seed of man upon the face of the whole earth. The great majority of those who are now before me are the descendants of that Joseph who was sold."[13]

The special mission of Joseph's seed to nourish the remainder of the family of Israel is also spoken of in a blessing that the patriarch Jacob gave to his son Joseph, as recorded in the Joseph Smith Translation of Genesis 48:8–11:

"Therefore, O my son, he hath blessed me in raising thee up to be a servant unto me, in saving my house from death;

"In delivering my people, thy brethren, from famine which was sore in the land; wherefore the God of thy fathers shall bless thee, and the fruit of thy loins, that they shall be blessed above thy brethren, and above thy father's house;

"For thou hast prevailed, and thy father's house hath bowed down unto thee, even as it was shown unto thee, before thou was sold into Egypt by the hands of thy brethren; wherefore thy brethren shall bow down unto thee, from generation to generation, unto the fruit of thy loins for ever;

"For thou shalt be a light unto my people, to deliver them in the days of their captivity, from bondage; and to bring salvation unto them, when they are altogether bowed down under sin."

This blessing was given to Joseph while he was in Egypt, before the Israelites became slaves to the Egyptians. The famine spoken of in verse 9 we are familiar with, but please note that the bondage spoken of in verse 11 cannot be the bondage of Egypt, for it was Moses who freed Israel from Egyptian bondage, and Moses was not a descendant of Joseph. The prophecy speaks of Joseph's seed delivering Israel from "the bondage of sin," so that must be a latter-day bondage of apostasy and false philosophy; Joseph's seed will rescue and reclaim many of the house of Israel from this apostasy by declaring the gospel of Jesus Christ among them.

That mission is also referred to in Genesis 49:24 in Jacob's blessing of Joseph, which includes the statement: "From thence is the shepherd, the stone of Israel." That passage may seem puzzling because Christ, the Shepherd, the Stone (D&C 50:49), was not of Joseph's lineage but of Judah's. Knowing the lineage of the Prophet Joseph Smith and most of the Latter-day Saints, however, we can see that through Joseph's lineage Christ and his gospel have been made manifest to the rest of Israel in the last days. There is harmony among all these passages and complete accord with President Young's statements.

In 1977 President Spencer W. Kimball proclaimed the blood descent from Joseph of present-day Church members: "The Lamanite is a chosen child of God, but he is not the only chosen one. There are many other good people including the Anglos, the French, the German, and the English, who are also of Ephraim and Manasseh. They, with the Lamanites, are also chosen people, and they are a remnant of Jacob. The Lamanite is not wholly and exclusively the remnant of Jacob which the Book of Mormon talks about. We are *all* of Israel! We are of Abraham and Isaac and Jacob and Joseph through Ephraim and Manasseh. We are *all of us* remnants of Jacob."[14]

Why the emphasis on Ephraim?

In the Church today it is a special time of Ephraim and Manasseh, the sons of Joseph. Ephraim was given the birthright in the house of Israel (1 Chronicles 5:1–2; Jeremiah 31:9), which is the right of presidency. It was necessary that he have the gospel first in this last dispensation, because he must teach it to all others. The Church today is growing more rapidly than ever before in this dispensation, but where are the converts coming from? Statistics published in 1989 show that from among the then most recent one million converts to the Church, approximately 65 percent had come from the countries of Mexico, Central and South America, and the Pacific Islands.[15] These are descendants of Lehi. Patriarchal blessings declare many of them to be of Manasseh (as was Lehi himself), whereas others are from Ephraim (as was Ishmael).[16]

Through the extensive scattering of Israel during the past twenty-seven hundred years, the house of Israel is now found among all nations. Nephi said that "the house of Israel, sooner or later, will be scattered upon all the face of the earth, and also among all nations" (1 Nephi 22:3). That means not only that they are situated all over the earth but also that they have intermarried with all peoples. It is likely, of course, that intermarriage has taken place more completely among some peoples than among others, so that all nations are not a uniform mixture.

Because the tribe of Ephraim has the birthright in Israel, it was and is Ephraim's responsibility to have the priesthood, the covenant of Abraham, and the fulness of the gospel of Jesus Christ first in the last days, which is the time of restoration. This responsibility requires Ephraim to extend that same covenant and priesthood to the other tribes of Israel and thus to the world. Moses referred to that privilege when he said that Joseph's family would prevail in Israel generation after generation and would "push the people together to the ends of the earth: and they are the ten thousands of Ephraim, and they are the thousands of Manasseh" (Deuteronomy 33:17). "Pushing together" sounds like a gathering. The Lord speaks of Ephraim's special situation in Doctrine and Covenants 133:34, where, after recounting the doctrine of the gathering, he says, "This is the blessing of the everlasting God upon the tribes of Israel, and the richer blessing upon the head of Ephraim and his fellows."

Church Patriarch Hyrum G. Smith, speaking in general conference on 7 April 1929, explained the role of Ephraim: "It is the policy and order of the Church at the present time to have at least one patriarch, who is authorized to bless the members of the stake, and in so doing, declare their lineage, in a similar way to the manner in which Jacob blessed his grandsons, and his own sons. At the present time in the Church the great majority of those receiving their blessings are declared to be of the house and lineage of Ephraim, while many others are designated as members of the house of Manasseh; but up to the present time we have discovered that those who are leaders in Israel, no matter where they come from, no matter what nation they have come out of, are of Ephraim; while the blood of Manasseh is found in the tribes and nations of the Indians of North and South America. They are great, they are wonderfully blessed, but Ephraim seems to prevail in the greater blessings, greater in responsibility, and in faithfulness to the Lord's work. And so people have wondered about it. Why do the patriarchs declare that most of us are of Ephraim?

"It is my testimony that 'today' is the day of Ephraim. It is the day which the Lord has set to fulfil his promises made in the times of the ancient patriarchs, when he said that he would scatter Israel to the four corners of the world, and that Ephraim should be scattered in all the nations, and then in the 'last days' be gathered out again. Many are being gathered out by our missionaries, as 'one of a family and two of a city'; and they are found here, gathered into a gathering place appointed of the Lord, and they are receiving his blessings. This is why so many of us are declared to be of Ephraim. If there were time I would like to speak further about our blessings. The Prophet Joseph Smith, was declared to be of this house of Joseph, a chosen vessel. . . .

" . . . the Prophet Joseph Smith was a prophet in very deed, the descendant of Joseph who was sold into Egypt, through the lineage of Ephraim, a promised vessel in the hands of the Lord."[17]

It is a matter of interest that Patriarch Hyrum G. Smith gave blessings to more than twenty-two thousand people, all of whom were of Ephraim, Manasseh, or Judah.[18]

What do patriarchs say about Israel in various countries?

There are representatives in the Church from all twelve tribes of Israel; however, most members are from Ephraim, many from Manasseh, and a few from Judah and the other tribes.

A list was prepared by Elder Mark E. Petersen of the Quorum of the Twelve Apostles to illustrate what lineages patriarchs have been declaring. The context of the list shows clearly that Elder Petersen regarded these as declarations of biological inheritance, not merely assignments to a tribe. Here are his words, showing the role of Joseph's seed in the Church today: "For example, three different patriarchs in Great Britain report that of their blessings, very few indeed show a lineage other than that of Ephraim. One of those patriarchs has given more than six hundred blessings, another five hundred, and the third more than three hundred. Each reports that of all his blessings, not more than half a dozen declare lineage other than of Ephraim.

"This clearly shows that Great Britain is a land of Ephraim. But the same thing may be said of other European countries. They too are Ephraim. Converts by the thousands have come from there. It is not expected, of course, that all of the millions in Europe will join the Church. The scripture says that the way is strait and narrow 'and few there be that find it.' (Matthew 7:14.) But those who do come are primarily of Ephraim. And Ephraim is a son of Joseph.

"Throughout the Polynesian islands and Latin America the blood of Manasseh is dominant.

"In Mexico, patriarchs report that 75 percent of the blessings indicate the lineage of Manasseh and 25 percent, of Ephraim. Only two or three blessings out of hundreds given mention any other tribe.

"In Peru one patriarch in a given period gave 95 blessings, of which 90 indicated the blood of Manasseh, 3 of Ephraim, and 2 of Abraham.

"Another patriarch in the same area gave 347 blessings in a given period, of which 122 were of Ephraim, 130 of Manasseh, 90 of Joseph, 2 of Asher, 2 of Benjamin, and 1 of Levi.

"Another patriarch in that land has given over nine hundred

blessings, of which 90 percent are of Manasseh and the rest of Ephraim, except for a half dozen referring to other tribes.

"In New Zealand virtually all of the Europeans are declared to be of Ephraim and the Polynesians of Manasseh, with a few declared simply to be of Joseph.

"In Tonga the patriarchs report that 75 percent of their blessings show a lineage of Manasseh and 25 percent of Ephraim. Out of many blessings given, only 4 were related to other tribes.

"It is interesting to see how the blessings occur in still other lands. In Hong Kong, out of 326 blessings, 323 were of Ephraim and 3 of Manasseh.

"In Taiwan, out of a group of 210 blessings, all were of Ephraim. In the Philippines every blessing given by the patriarchs there declared a lineage of Ephraim.

"In Japan, out of 2,641 blessings, 1,326 were shown to be of Joseph, 444 specifically of Ephraim, and 871 of Manasseh. No other tribes were mentioned.

"In Italy, out of 150 blessings, all were declared of Ephraim. No exceptions.

"In France one patriarch reported on 300 blessings of which 280 were of Ephraim and the rest of Manasseh except a few of Judah.

"Another French patriarch gave 94 blessings, all showing a line of Ephraim except one of Judah. A third French patriarch just beginning his work said that all of his blessings thus far showed the line of Ephraim.

"In Argentina, out of 100 blessings given, 66 were of Ephraim and 33 of Manasseh, with one from another tribe.

"Out of 100 blessings in Chile, 60 were of Ephraim and 40 of Manasseh. From 100 blessings given in Uruguay, 21 were of Ephraim, 76 were of Manasseh, and 3 from other tribes. In North America nearly all Indians are shown to be of Manasseh. The sifting of the blood of Joseph and his sons Ephraim and Manasseh to all parts of the world is nothing short of miraculous. And it is likewise obviously an act of Providence that the Latter-day Saints being

brought into the Church in all parts of the world are overwhelm-
ingly of the blood of Joseph.

"It is highly significant in the light of the prophecies concerning Joseph and his latter-day mission."[19]

*Why is a gathering necessary? Why cannot the Lord save the right-
eous individually wherever they are?*

The gathering and restoration of Israel is the work of Jesus
Christ; it is his work as the Savior and Redeemer. The Prophet
Joseph Smith declared that the gathering is a matter "of the greatest
importance" and "one of the most important points" of our faith.[20]
He explained that one main purpose of the gathering is so that
temples can be built in which necessary ordinances for the living
and the dead can be administered.[21] He also explained that the
gathering of the faithful has been an activity of all of the prophets
in every age of the world and that greater blessings can be achieved
through group, rather than individual, effort.[22] Furthermore, the
gathering is for the protection and preservation of the Saints in the
time that burning and destruction are sent forth upon the world (see
D&C 115:6).[23]

How long will it take to gather Israel in the last days?

The gathering began with the beginning of this last dispensation
and will continue through the Millennium. The gigantic proportions
of the gathering are startling. Jeremiah stated (16:14–21) that the
gathering of Israel in the last days will be so dramatic, extensive,
and miraculous that it will greatly overshadow the much smaller and
quicker rescue of Israel from Egypt by Moses. Moses led more than
one million Israelites out of Egypt; the gathering in the last days
could involve billions of people.

*What kind of individual traits or callings are found within the house
of Israel?*

Although each of the tribes has its own individuality, as noted in Jacob's blessings recorded in Genesis 49 and in Moses' blessing recorded in Deuteronomy 33, three seem to have particular callings in the last days: Judah, Levi, and Ephraim. The promise was that from Judah would come most of the kings of Israel, and King David received the assurance that Israel would never fail of a king from his line (see Genesis 49:8–10; 1 Chronicles 5:2; Micah 5:2; 2 Samuel 7:13; Psalms 89:4; 132:11–12, 17; Jeremiah 33:15). That promise has been perfectly fulfilled in Jesus Christ as the King of kings.

The tribe of Levi, and more particularly the sons of Aaron, were given a priesthood "throughout all their generations" (D&C 84:18) to minister in temporal things and arrange the land inheritances both anciently and in the fulness of times (D&C 58:17; 68:14–21).[24] That is the work of the bishop. Thus far in the present dispensation the Lord has not identified a person of Aaron's lineage to fill the office.

The tribe of Ephraim was given the birthright and the keys of presidency in Israel, a calling fully manifested in the person of the Prophet Joseph Smith and his successors.

In the restoration of all things we shall no doubt see the complete fulfillment of all these ancient appointments.

What is the situation of persons of other tribes of Israel who come into the Church now, during the special time of Ephraim and Manasseh?

Help in answering this question may be found in the Prophet Joseph's Smith answer to a question Elder Orson Hyde asked him in 1840 about whether a converted Jew should gather to Jerusalem or to Zion in America. The Prophet declared that such are to come to Zion.[25] It would seem, therefore, that individuals of other tribes who have the courage and inspiration to join the Church in our day shall inherit the blessings of Ephraim, which is the richer blessing (see D&C 133:34).

Are other descendants of Abraham, who are not of Isaac and Jacob,
also heirs of the blessings of Abraham?

Elder Bruce R. McConkie responded to this question thus: "Yes.
. . . I think every one of Abraham's descendants would have it. Now,
there is this statement: 'In Isaac shall thy seed be called' [Genesis
21:12; see also 17:19], where one of Abraham's descendants is
involved. That is, there were special blessings to him. But the language here is that all of Abraham's descendants are going to have
the right to the priesthood. Everybody that was married to him in
celestial marriage, and that was Hagar and all the rest, . . .[includ-
ing] Keturah. They all are inheritors of the blessings of Abraham."[26]
We remember also that Moses received the priesthood from
Jethro, his father-in-law, who was apparently not an Israelite but a
Midianite (D&C 84:6–7; Exodus 3:1). Whether Jethro was a
descendant of Abraham is not clear, but he was certainly not an
Israelite.

In the early days of the Church there was considerable emphasis on
gathering. Has that emphasis ended?

The gathering develops in various phases. In the days of Joseph
Smith, gathering was centered on Missouri and the site for the New
Jerusalem. Later it was focused on the Rocky Mountains. The Holy
Land in the Near East is also a place for gathering. Today converts
stay in their home countries and gather to stakes of Zion. Surely
other phases will be inaugurated in their time. Missouri is still the
place of the New Jerusalem, and the gathering to the Old Jerusalem
has hardly even begun, at least according to the description in Ether
13:1–12.

IN THE PATHWAY TO ETERNAL FAME

Ancient Israel was scattered because of willful disobedience to
the commandments of the God of Israel as delivered by holy
prophets. That God was Jehovah, who is also Jesus Christ. To be
scattered was a punishment to Israel, but it has been a blessing to

the nations because it has infused the natural inheritance to the priesthood and the covenant among all peoples. The Lord has informed us that "the rebellious are not of the blood of Ephraim" (D&C 64:36). He who scattered Israel (Jesus) is now gathering them. The Lord is putting forth his hand "the second time" to restore the house of Israel to their promised blessings and lands. The first time was the restoration of the Jews to Palestine from Babylon. The second and latter-day restoration is an undertaking of worldwide proportions that will require centuries of time and involve billions of people. The gathering and restoration of Israel is one of the great projects of the dispensation of the fulness of times, overshadowing any previous gathering in the world. It is going to happen because the Lord has not forgotten his covenant to Abraham, Isaac, and Jacob.

Great interest arises in our hearts as we contemplate the enormous scope of the task and the privilege that is ours to be on the Lord's errand to assist in the work. The Lord has called prophets and apostles of Ephraim's lineage, given them authority, and commissioned them to inaugurate the work. From the time of the first vision of Joseph Smith in 1820 to the present, the foundation has been laid. Church statistics show that the work of the gathering and restoration is going forward with ever-increasing momentum. The Prophet Joseph Smith knew that this is the work of God, and he gave encouraging counsel to Elder Orson Hyde and John E. Page as they continued on their mission to Palestine in 1840:

"Although it appears great at present, yet you have but just begun to realize the greatness, the extent and glory of the same. If there is anything calculated to interest the mind of the Saints, to awaken in them the finest sensibilities, and arouse them to enterprise and exertion, surely it is the great and precious promises made by our heavenly Father to the children of Abraham; and those engaged in seeking the outcasts of Israel, and the dispersed of Judah, cannot fail to enjoy the Spirit of the Lord and have the choicest blessings of heaven rest upon them in copious effusions.

"Brethren, you are in the pathway to eternal fame, and immortal glory; and inasmuch as you feel interested for the covenant people of the Lord, the God of their fathers shall bless you. Do not be discouraged on account of the greatness of the work; only be humble and faithful, and then you can say, 'What art thou, O great mountain! before Zerubbabel shalt thou be brought down.' He who scattered Israel has promised to gather them; therefore inasmuch as you are to be instrumental in this great work, He will endow you with power, wisdom, might and intelligence, and every qualification necessary; while your minds will expand wider and wider, until you can circumscribe the earth and the heavens, reach forth into eternity, and contemplate the mighty acts of Jehovah in all their variety and glory."[27]

Although the foregoing was said in the context of the gathering of the Jews, equal interest and importance is attached to the restoration of all of the house of Israel, such as the descendants of Lehi and the lost tribes. It will go forward until the Lord says the work is done.

SUMMARY

The discussion in this chapter may be condensed into several fundamental concepts:

Israel is covenant-founded, temple-based, and Christ-centered. The work of Jesus Christ is the reason the covenant of Abraham exists. The Abrahamic covenant, which is the covenant of Israel, is in every way as significant in the last days as it was in any age of the past.

Jesus Christ is the Savior of all nations, yet by heavenly design and divine intent, he was born into the lineage of Israel through the house of David. Although he is God of the whole earth, he is precisely the Holy One of Israel.

The arrangement of nations and races is the work of the Lord, according to his foreknowledge and our own premortal existence. Thus God has a hand in the developments of history.

The Abrahamic covenant is a prototype or manifestation of the work and mission of Jesus Christ. Just as Jesus was an Israelite but extends his atonement to all nations, so also the Abrahamic covenant is centered in Israel but has provisions for reaching out to all nations. The covenant incorporates priesthood, the Holy Ghost, baptism, eternal marriage, posterity, land, and a blessing for all nations.

The literal, biological descendants of Abraham have a natural right to the priesthood and the fulness of the gospel of Christ. Ephraim holds the birthright, or keys of presidency, in the last days.

Jesus deliberately limited his personal ministry, both before and after his resurrection, to those nations biologically of Israel. Jesus manifests himself to the Gentiles through the Holy Ghost, as they are taught the gospel by prophets who are of the house of Israel.

The Gentile nations can obtain the blessings of the gospel through the preaching of the prophets of Israel. Whether one is Gentile or Israelite, the only way to obtain the blessings of the Abrahamic covenant is by faith in Jesus Christ, repentance, baptism, receiving the Holy Ghost, priesthood, and so forth.

The house of Israel has been scattered over all the world among all nations; therefore, most nations today have the blood of Israel in their veins to some extent or another.

Latter-day Saints are for the most part biologically descended from Joseph through Ephraim and Manasseh.

As descendants of Joseph, the members of the Church have a responsibility in the last days to feed the world the bread of life, that is, the gospel of Jesus Christ.

Joseph Smith was a legal heir to the priesthood and the keys of presidency through his lineage of Ephraim.

As far as individual salvation is concerned, a Gentile can be saved in the celestial kingdom as well as an Israelite can, but the process is for the Gentiles to obtain the gospel through the agency of Israelite prophets and teachers.

A primary purpose of the gathering is for the building of

temples so that sacred ordinances essential for salvation may be administered.

The building of temples is an indication that the blood of Israel is present in the land. That truth is especially noteworthy in view of the temples being built in Asia (Japan, Taiwan, Korea, Hong Kong, the Philippines, and so forth).

The holy scriptures are Israel's witness for Jesus Christ and will eventually consist of records of the Jews, the Nephites, and the ten tribes.

The tribes of Judah, Joseph, and Levi were each given special responsibilities of long-lasting significance, which will be fulfilled when Israel is restored to the lands of their inheritance.

The restoration of Israel in the last days is much more extensive than a mere gathering and is a work many times larger than the exodus from Egypt in Moses' time. The promises of restoration are beginning to be fulfilled even now but will not be fully accomplished until well into the Millennium.

The gathering progresses through various phases. The first phase was to Midwestern America and then to the Rocky Mountains. Currently the gathering is to the stakes of Zion wherever they may be. Other phases will come in their time.

To be engaged in the gathering and restoration of Israel was described by the Prophet Joseph Smith as being on the "pathway to eternal fame and immortal glory."

NOTES

1. Joseph Smith, *Teachings of the Prophet Joseph Smith,* sel. Joseph Fielding Smith (Salt Lake City: Deseret Book, 1938), 365.

2. Ibid., 264.

3. *The Books and the Parchments* (Great Britain: Revell, 1955), 199.

4. *One-Volume Bible Commentary* (New York: Macmillan, 1960), 792.

5. Smith, *Teachings of the Prophet Joseph Smith,* 149–50.

6. *Hymns of The Church of Jesus Christ of Latter-day Saints* (Salt Lake City: The Church of Jesus Christ of Latter-day Saints, 1985.)

7. *Hymns* (Salt Lake City: The Church of Jesus Christ of Latter-day Saints, 1948), no. 296.

8. Bruce R. McConkie, "The Patriarchal Order," address delivered to religion in class, Brigham Young University, Provo, Utah, 8 Aug. 1967.

9. Brigham Young, in *Journal of Discourses,* 26 vols. (London: Latter-day Saints' Book Depot, 1854–86), 7:289–90.

10. Ibid., 7:290.

11. *Utah Genealogical Magazine,* 11:107–8.

12. Brigham Young, in *Journal of Discourses,* 2:268–69.

13. Ibid., 7:290.

14. Spencer W. Kimball, *The Teachings of Spencer W. Kimball,* ed. Edward L. Kimball (Salt Lake City: Bookcraft, 1982), 600–601.

15. See *Encyclopedia of Mormonism,* ed. Daniel H. Ludlow, 4 vols. (New York: Macmillan, 1992), 4:1522.

16. See Alma 10:3; Erastus Snow, in *Journal of Discourses,* 23:184–85.

17. Hyrum G. Smith, in Conference Report, Apr. 1929, 123–25.

18. Letter of Eldred G. Smith, 1 Feb. 1994.

19. Mark E. Petersen, *Joseph of Egypt,* 15–17.

20. Smith, *Teachings of the Prophet Joseph Smith,* 83, 92.

21. Ibid., 308.

22. Ibid., 83, 183, 208.

23. Ibid., 101.

24. Ibid., 112.

25. Ibid., 180.

26. McConkie, 8 Aug. 1967.

27. Smith, *Teachings of the Prophet Joseph Smith,* 163.

ANNOTATED BIBLIOGRAPHY

Anderson, James H. *God's Covenant Race.* Salt Lake City: Deseret Book, 1941. Wide historical treatment but poorly documented.

Ballard, Melvin J. In Conference Report, 4 Apr. 1938, 42. Statement about "the times of the Gentiles."

Benson, Ezra Taft. *Teachings of Ezra Taft Benson.* Salt Lake City: Bookcraft, 1988, 94–98. Specifically discusses the restoration of Judah.

———. *A Message to Judah from Joseph.* Address delivered at Jubilee

Auditorium, Calgary, Alberta, Canada, 2 May 1976. Salt Lake City: The Church of Jesus Christ of Latter-day Saints.

Burton, Theodore M. In Conference Report, 5 Apr. 1975, 103. States that Ephraim has an inherited right to the priesthood.

Cowdery, Oliver. In *Messenger and Advocate,* vol. 1 (1835), nos. 5–7. Many Old Testament passages the angel Moroni quoted to Joseph Smith about Israel. Includes Psalms 100; 107; 144; Isaiah 1–2; Jeremiah 31.

Dunn, Loren C. In Conference Report, Apr. 1981, 27. Israel's blood is believing blood.

Encyclopedia of Mormonism. Edited by Daniel H. Ludlow. New York: Macmillan, 1992. "Temple Dedicatory Prayers (Excerpts)." 4:1741–49, appendix 11, identifies the people of the Pacific islands as descendants of Lehi. 2:705 references articles on Israel.

Grant, Heber J. In Conference Report, Apr. 1930, 3. Official statement of the First Presidency on the one-hundredth anniversary of the organization of the Church. Much information about the gathering of Israel and such terminology as "our father Jacob." Page 7 suggests descent from Jacob is literal.

Hymns. Salt Lake City: The Church of Jesus Christ of Latter-day Saints, 1948.

Hymns of The Church of Jesus Christ of Latter-day Saints. Salt Lake City: The Church of Jesus Christ of Latter-day Saints, 1985. Index of topics, 415–28, is helpful but not complete.

Information and Suggestions for Patriarchs. Salt Lake City: The Church of Jesus Christ of Latter-day Saints, n.d. [1980s]. Speaks of "literal descent," "genealogical ancestry," "blood lines," "father, son relationship."

Ivins, Anthony W. In Conference Report, Apr. 1930, 13. Extensive discussion of the actual blood relationship of Latter-day Saints to ancient Israel.

Kimball, Spencer W. *Teachings of Spencer W. Kimball.* Edited by Edward L. Kimball. Salt Lake City: Bookcraft, 1982, 600–601. States that we are all of Israel. Lamanites are only one part of the remnant. Israelite blood is believing blood.

———. In Conference Report, Apr. 1949, 106. The blood of Israel is believing blood.

Ludlow, Daniel H. "Of the House of Israel." *Ensign,* Jan. 1991, 51–55. Discussions of the terms *Israel* and *Gentile* and also the history and mission of the house of Israel.

Ludlow, Victor L. "Jeremiah's Prophecies Concerning the Gathering of the Jews in the Last Days." Sperry Lecture Series, Brigham Young University, 28 Mar. 1974, 2–6.

McConkie, Bruce R. "The Patriarchal Order." Address delivered to religion class, Brigham Young University, Provo, Utah, 8 Aug. 1967. Audiocassette in author's possession. Very specific about Israel, the Abrahamic covenant, and Latter-day Saints being of Israel.

———. *Households of Faith.* Brigham Young University Speeches of the Year, 1 Dec. 1970, 3. Latter-day Saints are of the blood lineage of Abraham.

————. "Come, Let Israel Build Zion." *Ensign,* May 1977, 115–18. Originally an address delivered at area conference in South America. Printed at the request of President Spencer W. Kimball. Outlines the development of this dispensation in three phases. Emphasizes present-day gathering to the stakes of Zion.

————. "To the Koreans and All the People of Asia." Address delivered 5 Mar. 1971. Published as chap. 15 in Spencer J. Palmer, *The Expanding Church,* Deseret Book, 1978. Emphasis on the growth of the Church in Asia.

————. *The Promised Messiah.* Salt Lake City: Deseret Book, 1978. Index is helpful in locating statements about Israel.

————. *The Millennial Messiah.* Salt Lake City: Deseret Book, 1982. Excellent source on all aspects of Israel and the Gentiles.

————. *A New Witness for the Articles of Faith.* Salt Lake City: Deseret Book, 1985. Excellent chapters defining the role of Israel in the latter days.

Millennial Star. Liverpool. "Jews in China." 13 (15 June 1851): 185. Reports isolated colonies of Jewish people in the land of China.

Millet, Robert L., and McConkie, Joseph Fielding. *Our Destiny: The Call and Election of the House of Israel.* Salt Lake City: Bookcraft, 1993. Extensive treatment of Israel's history, including the Millennium and the promises given to Israel.

Nelson, Russell M. "Thanks for the Covenant," in *Brigham Young University Speeches of the Year, 1988–89.* Provo, Utah: Brigham Young University, 1989, 53–61. Very informative discussion of our heritage from Abraham, Isaac, Jacob, and Joseph.

Nyman, Monte S. "The Second Gathering of the Literal Seed." In *Doctrines for Exaltation.* Salt Lake City: Deseret Book, 1989, 186–200. From an address delivered at the Nineteenth Annual Sperry Symposium. Excellent evidences showing Latter-day Saints to be of Israel by literal descent.

Penrose, Charles W. In Conference Report, Oct. 1922, 21–23. Israel has a special mission. Believing blood. Ephraim to be first in the last days.

————. "Lost Tribes and the Restoration." *Millennial Star* 71 (1909): 696–701.

Petersen, Mark E. *Joseph of Egypt.* Salt Lake City: Deseret Book, 1981, 11–17. Excellent treatment of the role of Joseph anciently and his posterity today.

Pratt, Orson. In *Journal of Discourses.* 26 vols. London: Latter-day Saints' Book Depot, 1854–86. 19:168–73 speaks of records of the lost tribes. 18:296 addresses land inheritances on the earth for restored Israel.

Proclamation of the Twelve Apostles. 1845. New York City and Liverpool. Many strong statements about the restoration of Israel.

Romney, Marion G. "The Restoration of Israel to the Lands of Their Inheritance." *Ensign,* May 1981, 16–17. The restoration of Israel to their promised lands depends upon their acceptance of Jesus Christ as their Redeemer.

Smith, Eldred G. *Improvement Era,* June 1960, 417–18. Patriarchal blessings.

Smith, Hyrum G. In Conference Report, Apr. 1929, 122–25. This is the day of Ephraim. Also discusses the tribes of Ephraim and Manasseh.

Smith, Joseph. *Teachings of the Prophet Joseph Smith.* Selected by Joseph Fielding
    Smith. Salt Lake City: Deseret Book, 1938, 14–15, 102. Only a relatively few
    Gentiles will be gathered, compared to the many who are literally of Israel.
    The seed of Joseph is now spreading the gospel in the earth.

Smith, Joseph F. *Gospel Doctrine.* Salt Lake City: Deseret Book, 1946, 115. The
    Church is almost universally of Ephraim.

Smith, Joseph Fielding. Address delivered at the dedication of the Joseph Smith
    Memorial Building, Brigham Young University, Provo, Utah, 16 Oct. 1941.
    Typescript in Harold B. Lee Library, BYU. Quotes President Brigham Young
    on lineage of Joseph Smith.

———. *Answers to Gospel Questions.* 5 vols. Salt Lake City: Deseret Book,
    1957–66, 3:63–64. Nearly all persons are of mixed lineage. Discusses being of
    two or more tribes of Israel and also of Gentile blood.

Snow, Erastus. In *Journal of Discourses.* 26 vols. London: Latter-day Saints' Book
    Depot, 1854–86, 23:181–87. Ishmael of Ephraim; Ephraim heir to holy priest-
    hood. Traits of blood Israel. Ephraim inherits keys of presidency; a kingdom
    of priests.

Taylor, John. In *Journal of Discourses.* 26 vols. London: Latter-day Saints' Book
    Depot, 1854–86, 18:324–25. Future land inheritances on the earth.

———. "The Seer, Joseph, the Seer." In *Hymns.* Salt Lake City: The Church of
    Jesus Christ of Latter-day Saints, 1948, no. 296. States that Joseph Smith was
    of noble seed.

Whitehead, E. L. *The House of Israel.* Provo, Utah, 1955. A wide treatment of
    Israel historically but poorly documented.

Woodruff, Wilford. In *Journal of Discourses.* 26 vols. London: Latter-day Saints'
    Book Depot, 1854–86, 2:191–201. Latter-day Saints are Gentiles by political
    identification even though actually of Israel. Meaning of the phrase "fulness of
    the Gentiles."

Young, Brigham. In *Journal of Discourses.* 26 vols. London: Latter-day Saints'
    Book Depot, 1854–86. 10:288, 2:268–69 identify Ephraim as the Anglo-
    Saxon race. 7:290 discusses mission of the seed of Joseph of Egypt in the last
    days.

———. In *Utah Genealogical Magazine,* 11:104–17. Address originally delivered
    in 1845 in Nauvoo, Illinois. Lineage of Joseph Smith. Early Church families
    are closely related. Ephraim is heir to the priesthood because of lineage.

CHAPTER FIVE

ESTABLISHING ZION IN PREPARATION FOR THE SECOND COMING

RICHARD NEITZEL HOLZAPFEL

To establish Zion is among the noblest aspirations that humankind have dreamt and written about from the days of the early patriarchs to the present.[1] "The building up of Zion is a cause that has interested the people of God in every age," Joseph Smith wrote in 1842. "It is a theme upon which prophets, priests and kings have dwelt with peculiar delight; they have looked forward with joyful anticipation of the day in which we live."[2]

One consistent theme in scripture and in the teachings of Church leaders is that "before the coming of Christ and the general destruction of the wicked, God will gather his Saints together from every nation, tongue, language and kindred, under the whole heaven unto places before appointed."[3] These places include Jerusalem in the Old World as well as Zion, or the New Jerusalem, in the New World. These places were designated by the Lord so the Latter-day Saint converts could gather "for a defense, and for a refuge from the storm, and from wrath when it shall be poured out without mixture upon the whole earth" (D&C 115:6). The Prophet Joseph Smith stated, "Zion and Jerusalem must both be built up before the coming of Christ . . . and when these cities are built then shall the coming of the Son of man be."[4] Elder Orson Pratt reemphasized the Prophet's teachings on this matter when he said, "Before [the Lord] appears in his glory he is going to build up Zion, that is, Zion must again be built up on the earth: and if there is not a Zion built up on the earth before he comes,

---

Richard Neitzel Holzapfel is assistant professor of Church history and doctrine at Brigham Young University.

or in other words, if there never is to be another Zion built up on the earth, then he never will come" (see also Isaiah 59).[5] As can be seen from those statements, the gathering of Israel, the building of Zion, and the Second Coming are closely related.[6]

The desire to establish Zion, born out of faith and commitment to the Lord, caused the early Saints of this dispensation to gather to geographical locations identified by the Lord through the prophet in an attempt to establish Zion during the first three decades of the Church's existence. The Saints wanted to enjoy the benefits of a Zion society, and they knew that establishing Zion was part of the great event that will occur before the second coming of Jesus Christ (the restoration of the gospel itself is the great event prophesied in scripture).

TWO MILLENNIAL CAPITALS

Anciently, the prophet Isaiah spoke of a day "when the Lord of hosts shall reign in mount Zion, and in Jerusalem, and before his ancients gloriously" (Isaiah 24:23). The first bishop of the Church, Edward Partridge, explained, "Thus we see that the Lord is not only to reign in Jerusalem, but in mount Zion, also, which shows that Jerusalem and Zion are two places."[7] Early Church leaders taught that Zion was a special gathering place for the Church in North America, whereas Jerusalem was reserved for the Jews and other tribes of Israel. As one early revelation expressed it, "Let them, therefore, who are among the Gentiles flee unto Zion. And let them who be of Judah flee unto Jerusalem, unto the mountains of the Lord's house" (D&C 133:12–13). The early Saints of this dispensation concentrated their efforts on building the gathering place in America and sought to gather another group of the Lord's covenant people, the children of Father Lehi. Gathering was at the heart of the message of the Restoration.[8] Gathering to Zion in America was the principal goal of the Saints.

The Book of Mormon, published in March 1830, just weeks before the Church was organized in Fayette, New York, announced that a New Jerusalem would be built in the New World. The writings of Ether, abridged by Moroni in the Book of Mormon, prophesied of the preparations for the coming of the Messiah and of a New Jerusalem in the Western Hemisphere:

"Behold, Ether saw the days of Christ, and he spake concerning a New Jerusalem upon this land.

"And he spake also concerning the house of Israel, and the Jerusalem from whence Lehi should come—after it should be destroyed it should be built up again, a holy city unto the Lord; wherefore, it could not be a new Jerusalem for it had been in a time of old; but it should be built up again, and become a holy city of the Lord; and it should be built unto the house of Israel—

"And that a New Jerusalem should be built up upon this land, unto the remnant of the seed of Joseph. . . .

"Wherefore, the remnant of the house of Joseph shall be built upon this land; and it shall be a land of their inheritance; and they shall build up a holy city unto the Lord, like unto the Jerusalem of old; and they shall no more be confounded, until the end come when the earth shall pass away" (Ether 13:4–6, 8). Thus the Book of Mormon clarifies biblical prophecy about the New Jerusalem: it will be built in America.

THE CALL TO ESTABLISH ZION

Even before the founding of the Church, the Lord commanded Oliver Cowdery and others to "seek to bring forth and establish the cause of Zion" (D&C 6:6).[9] The Lord said on the very day the Church was organized: "For thus saith the Lord God: Him [Joseph Smith] have I inspired to move the cause of Zion. . . . Yea, his weeping for Zion I have seen, and I will cause that he shall mourn for her no longer; for his days of rejoicing are come" (D&C 21:7–8). The command and the desire to establish Zion were present at the very beginning of this final great dispensation.

Joseph Smith began work on another "branch of his calling,"[10] the inspired translation of the King James Version of the Bible, after the Church was organized. During the making of this translation (known as the Joseph Smith Translation, or JST), the Prophet and the early Saints received additional information regarding Zion— past, present, and future. The restored biblical account (JST Genesis), the book of Moses, records that Enoch called the people to repentance, but the more wicked part of them ignored his warning and pleas. Destruction ensued, as Enoch had prophesied. The righteous, however, were separated out from among the wicked and thus avoided the chaos and ruin that ultimately consumed the ancient world (see Moses 6; JST Genesis 7:11–78):

"And the Lord called his people Zion, because they were of one heart and one mind, and dwelt in righteousness; and there was no poor among them.

"And Enoch continued his preaching in righteousness unto the people of God. And it came to pass in these days, that he built a city that was called the City of Holiness, even Zion. . . .

" . . . and lo, Zion, in process of time, was taken up into heaven" (Moses 7:18–19, 21).

Before being taken up, however, Enoch was privileged to see in vision the last days and to hear the Lord proclaim:

"And righteousness will I send down out of heaven; and truth will I send forth out of the earth, to bear testimony of mine Only Begotten; his resurrection from the dead; yea, and also the resurrection of all men; and righteousness and truth will I cause to sweep the earth as with a flood, to gather out mine elect from the four quarters of the earth, unto a place which I shall prepare, an Holy City, that my people may gird up their loins, and be looking forth for the time of my coming; for there shall be my tabernacle, and it shall be called Zion, a New Jerusalem.

"And the Lord said unto Enoch: Then shalt thou and all thy city meet them there, and we will receive them into our bosom, and they shall see us; and we will fall upon their necks, and they shall fall upon our necks, and we will kiss each other;

"And there shall be mine abode, and it shall be Zion, which

shall come forth out of all the creations which I have made; and for the space of a thousand years the earth shall rest.

"And it came to pass that Enoch saw the day of the coming of the Son of Man, in the last days, to dwell on the earth in righteousness for the space of a thousand years" (Moses 7:62–65).

These verses make clear that a New Jerusalem will be built before the Second Coming and that Enoch's Zion will join with that holy city, but the Lord had yet to reveal the specific location. The questions of where it would be built and when and who were to build it were in the minds of the Saints. Hiram Page, an early member of the Church in New York, claimed to be receiving revelations concerning these matters and "the order of the Church" (D&C 28, headnote). His revelations created some confusion among the Saints. Pleading for help in settling the matter, Joseph Smith received the revelation we now have as Doctrine and Covenants 28. In that revelation the Lord declared that "no man knoweth where the city Zion shall be built" but that it would be "on the borders by the Lamanites" (D&C 28:9).[11] More important, the revelation emphasized that it was the Lord who directed the affairs of the kingdom, including the building up of Zion, through his appointed spokesman, the prophet (D&C 28:12–13).

Despite the uncertainty over the specific location of the city, the mission of the infant Church was explicit: "Ye are called to bring to pass the gathering of mine elect; for mine elect hear my voice and harden not their hearts; wherefore the decree hath gone forth from the Father that they shall be gathered in unto one place upon the face of this land, to prepare their hearts and be prepared in all things against the day when tribulation and desolation are sent forth upon the wicked" (D&C 29:7–8).

From the Book of Mormon, the Bible, and revelations to the Prophet Joseph, it is evident that the prophets have always labored to prepare Zion. Sometimes people embrace Zion; most often they do not. But in the last dispensation, the Lord was determined to find a people prepared to accept Zion, thus preparing the way for his second coming.

THE SAINTS MOVE TO OHIO

At a conference of the Church on 2 January 1831, the Lord commanded the New York Saints to relocate to Ohio. That revelation became the focus of the Saints' attention during the ensuing weeks and months (see D&C 38). The revelation promised the new converts "greater riches, even a land of promise, a land flowing with milk and honey, upon which there shall be no curse when the Lord cometh; And I will give it unto you for the land of your inheritance, if ye seek it with all your hearts" (D&C 38:18–19). By the first anniversary of the establishment of the restored Church, the small band of Saints were relocating from various New York sites to Kirtland, Ohio. Several revelations meanwhile assured the Saints that the exact location of Zion was soon to be revealed by the Lord, who also instructed the brethren to labor "in my vineyard for the last time—for the last time call upon the inhabitants of the earth. For in mine own due time will I come upon the earth in judgment, and my people shall be redeemed and shall reign with me on earth. For the great Millennium of which I have spoken by the mouth of my servants, shall come" (D&C 43:28–30).

One month later, the Lord told the Saints of an important purpose of gathering and building the city of Zion: "And it shall be called the New Jerusalem, a land of peace, a city of refuge, a place of safety for the saints of the Most High God; and the glory of the Lord shall be there. . . . And it shall come to past that the righteous shall be gathered out from among all nations, and shall come to Zion, singing with songs of everlasting joy" (D&C 45:66–67, 71).

Another revelation noted that "Zion shall flourish upon the hills and rejoice upon the mountains, and shall be assembled together unto the place which I have appointed" (D&C 49:25).

THE LOCATION OF THE NEW JERUSALEM

In the summer of 1831, the Prophet and other leading elders were commanded by the Lord to go to Missouri, where the land of their inheritance was to be made known.[12] After they arrived there in July, the Prophet asked the Lord, "When will Zion be built up in her glory, and where will Thy temple stand?"[13] The Lord responded, "This land, which is the land of Missouri, . . . is the land which I have appointed and consecrated for the gathering of the saints. Wherefore, *this is the land of promise, and the place for the city of Zion.* . . . *Behold the place which is now called Independence is the center place;* and a spot for the temple is lying westward, upon a lot which is not far from the courthouse. Wherefore, it is wisdom that the land should be purchased by the saints . . . that they may obtain it for an everlasting inheritance" (D&C 57:1–5; italics added). The Church leaders explored Jackson County, wrote a description of it for members of the Church, established the first settlement in Kaw Township (present-day Kansas City), dedicated the land for a gathering place, identified and dedicated the temple spot, and held the first Church conference in the area.[14]

When the Church leaders returned to Ohio with the news of the momentous announcement from the Lord and their own activities in the land of Zion, the Saints' enthusiasm grew understandably high. It took some persuasion and several revelations to convince them not to gather "in haste, lest there should be confusion" and that "the land of Zion shall not be obtained but by purchase" (D&C 63:24, 29).[15] The Lord reminded the Saints, "Behold, the land of Zion—I, the Lord, hold it in mine own hands" (D&C 63:25). Nor was it the Lord's will that Kirtland be abandoned yet, but the Saints from Colesville, New York, were appointed by revelation through the Prophet to be the first to proceed to western Missouri to establish the Latter-day Saints in Zion (see D&C 54:8).

Another reason for the Saints' singular interest in Jackson County, besides its designation as Zion, was the information Joseph

Smith gave about its ancient significance. During either his 1831 or his 1832 visit or both, the Prophet taught his companions that the Garden of Eden was also located in western Missouri.[16] The implication was that the ancient center place, the Garden of Eden, will again be a center place, the New Jerusalem, when the earth is renewed to its paradisiacal glory. This information made the early Saints reverential about the past and excited about the future.

THE FIRST LATTER-DAY SAINTS IN MISSOURI

Latter-day Saint converts who arrived in Jackson County spent the winter of 1831–32 struggling to survive on the harsh frontier. The Saints soon, however, established schools, businesses, including the first Church newspaper (*The Evening and the Morning Star*), and a store. Some five settlements absorbed the increasing number of Saints—more than eight hundred had arrived in Jackson County before the expulsion. On 25 June 1833 Joseph Smith sent a letter and a plat of the city of Zion to Church leaders in Missouri.[17] The city was to be one mile square with each square in the plat representing ten acres. It was intended that fifteen to twenty thousand people could live in the city. It was evident that not all the faithful could dwell in this one city of Zion. Hence, the Lord said, "I have other places which I will appoint unto them, and they shall be called stakes, for the curtains or the strength of Zion" (D&C 101:21).[18]

The side notes of the plat of Zion itself explain that it was to serve as a pattern: "Lay off another [city] in the same way, and so fill up the world in these last days; and let every man live in the city, for this is the city of Zion."[19] Evidently, the Prophet Joseph intended that numerous new cities would be built as they filled up with faithful Saints in the "stakes of Zion."

ZION, A TEMPLE CITY

The metaphor "stakes," which is associated with geographical areas of the Church, is from the prophet Isaiah: "Enlarge the place of thy tent [temple, tabernacle], and let them stretch forth the curtains of thy habitations: spare not, lengthen thy cords, and strengthen thy stakes" (Isaiah 54:2). The rich imagery of Isaiah associates the concept of "stake" with the tent pegs that firmly held the curtains around the tabernacle that Moses built, the central Israelite sanctuary and seat of the Lord.[20] In this sense, the great city of New Jerusalem is the "tent" of the Lord, the place of his temple and his throne. Zion is the temple city par excellence.

Marked on the plat map sent to the Saints in Zion are several public squares.[21] The map shows twenty-four temples in the very center of Zion—indicating the prominence of the temple in the community. "God gathers together His people in the last days," Joseph Smith taught, "to build unto the Lord a house," so that "He could reveal unto His people the ordinances of His house and the glories of His kingdom, and teach the people the way of salvation."[22]

The temple is at the heart of the New Jerusalem. "Verily this is the word of the Lord, that the city New Jerusalem shall be built by the gathering of the saints, beginning at this place, even the place of the temple" (D&C 84:4). Orson Pratt remarked that at the Second Coming, the Lord "will come and visit it; it will be a place where he will have his throne, where he will sit occasionally as King of Kings and Lord of Lords, and reign over his people who will occupy this great western continent; the same as he will have his throne at Jerusalem."[23]

A drawing of the center, or main, temple has also survived from this period. The Lord told the Saints, "A house should be built unto me in the land of Zion, like unto the pattern which I have given you." The revelation further stated that the temple was to be built by "tithing and . . . sacrifice" (D&C 97:10, 12).

ZION IS SCATTERED

Soon after the Saints received the Prophet's letter and the plat of Zion, their expectations of building the New Jerusalem were dashed as persecution from the old settlers increased. The story of the Saints' great trials in Missouri is well known; it need only be noted here that within two years of their original settlement near Independence, Missouri, the Saints had been driven from their homes, farms, and temple site. Many factors led to their expulsion from Jackson County, but the primary reason for the loss of the place called Zion was the Saints' inability to become a people who are pure in heart (see D&C 101:6–7, 46–49). The Lord held the enemies of the Church accountable as well, for he had allowed them to drive the Saints "that they might fill up the measure of their iniquities, that their cup might be full" (D&C 103:3).

While the Missouri Saints attempted to find temporary safety outside Jackson County, the Lord affirmed that other places were appointed for the gathering of the elect: "For I have consecrated the land of Kirtland . . . for a stake to Zion. For Zion must increase in beauty, and in holiness; her borders must be enlarged; her stakes must be strengthened; yea, verily I say unto you, Zion must arise and put on her beautiful garments" (D&C 82:13–14). "Zion" in this instance probably means something broader than Missouri, for the first stake of Zion was organized on 17 February 1834. The First Presidency of the Church was appointed as the presidency of the stake, and a high council was also organized at the same time. Later a second high council was organized in Clay County, Missouri, where the largest group of Missouri Saints had settled following their expulsion from Jackson County.

Zion in Jackson County, however, with all the scriptural prophecies and promises associated with it, always held a special place in the hearts of the early Saints, as it does for many today. That is poignantly illustrated in a conversation between several members of the Church at a dinner party in Kirtland in October 1835: "After being seated around the table Bishop Whitney observed to Bishop Partrige that [the] thought had just occurred to his mind that perhaps in about one yea[r] from this time they might be seated together around a table on the land of Zion. [My wife] observed that she hoped it might be the case that not only they but the rest of the company present might be seated around her table in the land of promise; the same sentiment was reciprocated from the company round the table and my heart responded amen God grant it."[24]

Such sentiments were held despite the near completion of the Church's first temple in Kirtland. As the pentecostal period descended upon the Saints in Ohio, the Lord revealed to the Prophet Joseph the destiny of Jackson County. He said of his 21 January 1836 vision: "I also beheld the redemption of Zion, and many things which the tongue of men cannot describe in full."[25]

At first the Jackson County Saints hoped that they would immediately return to their homes, shops, and temple site. Many Saints fled to Van Buren and Lafayette counties, but most settled across the Missouri River in Clay County and managed to coexist in peace with their neighbors for the next few years. By 1836, however, the Saints had once again been told to leave. This time they moved north and east within the state to sparsely settled areas and petitioned the legislature for incorporation as a county. When the request was granted, hundreds of Latter-day Saints poured into the new Caldwell County. A large settlement was established at Far West. Some went even farther north and laid out a settlement designated "Adam-ondi-Ahman, because, said [the Lord], it is the place where Adam shall come to visit his people, or the Ancient of Days shall sit, as spoken of by Daniel the prophet" (D&C 116:1).

In the fall of 1837 Bishop Newel K. Whitney and his counselors issued a circular at Kirtland "to the Saints scattered abroad" in which they announced, "Our hopes, our expectations, our glory and our reward, all depend on our building up Zion according to the testimony of the prophets. For unless Zion is built, our hopes perish, our expectations fail, our prospects are blasted, our salvation withers, and God will come and smite the whole earth with a curse." As if any of their readers might have wondered why that was the case, they explained that "this great work of building the zion of our God" was necessary so that "there may be a place of refuge for you, and for your children in the day of God's vengeance, when he shall come down on Idumea, or the world, in his fury, and stamp them down in his wrath, and none shall escape, but the inhabitants of zion."[26]

As a result of internal strife and persecution from without, Joseph Smith and nearly five thousand other faithful Saints abandoned their temple-city in Kirtland and settled in Missouri, the "land of promise," in 1838 (D&C 52:2). Despite persecution and sorrow, they rejoiced as they "gathered in unto one place upon the face of this land"—northwestern Missouri (D&C 29:8). Their rejoicing was brief, however, because the apostasy of disaffected Kirtland Saints spread to Missouri. By summer, the Saints found themselves plagued by enemies from within and without. Trouble began with the election-day disturbance at Gallatin, Missouri, and came to a head on 27 October 1838 with the issuance of the infamous extermination order by Missouri Governor Lilburn Boggs.

The Saints' desire to establish Zion, however, even in the midst of increased persecution, is revealed in a hymn composed by Elder Parley P. Pratt shortly after Far West fell to their enemies:

How long, O Lord, wilt Thou forsake
The Saints who tremble at Thy word?
Stretch forth Thy arm, O Lord! Awake
And teach the nations Thou art God.

Descend with all Thy holy throng,
The year of Thy redeemed bring near,
Haste, haste the day of vengeance on,
Bid Zion's children dry their tear.[27]

Joseph and Hyrum Smith and other Church leaders were arrested and incarcerated, and the Saints were exiled from the land of Zion. Yet, while in Liberty Jail, Joseph wrote that "Zion shall yet live, though she seem to be dead."[28] Some twelve thousand Saints crossed the Missouri prairies and the Mississippi River where they found temporary refuge from the storm that had overtaken them. Never again in the nineteenth century would the Saints return en masse to their Missouri Zion.

NAUVOO, A TEMPORARY HAVEN

Shortly after their wintertime exodus from their promised land of Zion, Church leaders negotiated the purchase of land on a gentle bend of the Mississippi River. This new gathering site became known as Nauvoo. The Prophet told a group of missionaries, including members of the Twelve, who were preparing to leave on missions, "We ought to have the building up of Zion as our greatest object. . . .

" . . .The time is soon coming, when no man will have any peace but in Zion and her stakes."[29]

In January 1841 the Lord told his Saints that their efforts to establish Zion in Missouri, particularly in Jackson County, were to be temporarily halted:

"Verily, verily, I say unto you, that when I give a commandment to any of the sons of men to do a work unto my name, and those sons of men go with all their might and with all they have to perform that work, and cease not their diligence, and their enemies come upon them and hinder them from performing that work, behold, it behooveth me to require that work no more at the hands of those sons of men, but to accept of their offerings. . . .

"Therefore, for this cause have I accepted the offering of those whom I commanded to build up a city and a house unto my name, in Jackson county, Missouri, and were hindered by their enemies, saith the Lord your God" (D&C 124:49–51).

Although the Saints' own weaknesses and transgressions were the main cause of their scattering from Jackson County, their expulsion was the work of their enemies. Now located in western Illinois, the Saints were to look forward, not backward. It seems that they were now prepared for the Lord to open the door to a broader interpretation of Zion.

A LARGER VIEW OF ZION REVEALED

Joseph Smith began teaching the Saints in Nauvoo that Zion

"consists of all N. and S. America but that any place where the Saints gather is Zion."[30] This was such a striking amplification of the Saints' understanding that Parley P. Pratt used seven exclamation points in reporting it to his brother Orson.[31]

Even with their enlarged concept of Zion and the understanding that wherever the Saints gather is part of Zion, the Saints remained committed to eventually building the City of Zion, the New Jerusalem. In 1842 the Prophet wrote the famous Wentworth Letter containing the Articles of Faith, of which the tenth declares that the New Jerusalem will be built upon the American continent. The Saints were still committed to building the city of Zion in North America.

In 1844 Joseph Smith reemphasized: "I have now a great proclamation for the Elders to teach the Church hereafter which is in relation to Zion. The whole of North and South America is Zion."[32] On 20 January 1844 the Prophet stated: "I have received instructions from the Lord that from henceforth wherever Elders of Israel shall build up churches and branches unto the Lord throughout the States, there shall be a stake of Zion. In the great cities, as Boston, New York, &c., there shall be stakes. It is a glorious proclamation."[33] He said that could happen once the Nauvoo Temple was finished "and the Elders endowed."[34]

At the death of the Prophet Joseph Smith and his brother Hyrum in 1844, many wondered what would become of the Church and the promised Zion. Yet the Twelve were committed to the vision the Lord had given them through their beloved prophet. The Council of the Twelve Apostles issued a proclamation in 1845, dealing with the events that were to occur before the Second Coming of Jesus Christ. They reinforced the Church's position regarding the connection between Zion, the gathering, and the Second Coming:

"He will assemble the Natives, the remnants of Joseph in America; and make them a great, and strong, and powerful nation: and he will civilize and enlighten them, and will establish a holy city, and temples and seat of government among them, which shall be called Zion.

"And there shall be his tabernacle, his sanctuary, his throne, and seat of government for the whole continent of North and South America for ever.

"In short, it will be to the western hemisphere what Jerusalem will be to the eastern. . . .

"The city of Zion, with its sanctuary and priesthood, and the glorious fulness of the gospel, will constitute a *standard* which will put an end to jarring creeds and political wranglings, by uniting the republics, states, provinces, territories, nations, tribes, kindred, tongues, people, and sects of North and South America in one great and common bond of brotherhood.

"While truth and knowledge shall make them free, and love cement their union. The Lord also shall be their king and their law-giver; while wars shall cease and peace prevail for a thousand years."[35]

A NEW GATHERING PLACE ESTABLISHED

With the exodus from Nauvoo, a new place of gathering was located, this time in the midst of the Rocky Mountains. The Saints had not forgotten that the "center place," the New Jerusalem, would one day be located in Jackson County, Missouri (D&C 57:3). But the persecutions and tragedies of Missouri and Illinois in the 1830s and 1840s had made it plain that the place Zion—the New Jerusalem—would not be established immediately. In the meantime, they would have to find another home. As the Saints prepared for their journey to the Salt Lake Valley from Winter Quarters, the Lord told them: "Zion [the center place] shall be redeemed in mine own due time. . . . My people must be tried in all things, that they may be prepared to receive the glory that I have for them, even the glory of Zion; and he that will not bear chastisement is not worthy of my kingdom" (D&C 136:18, 31). With the temporary failure to establish Zion in Missouri behind them, the Saints set their faces toward a new Zion.

Saints from all over the world gathered to the Intermountain West during the last half of the nineteenth century. The physical gathering of the Saints to specific geographical locations during the nineteenth century was remarkably successful. It allowed an increase in faith, devotion, and fellowship, as well as the possibility of beginning anew. It also allowed the Saints to demonstrate their devotion to the gospel and ultimately to build five temples (four in Utah by 1893). Tens of thousands of Saints gathered to the western American Zion during that period of Church history.

Still, the Saints dreamed of Zion in Missouri. They wrote about it, discussed it, sang about it, and often speculated about when they would gather to Jackson County. Among the questions they asked was whether the original 1833 plat of Zion and the original temple drawings would be used when the New Jerusalem is built. Elder Orson Pratt gave his opinion on this subject in 1873: "God intends to have a city built up that will never be destroyed nor overcome, but that will exist while eternity shall endure; and he will point out the pattern and show the order of architecture; he will show unto his servants the nature of the streets and the pavement thereof. . . .

" . . . Suffice it to say that God by revelation will inspire his servants and will dictate to them the order of that city—the number and width of the streets, the kind of houses, the character of the Temple that is to be built therein."[36]

Six years later, Elder Pratt noted: "The Lord our God will command his servants to build that Temple, in the most perfect order, differing very much from the Temples that are now being built. . . . From what has been revealed of this Temple to be erected we can readily perceive that it will differ from anything that we have had. . . . This house will be reared, then according to a certain plan, which God is to make known to his servant whom he will, in his own due time, raise up. And he will have to give more revelation on other things equally as important, for we shall need instructions how to build up Zion; how to establish the centre city; how to lay off the streets; the kind of ornamental trees to adorn the sidewalks, as well as everything else by way of beautifying it, and make it a city of perfection."[37] In 1880 he said: "We cannot suppose, as I was saying, that when the Lord shall thus enlarge the borders of Zion and multiply her Stakes, that He will be obliged to confine Himself to those circumstances and that condition of things that existed when we were a little handful of people. . . . New circumstances require new power, new knowledge, new additions, new strength."[38] The Lord has wisely placed in the kingdom prophets and apostles to whom he could reveal his mind and will concerning all things, including the establishment of Zion preceding his Second Coming.

Just months before his death, President Brigham Young tried to put the Saints' minds at ease concerning Zion and also to broaden their perspective of the Lord's plan:

"It has been asked if we intend to settle more valleys. Why certainly we expect to fill the next valley and then the next, and the next, and so on. It has been the cry of late, through the columns of the newspapers, that the 'Mormons' are going into Mexico! That is quite right, we calculate to go there. Are we going back to Jackson County? Yes. When? As soon as the way opens up. Are we all going? O no! of course not. The country is not large enough to hold our present numbers. When we do return there, will there be any less remaining in these mountains than we number today? No, there may be a hundred then for every single one that there is now. It is folly in men to suppose that we are going to break up these our hard earned homes to make others in a new country. We intend to hold our own here, and also penetrate the north and the south, the east and the west, there to make others and to raise the ensign of truth. This is the work of God, that marvelous work and a wonder referred to by ancient men of God, who saw it in its incipiency, as a stone cut out of the mountains without hands, but which rolled and gathered strength and magnitude until it filled the whole earth. . . .

"We have no business here other than to build up and establish the Zion of God. It must be done according to the will and law of God, after that pattern and order by which Enoch built up and perfected the former-day Zion, which was taken away to heaven. . . . By and by it will come back again, and as Enoch prepared his people to be worthy of translation, so we through our faithfulness must prepare ourselves to meet Zion from above when it shall return to earth, and to abide the brightness and glory of its coming.[39]

For nearly sixty years, gathering to Utah and to other Latter-day Saint settlements in Canada, Mexico, Colorado, Arizona, Idaho, Wyoming, and Nevada still remained a high priority for Church leaders. This changed, however, during the beginning of the twentieth century partly because of economic and political reasons in the United States.[40] Yet the Brethren saw the hand of the Lord in these events and began to unfold a much larger view of the Latter-day Saints' responsibility of establishing stakes of Zion throughout the world.

A WORLDWIDE VIEW OF ZION

In the twentieth century the prophets and apostles expanded further the Saints' understanding of the notion of Zion—Zion could be wherever pure Saints congregated to live and worship, including foreign lands. That view reflects the Lord's words to Joseph Smith: "Therefore, verily, thus saith the Lord, let Zion rejoice, for this is Zion—The Pure in Heart" (D&C 97:21). Forsaking Babylon and gathering to Zion now became as much of a spiritual as a geographical phenomenon. Ultimately, it involved changing one's heart, not necessarily one's place of residence. Lifestyle, therefore, in addition to locale, came to be an important distinguishing characteristic of Zion. In 1907, for example, the First Presidency sent a letter of greeting to the Saints in the Netherlands Mission, stating, "The policy of the Church is not to entice or encourage people to leave their native lands; but to remain faithful and true in their allegiance to their governments, and to be good citizens."[41]

President Joseph F. Smith and other Church leaders did not,

however, allow their desire or commitment to the New Jerusalem to fade. They acquired several significant Church historical sites in the East and Midwest. One purchase, made on 14 April 1904, was a twenty-five acre tract in Independence, Jackson County, Missouri, the place identified by revelation as the future site of the latter-day city of Zion, the New Jerusalem. Later, the Church purchased property at Far West and Adam-ondi-Ahman in northern Missouri. Yet the spokesman of the Lord did not call for a gathering in Missouri during this time of preparation. The Saints were to remain where they were, building up the stakes of Zion in preparation for a future day.

This advice was reiterated in a 1921 editorial in the Church's British periodical, the *Millennial Star:* "The counsel of the General Authorities to the yet ungathered saints, is not to flock Zionward under existing conditions; but to remain in the countries where they now dwell. . . . Such as have homes and employment, especially, should stay and help build up the Lord's work in the various missions and conferences and branches, strengthening the hands of the elders and other missionaries labouring among them."[42]

SPIRITUAL PREPARATION NEEDED TO ESTABLISH ZION

Church leaders increasingly emphasized spiritual preparedness as the way to bring about a Zion society. In 1948, Elder Harold B. Lee cautioned the Saints in all lands to be guided by the living prophet, not by rumor or supposition, and "look forward to the instruction that shall come to them from the First Presidency of this Church as to where they shall be gathered and not be disturbed in their feelings until such instruction is given to them as it is revealed by the Lord to the proper authority."[43] Elder Harold B. Lee further admonished the Saints in 1968:

"In these days of our generation, many of you are asking: Where is safety?

"The word of the Lord is not silent. He has admonished us: 'But my disciples shall stand in holy places, and shall not be moved. . . .'

"The Lord has told us where these 'holy places' are: 'And it shall come to pass among the wicked, that every man that will not take his sword against his neighbor must needs flee unto Zion for safety.' (D&C 45:68.)

"Where is Zion?

"During the various periods of time or dispensations, and for specific reasons, the Lord's prophets, his 'mouthpieces,' as it were, have designated gathering places. . . .

"Thus, clearly the Lord has placed the responsibility of directing the work of gathering in the hands of his divinely appointed leaders. May I fervently pray that all Saints and truth-seekers everywhere will attune their listening ears to these prophet-leaders."[44]

In August 1972, Elder Bruce R. McConkie amplified and applied the scriptures relating to the gathering and Zion:

"Now what concerns us is the gathering of Israel in these last days and the part each of us should play with respect thereto. This gathering has commenced and shall continue until the righteous are assembled into the congregations of the Saints in all the nations of the earth.

"'I will gather the remnant of my flock . . . and will bring them again to their folds . . .' (Jeremiah 23:3).

"Nephi teaches this truth in these words: 'The Lord God will proceed to make bare his arm. . . . they shall be gathered together to *the lands of their inheritance*. . . .' (1 Nephi 22:11, 12. Italics added.) . . .

"The place of gathering for the Mexican Saints is in Mexico; the place of gathering for the Guatemalan Saints is in Guatemala; the place of gathering for the Brazilian Saints is in Brazil; and so it goes throughout the length and breadth of the whole earth. Japan is for the Japanese; Korea is for the Koreans; Australia is for the Australians; every nation is the gathering place for its own people."[45]

President Harold B. Lee, who had recently been sustained as president of the Church, sanctioned Elder McConkie's interpretation by quoting from it at the April 1973 general conference.[46]

MYTHS AND LEGENDS ABOUT JACKSON COUNTY

The dream of building a city in Jackson County continues to interest the Saints, and many rumors and speculations concerning the American New Jerusalem abound. Some years ago, Graham W. Doxey wrote an article for the *Ensign* entitled "Missouri Myths" in an attempt to calm the waters about Zion. Brother Doxey had been the mission president of the Missouri Independence Mission and was at the time serving in the general presidency of the Church's Young Men organization. "Missouri from the time of the settlement of Adam-ondi-Ahman," he wrote, "has been a place dear to the Saints' hearts, a place important in our history and important in our future." He noted that out of our turbulent history in Missouri have come rumors and myths that "parallel the prophecies of its future until it is difficult to untangle what the Lord has told us from 'things we've heard all our lives.'" Brother Doxey identified three myths that have been perpetuated among the Saints as faith-promoting rumors. First, "we're going to walk to Missouri to prepare for the Second Coming"; second, "the entire Church will be gathered to Missouri"; and finally, the destruction in Missouri preceding the Second Coming will be so "extensive that 'not a yellow dog will be left to wag his tail.'" He concluded: "Regardless of our human logic and limited point of view, regardless of what may have been previously repeated innumerable times, we can be sure that the Lord's will on this and all other subjects pertaining to our welfare will be made known through his living prophet. One thing we do know— there is no call to gather to Missouri. And above all, I know that the living prophet's vision is both perfect and sufficient for our day."[47]

A VISION OF ZION

In 1978 President Spencer W. Kimball spoke about Zion to the Saints: "Zion can be built up only among those who are the pure in heart, not a people torn by covetousness or greed, but a pure and selfless people. Not a people who are pure in appearance, rather a people who are pure in heart. Zion is to be in the world and not of the world, not dulled by a sense of carnal security, nor paralyzed by materialism. No, Zion is not things of the lower, but of the higher order, things that exalt the mind and sanctify the heart.

"Zion is 'every man seeking the interest of his neighbor, and doing all things with an eye single to the glory of God.' (D&C 82:19.) As I understand these matters, Zion can be established only by those who are pure in heart, and who labor for Zion, for 'the laborer in Zion shall labor for Zion; for if they labor for money they shall perish.' (2 Nephi 26:31.)

"As important as it is to have this vision in mind, defining and describing Zion will not bring it about. That can only be done through consistent and concerted daily effort by every single member of the Church. No matter what the cost in toil or sacrifice, we must 'do it.' "[48]

During 1981 the Church refined Article of Faith 10 to reflect not only an increasingly worldwide membership but the continuing belief in the future establishment of an actual holy city in western Missouri as well as an amplified understanding of the term *Zion*. The statement "we believe . . . that Zion will be built upon this the American continent" was replaced with "we believe . . . that *Zion (the New Jerusalem) will be built upon the American continent*" (Articles of Faith 1:10; italics added). Church leaders have carefully and cautiously explained the Lord's plan, without causing fear or anxiety among the faithful.[49]

Clearly, the emphasis for several decades has been and continues to be preparing for what the Lord will have us do, instead of worrying about when these events will occur. "If ye are prepared," the Lord said, "ye shall not fear" (D&C 38:30). President Ezra Taft Benson also admonished the Saints to become a Zion people in preparation for future events: "Only a Zion people can bring in a Zion society. And as the Zion people increase, so we will be able to incorporate more of the principles of Zion until we have a people prepared to receive the Lord."[50]

CONCLUSION

The Latter-day Saints today use the term *Zion* to identify groups of followers of the Lord (see D&C 97:21), any place or land appointed by the Lord through his leaders where such a group gathers (see D&C 101:16–22; 3 Nephi 20–22), and the "center place" where the city of New Jerusalem will be built (D&C 57:3). The gathering, whether it is spiritual or physical, is an effort to raise up a "pure people" who will "serve [God] in righteousness" (D&C 100:16). Hence, Zion is where the pure in heart live together in righteousness and peace. Geographical Church units are called "stakes. . . of Zion" (D&C 101:21). The Church and its stakes are called Zion because they are for gathering and purifying a people of God and a place to worship the Lord (D&C 43:8–11; Ephesians 4:11–13). Scriptures also refer to Zion as a "City of Holiness" (Moses 7:19) where the "sanctified" or "pure" dwell (Moroni 10:31–33; Alma 13:11–12) and as a "city of refuge" (D&C 45:66–67) where the Lord protects his Saints from the evil that will overtake the world.

The Lord, through his prophets and apostles, has revealed his broad and inclusive program of gathering the faithful in the last days. It is done in stages. Originally, he gathered his Saints to specific geographical locations where they could be strengthened and where they could unite their efforts and resources in building his kingdom. In these special places, the Lord required them to build a house of God, through sacrifice, so he could reveal sacred ordinances. Then, empowered from on high, the Saints were able to go out to the whole world and spread Zion's curtains throughout the nations of the earth. As the kingdom grew, it began to fulfill the vision of Nephi: "I beheld that the church of the Lamb, who were the saints of God, were also upon all the face of the earth" (1 Nephi 14:12).

President Brigham Young prophesied, "There will have to be not only one temple but thousands of them."[51] Several decades later,

President Joseph F. Smith reemphasized that "temples of God . . . will be erected in the diverse countries of the earth, for the gospel must be spread over all the world."[52] Only in this way could John the Revelator's vision recorded in the New Testament book of Revelation be fulfilled. In his great vision of the end times he saw a day when the Church was spread across the world and where could be found faithful Saints endowed with power from on high. John the Revelator wrote of Jesus Christ and the events preceding his Second Coming, "Thou art worthy to take the book, and to open the seals thereof: for thou wast slain, and hast redeemed us to God by thy blood out of every kindred, and tongue, and people, and nation; and hast made us unto our God kings and priests: and we shall reign on the earth" (Revelation 5:9–10). It seems clear that before the Lord returns, the missionaries will tread the soil of every nation, the gospel will be preached to every people, and from all kindreds and tongues the elect will gather to the kingdom of God in their own lands. They will progress in righteousness so that they enter holy temples spread across the earth and receive the ordinances of the priesthood that allow those called and chosen to receive the "fulness of the Melchizedek Priesthood."[53] All this will happen before Christ returns. This larger view of the Saints' current duty and obligation helps focus our attention on the here and now instead of on the there and then of building the city of New Jerusalem. Only if we are prepared can we inherit the blessings and promise of the Lord concerning Zion, the New Jerusalem.

The Lord promised the Saints in his preface to the compilation of revelations to Joseph Smith, "Search these commandments, for they are true and faithful, and the prophecies and promises which are in them shall all be fulfilled" (D&C 1:37). The modern Church can therefore have faith that the promises of Lord concerning the place called Zion, the New Jerusalem, will all be fulfilled in the Lord's due time.

Zion will be built by the gathering of the Saints (D&C 84:4). It is the Saints' inheritance (D&C 38:19–20); 101:18) reserved for the obedient (D&C 64:34–35). It will be built before the Second Coming (Moses 7:62), and it will eventually prosper (D&C 64:41; 82:14; 97:18). God's tabernacle will be there (Moses 7:62), and the glory of the Lord will be upon this holy city (D&C 45:67; 64:41; 97:19). The inhabitants will be the Lord's people and the Lord will be their God (D&C 42:9). Zion will be honored by the nations of the earth (D&C 97:19), which will acknowledge the sovereignty of Zion (D&C 105:32). It will be an ensign to the world (D&C 64:42), and God will protect it (D&C 97:19–20). Zion's redemption will come by power (D&C 103:15–18). Christ's presence will go before the Saints to help them possess it (D&C 103:20), and Enoch's Zion will join Zion on earth (D&C 84:99–100). Christ will dwell in the New Jerusalem during the Millennium (Moses 7:64) and speak from this holy city (D&C 133:20–21). The resurrected Saints will be with Christ in Zion (D&C 133:56). After the Millennium, Zion will, along with the earth, be celestialized, and there will be a "new heaven and a new earth" as the New Jerusalem comes again for the last time upon the earth (Ether 13:9–10). And finally, the Saints will possess it in eternity (D&C 38:20).

Joseph Smith and those who have succeeded him in the prophetic office have taught the Latter-day Saints that they can and must establish Zion. That vision inspires the labors of the Church today. Latter-day Saints believe that they are to be a light to humankind in establishing Zion (D&C 115:4–6) to usher in the millennial reign of Jesus Christ (Moses 7:60–65; D&C 43:29–30). During the Millennium, Zion will have two great centers— Jerusalem of old and a New Jerusalem in America—from which "the law" and the "word of the Lord" will go forth to the world (Isaiah 2:3; see also Ether 13:2–11).

Both current leaders of the Church and scripture indicate that our first obligation concerning Zion should be to establish it in our own hearts, families, and communities. The basic principle regarding the establishment of Zion today is that we must be possessed of the spirit of Zion before we can build the New Jerusalem at the place designated by the Lord. The Lord has been very clear about the preparation that the Latter-day Saints must make for the "center place" to be built up in preparation for the Second Coming. In answering the question, "Why was not Zion [the New Jerusalem in Missouri] redeemed?" the Lord outlined the preparation we must make for this dream to come about. First, the Saints "should wait for a little season for the redemption of Zion" (D&C 105:9). The waiting allows the Saints to "be prepared" (D&C 105:10). The Saints will be prepared when we are "taught more perfectly, and have experience, and know more perfectly concerning [our] duty, and the things which [the Lord will] require at [our] hands" (D&C 105:10). In addition, the Saints must be "endowed with power from on high" (D&C 105:11), and the "army of Israel" must become "very great" (D&C 105:26). It is not just that Church membership must increase, but "first let my army become very great, and let it be sanctified before me" (D&C 105:31). The Lord promised the Saints, "And inasmuch as they follow the counsel which they receive, they shall have power after many days to accomplish all things pertaining to Zion" (D&C 105:37). "Zion cannot be built up unless it is by the principles of the law of the celestial kingdom" (D&C 105:5).

The Lord has told his Saints where to look for direction concerning gathering and redeeming Zion: "And let the work of the gathering be not in haste, nor by flight; but let it be done as it shall be counseled by the elders of the church at the conferences, according to the knowledge which they receive from time to time" (D&C 58:56). Direction regarding the building of the place Zion—the New Jerusalem—will come from Church leaders through official communications and through the counsel given at general conference. "Therefore," the Lord declared, "let your hearts be comforted concerning Zion; for all flesh is in mine hands; be still and know that I am God. Zion [the city of the New Jerusalem] shall not be moved out of her place, notwithstanding her children are scattered" (D&C 101:16–17).

NOTES

1. See A. D. Sorensen, "Zion," in *Encyclopedia of Mormonism,* ed. Daniel H. Ludlow, 4 vols. (New York: Macmillan, 1992), 4:1624–26.

2. Joseph Smith, *History of The Church of Jesus Christ of Latter-day Saints,* ed. B. H. Roberts, 2d ed. rev., 7 vols. (Salt Lake City: The Church of Jesus Christ of Latter-day Saints, 1932–51), 4:609.

3. Sidney Rigdon articulated this position very early in Church history in a series of fourteen articles entitled "Millennium" appearing in the Church's periodical *The Messenger and Advocate* from December 1833 through May 1835; see, in particular, *Messenger and Advocate* 3 (November 1836): 403.

4. *Words of Joseph Smith: Contemporary Accounts of the Prophet's Nauvoo Discourses,* ed. Andrew F. Ehat and Lyndon W. Cook (Provo, Utah: Religious Studies Center, Brigham Young University, 1980), 417.

5. Orson Pratt, address delivered in Salt Lake City, 10 Mar. 1872; in *Journal of Discourses,* 26 vols. (London: Latter-day Saints' Book Depot, 1854–86), 14:348.

6. For a fuller discussion of the relationship of these three events, see Grant Underwood, "Millenarianism," in *Encyclopedia of Mormonism,* 2:905–6, and *The Millenarian World of Early Mormonism* (Urbana: University of Illinois Press, 1994).

7. *Messenger and Advocate* 1 (January 1835): 57.

8. See Ronald D. Dennis, "Gathering," in *Encyclopedia of Mormonism,* 2:536–37.

9. Hyrum Smith, Joseph Knight Sr., and David Whitmer received similar counsel from the Lord soon thereafter; see D&C 11:4–7; 12:3–9; 14:4–11.

10. Smith, *History of the Church,* 1:238.

11. The original revelation, recorded in section 30:8 of the Book of Commandments, did not use the word *Zion.* It was added later to clarify the meaning of the passage. Another important Book of Mormon passage regarding Zion is found in 3 Nephi: "And behold, this people will I establish in this land, unto the fulfilling of the covenant which I made with your father Jacob; and it shall be a New Jerusalem. And the powers of heaven shall be in the midst of this people; yea, even I will be in the midst of you" (3 Nephi 20:22).

12. See Clark V. Johnson and Leland H. Gentry, "Missouri," in *Encyclopedia of Mormonism,* 2:922–26.

13. Smith, *History of the Church,* 1:189.

14. Ibid., 1:189–202.

15. The Church purchased nearly sixty-three acres in Independence on 31 December 1831; see Richard Neitzel Holzapfel and T. Jeffery Cottle, *Old Mormon Kirtland and Missouri: Historic Photographs and Guide* (Santa Ana, Calif.: Fieldbrook Productions, 1991), 196–98.

16. This was a belief commonly held among the Saints. Brigham Young later recalled, "Joseph the Prophet told me that the garden of Eden was in Jackson

[County] Missouri"; see Wilford Woodruff Journal, 15 Mar. 1857, LDS Church Archives, Salt Lake City, Utah.

17. Smith, *History of the Church,* 1:357 ff.

18. Later the New Jerusalem came to be referred to as the "center place," or "center stake," though "center stake" is not technically correct. Orson Pratt explained: "Let me here take the liberty to say to this congregation that the City of Zion when it is built in Jackson County, will not be called a Stake. We can find no mention in all the revelations that God has given, that the City of Zion is to be the Centre Stake of Zion; the Lord never called it a Stake in any revelation that has been given. It is to be the head quarters, it is to be the place where the Son of Man will come and dwell, where He will have a Temple . . . ; it will be the great central city, and the outward branches will be called Stakes wherever they shall be organized as such"; in *Journal of Discourses,* 22:35.

19. Smith, *History of the Church,* 1:358.

20. See Stan L. Albrecht, "Stake," in *Encyclopedia of Mormonism,* 3:1411–14.

21. See plat map and temple drawings in Richard Neitzel Holzapfel and T. Jeffery Cottle, *A Window to the Past* (Salt Lake City: Bookcraft, 1993), 4–5.

22. Joseph Smith, *Teachings of the Prophet Joseph Smith,* sel. Joseph Fielding Smith (Salt Lake City: Deseret Book, 1976), 308.

23. Orson Pratt, address delivered 1 Nov. 1879, Logan, Utah; in *Journal of Discourses,* 21:154.

24. *Personal Writings of Joseph Smith,* comp. Dean C. Jessee (Salt Lake City: Deseret Book, 1984), 66–67.

25. Smith, *Teachings of the Prophet Joseph Smith,* 108.

26. This circular was issued as a broadside and reprinted in *Messenger and Advocate* 3 (September 1837): 561–64.

27. *Writings of Parley Parker Pratt,* ed. Parker Pratt Robinson (Salt Lake City: Parker Pratt Robinson, 1952), 381.

28. Smith, *Teachings of the Prophet Joseph Smith,* 129.

29. Ibid., 160–61.

30. Joseph Smith, address delivered 19 July 1840, Nauvoo, Illinois; in *Words of Joseph Smith,* 415.

31. Orson Pratt to George A. Smith, 21 January 1841, citing excerpts from a letter received from Parley P. Pratt, LDS Church Archives; see James B. Allen, Ronald K. Esplin, and David J. Whittaker, *Men with a Mission, 1837–1841: The Quorum of the Twelve Apostles in the British Isles* (Salt Lake City: Deseret Book, 1992), 87–88.

32. *Words of Joseph Smith,* 363.

33. Smith, *Teachings of the Prophet Joseph Smith,* 363.

34. Wilford Woodruff Diary, 8 Apr. 1844.

35. James R. Clark, comp., *Messages of the First Presidency of The Church of*

Jesus Christ of Latter-day Saints, 6 vols. (Salt Lake City: Bookcraft, 1965–75), 1:259–60; italics in original.

36. Orson Pratt, address delivered 9 Mar. 1873, Salt Lake City, Utah; in *Journal of Discourses,* 15:365.

37. Orson Pratt, address delivered 1 Nov. 1879, Logan, Utah; in *Journal of Discourses,* 21:153–54.

38. Orson Pratt, address delivered 10 Oct. 1880, Salt Lake City, Utah; in *Journal of Discourses,* 22:35–36.

39. Brigham Young, address delivered 6 Apr. 1877, St. George, Utah; in *Journal of Discourses,* 18:355–56.

40. See Thomas Alexander, *Mormonism in Transition* (Urbana: University of Illinois Press, 1986), 289–90.

41. "First Presidency to Netherlands Mission," 14 Dec. 1907; in Clark, *Messages of the First Presidency,* 4:165.

42. *Millennial Star* 83 (15 September 1921): 585.

43. Harold B. Lee, in Conference Report, Apr. 1948, 55.

44. Harold B. Lee, in Conference Report, Oct. 1968, 61.

45. Bruce R. McConkie, in Mexico and Central America Area Conference Report, Aug. 1972, 43–45.

46. See Harold B. Lee, in Conference Report, Apr. 1973, 6. President Spencer W. Kimball requested that another talk by Elder McConkie stating the same principles be published in the *Ensign;* see Bruce R. McConkie, "Come, Let Israel Build Zion," *Ensign,* May 1977, 115–18.

47. Graham W. Doxey, "Missouri Myths," *Ensign,* Apr. 1979, 64–65.

48. Spencer W. Kimball, "Becoming the Pure in Heart," *Ensign,* May 1978, 81.

49. See, for example, Bruce R. McConkie, *A New Witness for the Articles of Faith* (Salt Lake City: Deseret Book, 1985), 576–619.

50. Ezra Taft Benson, *The Teachings of Ezra Taft Benson* (Salt Lake City: Bookcraft, 1988), 124.

51. Brigham Young, address delivered 22 June 1856, Salt Lake City, Utah; in *Journal of Discourses,* 3:372.

52. Joseph F. Smith, in *Der Stern,* 38 (15 August 1906): 241–42.

53. See Smith, *Teachings of the Prophet Joseph Smith,* 322.

CHAPTER SIX

THE SECOND COMINGS OF THE LORD

LARRY E. DAHL

The Bible (both Old and New Testaments), the Book of Mormon, the Doctrine and Covenants, and the Pearl of Great Price all testify that the Lord Jesus Christ will return to the earth in power and glory at some future date: "Prepare ye, prepare ye, O inhabitants of the earth; for the judgment of our God is come. Behold, and lo, the Bridegroom cometh; go ye out to meet him" (D&C 88:92).[1] His coming will cleanse the earth of telestial wickedness and usher in the Millennium, a thousand-year period of peace and righteousness. At that time, "the earth will be renewed and receive its paradisiacal glory" (Articles of Faith 1:10). The destruction of the wicked at the beginning of the Millennium is called the "end of the world" (Joseph Smith–Matthew 1:4), as distinguished from the "end of the earth" (D&C 43:31), which will take place at the end of the Millennium, when the earth will be changed again, this time to a celestial glory (see D&C 43:30–33; 88:17–19, 25–26; 130:8–9). The Lord and his prophets have testified of his second coming, or, more accurately, second comings, as well as the events and conditions preceding that great event.

THE SAVIOR ANSWERS TWO QUESTIONS

Just a few days before Gethsemane and his crucifixion, the Savior stood with his disciples on the Temple Mount in Jerusalem. He told them that the temple would be destroyed, that "there shall not be left here, upon this temple, one stone upon another." They

---

Larry E. Dahl is professor of Church history and doctrine at Brigham Young University.

also understood that he would "come again on the earth, after that he was glorified and crowned on the right hand of God" (Joseph Smith–Matthew 1:3, 1). A short time later, as Jesus sat upon the Mount of Olives, "the disciples came unto him privately, saying: Tell us when shall these things be which thou hast said concerning the destruction of the temple, and the Jews; and what is the sign of thy coming, and of the end of the world, or the destruction of the wicked, which is the end of the world?" (Joseph Smith–Matthew 1:4).

We have three scriptural accounts of the Savior's answers to those questions: Matthew 24 (King James Version of the Bible), Joseph Smith–Matthew (Joseph Smith's inspired translation of Matthew 24, found in the Pearl of Great Price), and Doctrine and Covenants 45:15–59.

In Matthew 24, King James Version, the questions are addressed, but it is not clear which verses refer to the generation of A.D. 33–70 and which verses tell of events associated with the Lord's second coming. Hence, it can be confusing trying to decide the meaning of "this generation shall not pass, till all these things be fulfilled" (v. 34). Which generation? The generation of A.D. 33 or some later generation? Similarly, in which time period are there to be "wars and rumours of wars" and "famines, pestilences, and earthquakes"? (vv. 6–7). Also, who are those who will be betrayed, hated of all nations, and killed? (vv. 9–10). And why are false Christs mentioned twice? (vv. 4–5, 23–26).

Thankfully, both Joseph Smith–Matthew and Doctrine and Covenants 45 help sort things out. In each of those two accounts a transition verse tells us when the scene changes from the generation of A.D. 33–70 to a description of later generations, especially the generation that will be living immediately prior to the Lord's second advent. In Joseph Smith–Matthew the transition is made in verse 21, which reads, "Behold, these things I have spoken unto you concerning the Jews; and again, after the tribulation of those days which shall come upon Jerusalem, if any man shall say unto you, Lo, here is Christ, or there, believe him not." In Doctrine and Covenants 45 the transition occurs in verse 24, which begins, "And this I have told you concerning Jerusalem." The intent seems clear that what precedes the transition verses in both Joseph Smith–Matthew and Doctrine and Covenants 45 refers to the generation of A.D. 33–70 and what follows speaks of later times. Some conditions are unique to the meridian of time: the temple being destroyed, believers being betrayed and killed, and days being shortened. Other conditions are unique to the last days: the elect being gathered; wars and rumors of wars; famines, pestilences, earthquakes; the gospel being taught in all the world; the sun, moon, and stars phenomena; and the sign of the Son of Man. At least three items are common to both eras: false Christs and false prophets, love waxing cold because iniquity shall abound, and the abomination of desolation. Doctrine and Covenants 45 also contains information that is either not mentioned or not clearly explained in the other two accounts: the scattering of the Jews at the destruction of Jerusalem, the times of the Gentiles coming in and being fulfilled, disciples standing in holy places, and a believing remnant being gathered at Jerusalem looking for the coming of Christ.

Examining the three accounts of the Savior's instruction to his disciples concerning his second coming, in light of other pertinent scriptures and prophetic commentary, can help us better understand and prepare for that great day. Let us consider some of the scriptural terms relating to the Second Coming.

THE ABOMINATION OF DESOLATION

According to Joseph Smith–Matthew 1:12, 32, "the abomination of desolation" was to happen twice—once in the generation of Jews living in A.D. 33–70 and again in the generation living when the Savior comes in glory. Just what is "the abomination of desolation"?

A number of scriptural references use the words *abomination* and *desolation* in connection with each other, referring to the same principle or scenario. "Abomination of desolation" appears in Matthew 24:15; Mark 13:14; and Joseph Smith–Matthew 1:12, 32. "Desolation of abomination" appears in Doctrine and Covenants 84:117 and 88:85. Daniel adds a few words, rendering the phrase "for the overspreading of abominations he shall make it desolate" (Daniel 9:27) and "the abomination that maketh desolate" (Daniel 11:31). Considering all these references and adding other scriptures that speak of "abomination" and/or "desolation," either by those words or other words that mean the same thing ("wickedness," "iniquity," etc., and "destruction," "desolating scourge," etc.), help us understand what is meant by the "abomination of desolation," or the "desolation of abomination," or the "abomination which maketh desolate."[2] In clear and simple language these terms mean "wickedness brings destruction, or devastation, or desolation."

This principle is true for both individuals and nations. A Book of Mormon prophet said, "Wickedness never was happiness" (Alma 41:10). And a modern prophet, referring to that statement, declared, "It is an absolute formula; your chances of reversing that are zero."[3] It is true the Lord is patient, allowing time for learning and repentance. But to the ungodly and unrepentant the principle of restoration will be realized (see Alma 41). Sooner or later, "either in life or in death" (D&C 50:8), perhaps not until they are "fully ripe" (2 Nephi 28:16), wicked and rebellious souls will reap the inevitable and unhappy consequences of their willful disobedience. Vivid testimony of that truth is seen in the destruction of the Jews and Jerusalem in A.D. 70. And as the Lord affirmed in 1829 concerning the cleansing of the earth in the last days, "Behold, I tell you these things, even as I also told the people of the destruction of Jerusalem; and my word shall be verified at this time as it hath hitherto been verified" (D&C 5:20).

The sense of the scriptural warnings about desolation coming because of abominations in the last days is captured in Doctrine and Covenants 97:22–24: "For behold, and lo, vengeance cometh speedily upon the ungodly as the whirlwind; and who shall escape it? The Lord's scourge shall pass over by night and by day, and the report thereof shall vex all people; yea, it shall not be stayed until the Lord come; for the indignation of the Lord is kindled against their abominations and all their wicked works."

The covenant people of this dispensation have been called to raise a warning voice by precept and example, inviting all to come unto Christ, "setting forth clearly and understandingly the desolation of abomination in the last days" (D&C 84:117; see also 88:77–82; Moroni 10:32). The object of that warning and invitation is "that their souls may escape the wrath of God, the desolation of abomination which awaits the wicked, both in this world and in the world to come" (D&C 88:85).

THE TIMES OF THE GENTILES

What is meant by "the times of the Gentiles"? What signals the "coming in" of those times, and when will the times of the Gentiles "be fulfilled"? What is the relationship of the "times of the Gentiles" and the "fulness of the Gentiles"? Because only a few scriptural verses use these terms, let us consider each verse in context and then draw some conclusions.

Joseph Smith Translation Luke 21:19–25, 32. "And when ye shall see Jerusalem compassed with armies, then know that the desolation thereof is nigh.

"Then let them who are in Judea flee to the mountains; and let them who are in the midst of it, depart out; and let not them who are in the countries, return to enter into the city.

"For these be the days of vengeance, that all things which are written may be fulfilled.

"But woe unto them who are with child, and to them who give suck, in those days! For there shall be great distress in the land, and wrath upon this people.

"And they shall fall by the edge of the sword, and shall be led away captive into all nations; and Jerusalem shall be trodden down of the Gentiles, until *the times of the Gentiles be fulfilled.*

"Now these things he spake unto them, concerning the destruction of Jerusalem. And then his disciples asked him, saying, Master, tell us concerning thy coming?

"And he answered them, and said, In the generation in which *the times of the Gentiles* shall *be fulfilled,* there shall be signs in the sun, and in the moon, and in the stars; and upon the earth distress of nations with perplexity, like the sea and the waves roaring. The earth also shall be troubled, and the waters of the great deep. . . .

"Verily I say unto you, this generation, the generation when *the times of the Gentiles be fulfilled,* shall not pass away till all be fulfilled" (italics added).

Doctrine and Covenants 45:24–31. "And this I have told you concerning Jerusalem; and when that day shall come, shall a remnant be scattered among all nations;

"But they shall be gathered again; but they shall remain until *the times of the Gentiles be fulfilled.*

"And in that day shall be heard of wars and rumors of wars, and the whole earth shall be in commotion, and men's hearts shall fail them, and they shall say that Christ delayeth his coming until the end of the earth.

"And the love of men shall wax cold, and iniquity shall abound.

"And when *the times of the Gentiles* is *come in,* a light shall break forth among them that sit in darkness, and it shall be the fulness of my gospel;

"But they receive it not; for they perceive not the light, and they turn their hearts from me because of the precepts of men.

"And in that generation shall *the times of the Gentiles be fulfilled.*

"And there shall be men standing in that generation, that shall not pass until they shall see an overflowing scourge; for a desolating sickness shall cover the land" (italics added).

Now let us consider the scriptural references to "the fulness of the Gentiles":

Romans 11:25. "For I would not, brethren, that ye should be ignorant of this mystery, lest ye should be wise in your own conceits; that blindness in part is happened to Israel, until *the fulness of the Gentiles* be *come in*" (italics added).

1 Nephi 15:13. "And now, the thing which our father meaneth concerning the grafting in of the natural branches through *the fulness of the Gentiles,* is, that in the latter days, when our seed shall have dwindled in unbelief, yea, for the space of many years, and many generations after the Messiah shall be manifested in body unto the children of men, then shall the fulness of the gospel of the Messiah come unto the Gentiles, and from the Gentiles unto the remnant of our seed" (italics added).

3 Nephi 16:4. "And I command you that ye shall write these sayings after I am gone, that if it so be that my people at Jerusalem, they who have seen me and been with me in my ministry, do not ask the Father in my name, that they may receive a knowledge of you by the Holy Ghost, and also of the other tribes whom they know not of, that these sayings which ye shall write shall be kept and shall be manifested unto the Gentiles, that through *the fulness of the Gentiles,* the remnant of their seed, who shall be scattered forth upon the face of the earth because of their unbelief, may be brought in, or may be brought to a knowledge of me, their Redeemer" (italics added).

Joseph Smith–History 1:41. "He [Moroni] also quoted the second chapter of Joel, from the twenty-eighth verse to the last. He also said that this was not yet fulfilled, but was soon to be. And he further stated that *the fulness of the Gentiles* was soon to *come in.* He quoted many other passages of scripture, and offered many explanations which cannot be mentioned here" (italics added).

It seems clear from examining the phrases "times of the Gentiles" and "fulness of the Gentiles" in context that they mean the same thing. They are interchangeable. And they both refer to a particular period of time in earth's history—the time between the restoration of the gospel and the second coming of the Lord. The times (fulness) of the Gentiles *come in* when "a light shall break forth among them that sit in darkness, and it shall be the fulness of my gospel" (D&C 45:28). Or, as Nephi explained, "Then shall the fulness of the gospel of the Messiah come unto the Gentiles, and from the Gentiles unto the remnant of our seed" (1 Nephi 15:13). The coming forth of the fulness of the gospel began with Joseph Smith's first vision, in the Sacred Grove near Palmyra, New York, in the spring of 1820. That marked the beginning of the times (fulness) of the Gentiles. The times (fulness) of the Gentiles will be *fulfilled* in that generation that turns "their hearts from [the Savior] because of the precepts of men" (D&C 45:29–30), the same generation that "shall see an overflowing scourge; for a desolating sickness shall cover the land" (D&C 45:31), which scourge "shall not be stayed until the Lord come" (D&C 97:23), the same generation that will see "signs in the sun, and in the moon, and in the stars" (Luke 21:25), the same generation that "shall not pass away, till all be fulfilled" (Luke 21:32). Clearly, that generation is the one that will be living on the earth when the Savior comes to usher in the Millennium.

What is the meaning of *Gentile* in all of this? "The word *gentile* means the nations, and eventually came to be used to mean all those not of the house of Israel. . . . As used throughout the scriptures it has a dual meaning, sometimes to designate peoples of non-Israelite lineage, and other times to designate nations that are without the gospel, even though there may be some Israelite blood therein. This latter usage is especially characteristic of the word as used in the Book of Mormon."[4] Also, a common meaning of *Gentile* is anyone who is not a Jew. This usage was applied in New Testament times, when a distinction was made between Jew and Gentile (Romans 2:10; 3:9), or Jew and Greek (Romans 1:16; Galatians 3:28). Perhaps *Jew* was used rather than *Israel* at that time because the Jews were the only Israelites in the Holy Land.

The other tribes of Israel had been captured and taken away into the north countries centuries before.

What, then, is the meaning of *Gentile* in the terms "times of the Gentiles" and "fulness of the Gentiles"? And what does the title page of the Book of Mormon mean in saying that the record of the Nephites would be "hid up unto the Lord, to come forth in due time by way of the Gentile"? The Book of Mormon and the restoration of the gospel came through Joseph Smith. He was of the blood of Israel, a descendant of Joseph through the loins of Ephraim,[5] but he was a cultural-political Gentile because he lived in the United States of America, a nation referred to in the Book of Mormon as a gentile nation. Gentiles would scatter and afflict the descendants of Lehi, but also through them would come the fulness of the gospel, and they would serve as nursing fathers and mothers to the remnants of Lehi as well as other remnants of scattered Israel (see 1 Nephi 13:33–35; 21:15, 22–23; 22:1–12). Thus the gospel came in these last days "by way of the Gentile," that is, through the Lord's servants who were "identified with the Gentiles" (D&C 109:60) culturally and politically but whose lineage was of Israel.

During the period designated as the times of the Gentiles, the gospel is to be taken to all the Gentile nations of the earth. In those nations will be found those of the blood of Israel who have been scattered to the four corners of the earth. The gospel of Jesus Christ will ring true to many of them, as sheep recognize the voice of their Master. Also responding to the message of the restored gospel will be those who are not of the lineage of Israel but who become such through covenant adoption. The apostle Paul taught, "For as many of you as have been baptized into Christ have put on Christ. There is neither Jew nor Greek, there is neither bond nor free, there is neither male nor female: for ye are all one in Christ Jesus. And if ye be Christ's, then are ye Abraham's seed, and heirs according to the promise" (Galatians 3:27–29).

And what of the Jews during this time? Perhaps the phrases "begin to believe in Christ" and "begin to gather in" best describe their response during the times of the Gentiles. Nephi wrote: "And it shall come to pass that the Jews which are scattered also shall begin to believe in Christ; and they shall begin to gather in upon the face of the land; and as many as shall believe in Christ shall also become a delightsome people" (2 Nephi 30:7).

The context of that statement is the time just previous to the Millennium. That the Jews will wait until that time to be gathered into the gospel net is consistent with the prophetic declaration that in the last days, the last would be first and the first would be last. In the dispensation of the meridian of time, the gospel was first taken to the Jews. Then the gospel was preached also to the Gentiles, the story of Cornelius illustrating the shift in focus (Acts 10). As both Jew and Gentile converts fell into apostasy and the apostles were killed, the "tares" among the early Christians choked the "wheat," driving the Church "into the wilderness" (D&C 86:3). The world was plunged into relative spiritual darkness, which continued for nearly two thousand years.

Now, in the last days, the Church has been called "out of the wilderness of darkness" (D&C 109:73) to be spread throughout all the world. But that spreading is to take place in an orderly manner. In our day, in the dispensation of the fulness of times, the Gentiles, including the blood of Israel scattered among the Gentile nations of the earth, will be afforded the first opportunity to hear and embrace the gospel of Jesus Christ. Then the message will be taken to the Jews (Romans 2:9–11; 1 Nephi 13:42; Ether 13:11–12; D&C 90:9; 107:33–35; 133:8). But even during "the times of the Gentiles" there will be Jews who will be drawn to the gospel. It appears that there will be a "remnant" of the Jews, believing Jews, gathered in Jerusalem, looking for the Savior to come "in the clouds of heaven, clothed with power and great glory; with all the holy angels" (D&C 45:44). And two prophets will be "raised up to the Jewish nation in the last days, at the time of the restoration, . . . to prophesy to the Jews after they are gathered and have built the city of Jerusalem in the land of their fathers" (D&C 77:15; see also Revelation 11:1–13).[6]

Perhaps the great conversion of the Jews as a people to Christ and his gospel will await his appearance on the Mount of Olives, one of several appearances collectively referred to as his second coming. That event at the Mount of Olives will take place either during "the times of the Gentiles" or after that time is fulfilled. What a tender scene will there take place between the Savior and the Jews!

"Then shall the Lord set his foot upon this mount, and it shall cleave in twain, and the earth shall tremble, and reel to and fro, and the heavens also shall shake. . . .

"And then shall the Jews look upon me and say: What are these wounds in thine hands and in thy feet?

"Then shall they know that I am the Lord; for I will say unto them: These wounds are the wounds with which I was wounded in the house of my friends. I am he who was lifted up. I am Jesus that was crucified. I am the Son of God.

"And then shall they weep because of their iniquities; then shall they lament because they persecuted their king" (D&C 45:48–53).

FALSE CHRISTS AND FALSE PROPHETS
VS. THE VERY ELECT

Through the years I have heard many times the notion that in the last days false Christs and false prophets would deceive the very elect. That is a troublesome idea—can even the very elect really be victimized by false Christs and false prophets? I have been heartened by a careful examination of the Savior's words on this point. Three scriptural verses deal directly with the question:

Matthew 24:24 (KJV). "For there shall arise false Christs, and false prophets, and shall shew great signs and wonders; insomuch that, *if it were possible,* they shall deceive the very elect" (italics added).

Mark 13:22 (KJV). "For false Christs and false prophets shall rise, and shall shew signs and wonders, to seduce, *if it were possible,* even the elect" (italics added).

Joseph Smith–Matthew 1:22. "For in those days there shall also arise false Christs, and false prophets, and shall show great signs and wonders, insomuch, that, *if possible,* they shall deceive the very elect, who are the elect according to the covenant" (italics added).

Joseph Smith–Matthew is Joseph Smith's translation (JST) of Matthew 24:24 in the King James Version. Joseph Smith Translation Mark 13:25, the inspired version of Mark 13:22, is worded the same as Joseph Smith–Matthew 1:22.

In each case the qualifying phrase "if possible" or "if it were possible" appears. That seems to say that it is not possible to deceive the "very elect, who are the elect according to the covenant" (Joseph Smith–Matthew 1:22). The real question, then, seems to be, How can we become one of the very elect?

Consider the words of some latter-day prophets:

Joseph Smith: "Woe, woe be to that man or set of men who lift up their hands against God and His witness in these last days: for they shall deceive *almost* the very chosen ones! . . .

". . . False prophets always arise to oppose the true prophets and they will prophesy so very near the truth that they will deceive *almost* the very chosen ones."[7]

Brigham Young: "Were your faith concentrated upon the proper object, your confidence unshaken, your lives pure and holy, every one fulfilling the duties of his or her calling . . . you would be filled with the Holy Ghost, and it would be as impossible for any man to deceive and lead you to destruction as for a feather to remain unconsumed in the midst of intense heat."[8]

Joseph F. Smith: "The faithful Latter-day Saint is given the right to know the truth, as God knows it; and no power beneath the celestial kingdom can lead him astray, darken his understanding, becloud his mind or dim his faith or his knowledge of the principles of the gospel of Jesus Christ."[9]

Those are reassuring words. We can indeed protect ourselves against being deceived by becoming the Lord's elect people. And who are they? The Lord revealed that "mine elect hear my voice and harden not their hearts" (D&C 29:7). Further, he said, "Whoso is faithful unto the obtaining these two priesthoods [Aaronic and Melchizedek] of which I have spoken, and the magnifying of their calling . . . become . . . the elect of God" (D&C 84:33–34). The Lord promised Joseph Smith and Sidney Rigdon, referring to the Joseph Smith Translation, "The scriptures shall be given, even as they are in mine own bosom, to the salvation of mine own elect; for they [mine own elect] will hear my voice, and shall see me, and shall not be asleep, and shall abide the day of my coming; for they shall be purified, even as I am pure" (D&C 35:20–21). It is the elect who will be gathered "from the four quarters of the earth, unto a place which I shall prepare, an Holy City, that my people may gird up their loins, and be looking forth for the time of my coming; for there shall be my tabernacle, and it shall be called Zion, a New Jerusalem" (Moses 7:62; Joseph Smith–Matthew 1:27). And it is the elect who, by correctly reading the signs of the times, will "know that he is near, even at the doors" (Joseph Smith–Matthew 1:39).

These reassurances from the Lord and his prophets about the elect should not, however, cause us to become complacent. We must be constantly vigilant. Joseph Smith taught that "the nearer a person approaches the Lord, a greater power will be manifested by the adversary to prevent the accomplishment of His purposes."[10] The Prophet also said, "The devil will use his greatest efforts to trap the Saints."[11] To help the Saints avoid the adversary's traps, the Lord has revealed some important guidelines. Four of them follow. In each case, the Lord himself said he was giving the instruction that his people might not be deceived.

1. *Treasure up the word of the Lord, the scriptures.* "And whoso treasureth up my word, shall not be deceived" (Joseph Smith–Matthew 1:37).

"And they said unto me: What meaneth the rod of iron which our father saw, that led to the tree?

"And I said unto them that it was the word of God; and whoso would hearken unto the word of God, and would hold fast unto it, they would never perish; neither could the temptations and the fiery darts of the adversary overpower them unto blindness, to lead them away to destruction" (1 Nephi 15:23–24).

"Yea, we see that whosoever will may lay hold upon the word of God, which is quick and powerful, which shall divide asunder all the cunning and the snares and the wiles of the devil, and lead the man of Christ in a strait and narrow course across that everlasting gulf of misery which is prepared to engulf the wicked—

"And land their souls, yea, their immortal souls, at the right hand of God in the kingdom of heaven, to sit down with Abraham, and Isaac, and with Jacob, and with all our holy fathers, to go no more out" (Helaman 3:29–30; see also 2 Timothy 3:12–17).

2. *Follow the living prophet and apostles.* "Wherefore, meaning the church, thou shalt give heed unto all his [Joseph Smith, as president of the Church] words and commandments which he shall give unto you as he receiveth them, walking in all holiness before me;

"For his word ye shall receive, as if from mine own mouth, in all patience and faith.

"For by doing these things the gates of hell shall not prevail against you; yea, and the Lord God will disperse the powers of darkness from before you, and cause the heavens to shake for your good, and his name's glory" (D&C 21:4–6).

"And this ye shall know assuredly—that there is none other [than Joseph Smith] appointed unto you to receive commandments and revelations until he be taken, if he abide in me. . . .

"And this shall be a law unto you, that ye receive not the teachings of any that shall come before you as revelations or commandments;

"And this I give unto you that you may not be deceived, that you may know they are not of me" (D&C 43:3–6).

These revelations were given in 1830 and 1831, when there were no counselors in a Quorum of the First Presidency and no Quorum of Twelve Apostles to share with the prophet the keys of the kingdom of God. Today those quorums are in place and, always subject to the authority and direction of the president of the Church (see D&C 132:7), they are the channel through which the revelations of heaven, the mind and will of the Lord, are communicated to the Church (see D&C 81:2; 90:6–7; 112:30–32). The path of safety against deception lies in following their counsel and direction.[12]

3. *Measure our teachers by gospel standards.* "And again, I will give unto you a pattern in all things, that ye may not be deceived; for Satan is abroad in the land, and he goeth forth deceiving the nations—

"Wherefore he that prayeth, whose spirit is contrite, the same is accepted of me if he obey mine ordinances.

"He that speaketh, whose spirit is contrite, whose language is meek and edifieth, the same is of God if he obey mine ordinances.

"And again, he that trembleth under my power shall be made strong, and shall bring forth fruits of praise and wisdom, according to the revelations and truths which I have given you.

"And again, he that is overcome and bringeth not forth fruits, even according to this pattern, is not of me.

"Wherefore, by this pattern ye shall know the spirits in all cases under the whole heavens" (D&C 52:14–19).

The standard is not whether one prays, or appears contrite, or even uses language that is "meek and edifieth." The standard is whether the one who teaches us—influences our thoughts and feelings—"obey[s] mine ordinances" and "brings forth fruits . . . according to the revelations and truths" which the Lord has given. Is the teacher living the gospel? Does he or she attend and serve in the Church, pay an honest tithing, attend the temple, live a chaste life, love and serve others, sustain the Lord's appointed servants, honor marriage and family covenants, and so on? In this same spirit, Alma counseled, "And also trust no one to be your teacher nor your minister, except he be a man of God, walking in his ways and keeping his commandments" (Mosiah 23:14).

How unfruitful it seems therefore for someone who has honest questions about the gospel or the Church, and who is concerned about being deceived, to seek answers from enemies of the Church or from dissident, disgruntled members or apostates or even from casual, inactive members. The "pattern" given by the Lord to measure our mentors by the standard of obedience to the Lord's ordinances or commandments is an important one in a day when many divergent voices vie for our attention and allegiance.

4. *Seek earnestly the best gifts.* "But ye are commanded in all things to ask of God, who giveth liberally; and that which the Spirit testifies unto you even so I would that ye should do in all holiness of heart, walking uprightly before me, considering the end of your salvation, doing all things with prayer and thanksgiving, that ye may not be seduced by evil spirits, or doctrines of devils, or the commandments of men; for some are of men, and others of devils.

"Wherefore, beware lest ye are deceived; and that ye may not be deceived seek ye earnestly the best gifts, always remembering for what they are given.

"For verily I say unto you, they are given for the benefit of those who love me and keep all my commandments, and him that seeketh so to do; that all may be benefited that seek or that ask of me, that ask and not for a sign that they may consume it upon their lusts" (D&C 46:7–9).

"That ye may not be deceived, seek ye earnestly the best gifts." The Prophet Joseph Smith said, "The greatest, the best, the most useful gifts would be known nothing about by an observer."[13] That standard seems to rule out miracles, tongues, prophecy, and other outwardly manifested gifts. It points to such quiet, inner gifts as testimony, faith, peace, love, and the gift of discerning truth from error, right from wrong, true prophets from false ones. Some specifics in earnestly seeking such gifts include asking God for direction from the Spirit, doing that which the Spirit prompts us to do, walking uprightly before God, considering the end of our salvation, and doing all things with prayer and thanksgiving.

Obviously, if we have the companionship of the Holy Ghost, we will not be deceived. But the Holy Ghost is not the only source of revelation. The devil and his agents can also reveal things to mortals. "We get our answers from the source of the power we list to obey," said President Harold B. Lee. "If we're following the ways of the devil, we'll get answers from the devil. If we're keeping the commandments of God, we'll get our answers from God."[14] Then, too, at times we may conclude that some notion that has sprung into our minds is revelation from God, when it is not. Hence the wisdom of the Lord's giving us several guidelines that can act as checks upon one another, all of them together providing a secure foundation against being deceived by the misapplication of one or more of them. Surely, if the scriptures, the living prophets, a mentor who is obeying the ordinances of God, and the Spirit all agree, we are on solid gospel sod. If our lives are in harmony with those four sources, we could certainly be considered as among the Lord's elect, even the very elect. And we will not be deceived.

AS IN THE DAYS OF NOAH

"But as it was in the days of Noah, so it shall be also at the coming of the Son of Man;

"For it shall be with them, as it was in the days which were before the flood; for until the day that Noah entered into the ark they were eating and drinking, marrying and giving in marriage;

"And knew not until the flood came, and took them all away; so shall also the coming of the Son of Man be" (Joseph Smith–Matthew 1:41–43).

It appears there are two points of similarity, in addition to the fact of their destruction, between the last generation living before Christ comes and the generation of Noah's day: they do not expect what is about to happen to them, and they are extremely wicked. Those who do not expect the Second Coming fall into at least two different camps. There are those who are so captured by "surfeiting, and drunkenness, and cares of this life," that they do not make the effort to find out about the Savior and his promised return. Hence, they are caught "unawares" (Luke 21:34). There are others who may know of his promise but do not believe it. They are the willingly ignorant scoffers of the last days who ask, "Where is the promise of his coming? for since the fathers fell asleep, all things continue as they were from the beginning of the creation" (2 Peter 3:3–5). Neither group will be prepared. To them "the day of the Lord will come as a thief in the night" (2 Peter 3:10).

The second similarity, the level of wickedness, is truly a sad commentary upon both generations. The scriptural record reports that in the days of Noah "the wickedness of men had become great in the earth; and every man was lifted up in the imagination of the thoughts of his heart, being only evil continually" (Moses 8:22). Viewing in vision the wickedness of men on the earth in Noah's day, with the Lord standing beside him, Enoch "beheld Satan; and he had a great chain in his hand, and it veiled the whole face of the earth with darkness; and he looked up and laughed, and his angels rejoiced" (Moses 7:26). The Lord wept at their wickedness and consequent spiritual bondage. Enoch asked, "How is it that thou canst weep, seeing thou art holy, and from all eternity to all eternity," and have innumerable creations? (Moses 7:29.) The Lord answered: "Behold these thy brethren; they are the workmanship of mine own hands, and I gave unto them their knowledge, in the day I created them; and in the Garden of Eden, gave I unto man his agency;

"And unto thy brethren have I said, and also given commandment, that they should love one another, and that they should choose me, their Father; but behold, they are without affection, and they hate their own blood;

"And the fire of mine indignation is kindled against them; and in my hot displeasure will I send in the floods upon them, for my fierce anger is kindled against them. . . .

"Wherefore, I can stretch forth mine hands and hold all the creations which I have made; and mine eye can pierce them also, and *among all the workmanship of mine hands there has not been so great wickedness as among thy brethren*" (Moses 7:32–36; italics added).

If mankind were that wicked in the days of Noah and will again be that wicked in the generation that is living when Christ comes, where are we today? Joseph Smith said that his generation of one hundred sixty years ago was "as corrupt as the generation of the Jews that crucified Christ; and if He were here to-day, and should preach the same doctrine He did then, they would put Him to death."[15] A generation ago, President Joseph Fielding Smith taught: "Our Savior promised that the days preceding his second coming will be typical of the days of the flood. . . . This comparison is not to be taken figuratively, but literally, as it is given. The world today is corrupt and filled with violence as it was at that earlier day, for now as then, all flesh has corrupted its way upon the earth."[16]

President Spencer W. Kimball added his witness by quoting in general conference in 1975 a magazine writer's assessment that "morality in public life has plunged to the lowest level, the lowest level in history."[17] And what has happened since Joseph Smith's day, or Joseph Fielding Smith's, or Spencer W. Kimball's? Even a casual look at our present world indicates that violence, evil imaginations, and general wickedness continue to escalate at ever-increasing rates. If we are not already there, the direction we are headed will soon drench the world in sin "as it was in the days of Noah" (Joseph Smith–Matthew 1:41).

As the covenant people of the Lord, what are we to do? Is there a way to escape the judgments, that desolation which is the inevitable consequence of such abomination?

THE SAINTS SHALL HARDLY ESCAPE

When the desolations come in the form of social and political conflict,[18] famines and pestilences,[19] and extensive natural calamities,[20] what will happen to the people of the Lord? The answer to that question is both good news and bad news. The good news is that many of the Saints will be protected by the power of God through their faith and obedience. The bad news is that not all the Saints will be spared. Let us consider a few scriptures and some prophetic commentary on this point. In 1831 the Lord revealed: "I, the Lord, am angry with the wicked; I am holding my Spirit from the inhabitants of the earth.

"I have sworn in my wrath, and decreed wars upon the face of the earth, and the wicked shall slay the wicked, and fear shall come upon every man;

"And *the saints also shall hardly escape;* nevertheless, I, the Lord, am with them, and will come down in heaven from the presence of my Father and consume the wicked with unquenchable fire.

"And behold, this is not yet, but by and by" (D&C 63:32–35; italics added).

The Prophet Joseph Smith taught: "I explained concerning the coming of the Son of Man; also that it is a false idea that the Saints will escape all the judgments, whilst the wicked suffer; for all flesh is subject to suffer, and 'the righteous shall hardly escape'; still many of the Saints will escape, for the just shall live by faith; yet many of the righteous shall fall a prey to disease, to pestilence, etc., by reason of the weakness of the flesh, and yet be saved in the Kingdom of God. So that it is an unhallowed principle to say that such and such have transgressed because they have been preyed upon by disease or death, for all flesh is subject to death; and the Savior has said, 'Judge not, lest ye be judged.'"[21]

Realizing that there is no absolute guarantee but that there is the promise of "many" Saints being protected, how can we make the most of the situation? First, we can gather with other Saints.

The Savior told his disciples that as the end nears, his elect would be "gathered from the four quarters of the earth" (Joseph Smith–Matthew 1:27). First is a spiritual gathering from Babylon into the kingdom of God. Then, those thus gathered are instructed to gather geographically to "Zion" and "other places which I will appoint unto them, and they shall be called stakes, for the curtains or the strength of Zion" (D&C 101:21). The Lord commanded:

"Behold, it is my will, that all they who call on my name, and worship me according to mine everlasting gospel, should gather together, and stand in holy places;

"And prepare for the revelation which is to come, when the veil of the covering of my temple, in my tabernacle, which hideth the earth, shall be taken off, and all flesh shall see me together" (D&C 101:22–23).

"The time is soon coming," said Joseph Smith, "when no man will have any peace but in Zion and her stakes."[22] Presumably, the stakes are also included as part of the "Zion" to which "every man that will not take his sword against his neighbor must needs flee unto Zion for safety;" and it is to be hoped that the Saints in those stakes will be numbered among "the only people that shall not be at war one with another" (D&C 45:68–69).

STAND IN HOLY PLACES AND BE NOT MOVED

Repeatedly the Lord has instructed his Saints to "stand ye in holy places, and be not moved" during the days of turmoil, when by "the sword and by bloodshed . . . famine, and plague, and earth-quake . . . shall the inhabitants of the earth be made to feel the wrath, and indignation, and chastening hand of an Almighty God, until the consumption decreed hath made a full end of all nations" (D&C 87:8, 6).

Where are the holy places? And what does it mean to "stand"? The revelations and the Prophet Joseph Smith designate Zion and her stakes as holy places.[23] President Ezra Taft Benson added the following insight: "Holy places consist of our temples, our chapels, our homes, and the stakes of Zion, which are, as the Lord declares, 'for a defense, and for a refuge from the storm, and from wrath when it shall be poured out without mixture upon the whole earth.' (Doctrine and Covenants 115:6.)"[24]

To "stand" and to "be not moved" mean to be resolute and faithful, firmly grounded, solidly committed to the Lord and his commandments. In Paul's words: "Wherefore take unto you the whole armour of God, that ye may be able to *withstand* in the evil day, and having done all, to *stand.*

"*Stand* therefore, having your loins girt about with truth, and having on the breastplate of righteousness;

"And your feet shod with the preparation of the gospel of peace;

"Above all, taking the shield of faith, wherewith ye shall be able to quench all the fiery darts of the wicked.

"And take the helmet of salvation, and the sword of the Spirit, which is the word of God:

"Praying always with all prayer and supplication in the Spirit, and watching thereunto with all perseverance and supplication for all saints" (Ephesians 6:13–18; italics added; see also D&C 27:15–18).

Living among covenant people of the Lord who wear the whole armor of God will do much to allay the social conflict and fear that will characterize the rest of the world. Keeping the Word of Wisdom and other health-related commandments will help the Saints avoid many sicknesses. Keeping the Lord's law of chastity will keep the Saints from sexually transmitted diseases. Added to these measures is the Lord's promise that his power and glory will attend his people who gather and are righteous. "Wherefore, stand ye in holy places, and be not moved" (D&C 87:8).

"UPON MY HOUSE SHALL IT BEGIN"

It should be emphasized that there is no promise of protection in simply gathering with the Saints. In fact, gathering with the

Saints, claiming loyalty to the kingdom of God while at the same time undermining it, may entail a serious liability. For those who profess the name of the Lord but who refuse to obey him, the Lord has reserved "the heaviest of all cursings" (D&C 41:1). And when it comes time to cleanse the earth in the last days, the Lord has said he will begin within the Church:

"Verily, verily, I say unto you, darkness covereth the earth, and gross darkness the minds of the people, and all flesh has become corrupt before my face.

"Behold, vengeance cometh speedily upon the inhabitants of the earth, a day of wrath, a day of burning, a day of desolation, of weeping, of mourning, and of lamentation; and as a whirlwind it shall come upon all the face of the earth, saith the Lord.

"And upon my house shall it begin, and from my house shall it go forth, saith the Lord;

"First among those among you, saith the Lord, who have professed to know my name and have not known me, and have blasphemed against me in the midst of my house, saith the Lord" (D&C 112:23–26).

As we consider the conditions that will be in the world as the Savior's return draws near, we need not fear "if [we] are prepared" (D&C 38:30). If we are among those of the Saints who are shielded from many of the judgments, praise the Lord. If, however, we get caught in the cross fire, so to speak, and fall prey to disease, or violence, or natural calamity, we can take courage in the Lord's assurance that "blessed is he that keepeth my commandments, whether in life or in death; and he that is faithful in tribulation, the reward of the same is greater in the kingdom of heaven.

"Ye cannot behold with your natural eyes, for the present time, the design of your God concerning those things which shall come hereafter, and the glory which shall follow after much tribulation" (D&C 58:2–3).

THE SIGN OF THE SON OF MAN

Among the last of the signs of his coming, perhaps the very last sign is the "sign of the Son of man" (Matthew 24:30; see also Joseph Smith–Matthew 1:36; D&C 88:93). Of that sign, Joseph Smith said: "Mr. Redding thinks that he has seen the sign of the Son of Man. But I shall use my right, and declare that, notwithstanding Mr. Redding may have seen a wonderful appearance in the clouds one morning about sunrise (which is nothing very uncommon in the winter season) he has not seen the sign of the Son of Man, as foretold by Jesus; neither has any man, nor will any man, until after the sun shall have been darkened and the moon bathed in blood; for the Lord hath not shown me any such sign; and as the prophet saith, so it must be—'Surely the Lord God will do nothing, but He revealeth His secret unto His servants the prophets.' (See Amos 3:7.) Therefore, hear this, O earth: The Lord will not come to reign over the righteous, in this world, in 1843, nor until everything for the Bridegroom is ready."[25]

On another occasion the Prophet outlined some things that must happen in preparation for the coming of the Bridegroom: "Judah must return, Jerusalem must be rebuilt, and the temple, and water come out from under the temple, and the waters of the Dead Sea be healed. It will take some time to rebuild the walls of the city and the temple, &c.; and all this must be done before the Son of Man will make His appearance. There will be wars and rumors of wars, signs in the heavens above and on the earth beneath, the sun turned into darkness and the moon to blood, earthquakes in divers places, the seas heaving beyond their bounds; then will appear one grand sign of the Son of Man in heaven. But what will the world do? They will say it is a planet, a comet, etc. But the Son of man will come as the sign of the coming of the Son of Man, which will be as the light of the morning cometh out of the east."[26]

What is the sign of the Son of Man? Elder Bruce R. McConkie declared, "We do not know."[27] What we do know is that it will be among the last of the signs before the Savior comes, that it will come out of the east, that it will be seen by all people together but not be understood by many. The Lord's servants, however, will understand, for he promised, "Unto you it shall be given to know the signs of the times, and the signs of the coming of the Son of Man" (D&C 68:11).

THE COMINGS OF THE LORD

The plural word *comings* is used purposely, for what we generally refer to as the Lord's second coming involves several appearances to various groups of people. The scriptures tell of his coming to three groups—the Saints, the Jews, and then the whole world. The sequence of events in these several comings is not always clear, and the same is true about how much time will elapse between some of the events. Elder Bruce R. McConkie has written:

"It is not possible for us, in our present relatively low state of spiritual understanding, to specify the exact chronology of all the events that shall attend the Second Coming. Nearly all of the prophetic word relative to our Lord's return links various events together without reference to the order of their occurrence. Indeed, the same scriptural language is often used to describe similar events that will take place at different times."[28]

THE LORD'S APPEARANCES TO THE SAINTS

To his covenant people of the last dispensation the Lord has appeared and will yet appear several times. The dispensation of the fulness of times burst open with the appearance of the Father and the Savior to the young Prophet Joseph Smith in the spring of 1820 (Joseph Smith–History 1:7–20). In 1832, Joseph Smith and Sidney Rigdon "saw" and "conversed" with the Savior in heavenly vision (D&C 76:14). Four years later, in 1836, Joseph Smith and Oliver Cowdery "saw the Lord" and heard his voice, "even the voice of Jehovah," as he appeared in the Kirtland Temple to accept that holy edifice (D&C 110:1, 3). Promised future appearances include a grand council at Adam-ondi-Ahman and his coming to the city of Zion, the New Jerusalem, yet to be built in Independence, Missouri.

THE COUNCIL AT ADAM-ONDI-AHMAN

We know of two special meetings at Adam-ondi-Ahman—one three years before the death of Adam, and another just prior to the second coming of the Lord.

Three years before his death, Adam called his righteous posterity to a special meeting at a place called Adam-ondi-Ahman "and there bestowed upon them his last blessing." The Lord appeared to those gathered, "administered comfort unto Adam, and said unto him: I have set thee to be at the head; a multitude of nations shall come of thee, and thou art a prince over them forever" (D&C 107:53, 55). By revelation, Joseph Smith identified Spring Hill, Daviess County, Missouri, as the location of Adam-ondi-Ahman. That revelation also says that "it is the place where Adam shall come to visit his people, or the Ancient of Days shall sit, as spoken of by Daniel the prophet" (D&C 116). Explaining something of that event, Joseph Smith taught:

"Daniel in his seventh chapter speaks of the Ancient of Days; he means the oldest man, our Father Adam, Michael, he will call his children together and hold a council with them to prepare them for the coming of the Son of Man. He (Adam) is the father of the human family, and presides over the spirits of all men, and all that have had keys must stand before him in this grand council. This may take place before some of us leave this stage of action. The Son of Man stands before him, and there is given him glory and dominion. Adam delivers up his stewardship to Christ, that which was delivered to him as holding the keys of the universe, but retains his standing as head of the human family."[29]

Interesting details of this second gathering at Adam-ondi-Ahman are provided by President Joseph Fielding Smith: "Not many years hence there shall be another gathering of high priests and righteous souls in this same valley of Adam-ondi-Ahman. At

this gathering Adam, the Ancient of Days, will again be present.
. . . There will stand before him those who have held the keys of all
dispensations, who shall render up their stewardships to the first
Patriarch of the race, who holds the keys of salvation . . .

". . . In this council Christ will take over the reigns of government, officially, on this earth. . . .

"Until this grand council is held, Satan shall hold rule in the
nations of the earth; but at that time thrones are to be cast down and
man's rule shall come to an end—for it is decreed that the Lord
shall make an end of all nations. (D&C 87:6.) . . .

"This council in the valley of Adam-ondi-Ahman is to be of
the greatest importance to this world. At that time there will be a
transfer of authority from the usurper and impostor, Lucifer, to the
rightful King, Jesus Christ. . . .

"When this gathering is held, the world will not know of it; the
members of the Church at large will not know of it, yet it shall be
preparatory to the coming in the clouds of glory of our Savior Jesus
Christ as the Prophet Joseph Smith has said. The world cannot know
of it. The Saints cannot know of it—except those who officially
shall be called into this council—for it shall precede the coming of
Jesus Christ as a thief in the night, unbeknown to all the world."[30]

THE SAVIOR'S APPEARANCE IN ZION

As to the Savior's appearance in Zion, the Lord promised
that his presence would be in the temple there and "all the pure in
heart that shall come into it shall see God" (D&C 97:16). Elder
Charles W. Penrose, commenting on this promise, wrote: "He will
come to the Temple prepared for him, and his faithful people will
behold his face, hear his voice, and gaze upon his glory. From his
own lips they will receive further instructions for the development
and beautifying of Zion and for the extension and sure stability of
his kingdom."[31]

In more recent times, President Ezra Taft Benson spoke of the
Lord's appearing to his Saints in Zion:

"But to an otherwise gloomy picture there is a bright side—the coming of our Lord in all his glory. His coming will be both glorious and terrible, depending on the spiritual condition of those who remain.

"One appearance will be to the righteous Saints who have gathered to the New Jerusalem here in America. In this place of refuge they will be safe from the wrath of the Lord which will be poured out without measure on all nations."[32]

THE SAVIOR'S APPEARANCE TO THE JEWS

Earlier in this chapter is the account of the Savior's appearance to the Jews as recorded in Doctrine and Covenants 45:48–53. Zechariah 12–14 also makes reference to that event. It will come at a time when "all nations" are gathered "against Jerusalem." The city is besieged and then taken. The Lord will stand on the Mount of Olives, which is just a few blocks east of the city of Jerusalem, through the Kidron Valley. The Mount of Olives will "cleave in the midst thereof . . . and there shall be a very great valley; and half of the mountain shall remove toward the north, and half of it toward the south" (Zechariah 14:4). It is there that the Jews will see the Savior and query him concerning the wounds in his hands and feet. He will tell them that he is their Messiah, the Son of God, the Lord and Redeemer, even Jesus Christ, who was rejected and wounded in the house of his friends, their forefathers. "And then shall they weep because of their iniquities; then shall they lament because they persecuted their king" (D&C 45:53). A long-awaited reconciliation between the Savior and a loved but beleaguered portion of his ancient covenant people, the Jews, will be realized.

THE SAVIOR'S APPEARANCE TO THE WORLD

The Savior's appearance to the whole world is what usually comes to mind when people speak of the "Second Coming." At that time he will come "in the clouds of heaven, clothed with power and great glory; with all the holy angels" (D&C 45:44). "The curtain of heaven [shall] be unfolded, as a scroll is unfolded after it is rolled up, and the face of the Lord shall be unveiled" (D&C 88:95), "and all flesh shall see [him] together" (D&C 101:23). "The Lord shall utter his voice, and all the ends of the earth shall hear it; and the nations of the earth shall mourn, and they that have laughed shall see their folly. And calamity shall cover the mocker, and the scorner shall be consumed; and they that have watched for iniquity shall be hewn down and cast into the fire" (D&C 45:49–50). "And the saints that are upon the earth, who are alive, shall be . . . caught up to meet him" (D&C 88:96). These Saints will return to the earth with the Savior and "shall reign with [him] on earth" (D&C 43:29), as he ushers in the Millennium.

WHEN WILL HE COME?

In response to the question of when he will come, the Lord told his disciples, "Of that day, and hour, no one knoweth; no, not the angels of God in heaven, but my Father only" (Joseph Smith–Matthew 1:40). He also said, "In such an hour as ye think not, the Son of Man cometh" (Joseph Smith–Matthew 1:48). Paul wrote that his coming will be "as a thief in the night" (1 Thessalonians 5:2). It seems obvious that the precise time of his coming has been left deliberately and purposefully obscure (Matthew 24:42–51). Joseph Smith said: "Jesus Christ never did reveal to any man the precise time that He would come. Go and read the Scriptures, and you cannot find anything that specifies the exact hour He would come; and all that say so are false teachers."[33]

The Prophet made that statement in March 1844. He could speak with some confidence because of his own experience with the question some time earlier, as recorded in Doctrine and Covenants 130:14–17:

"I was once praying very earnestly to know the time of the coming of the Son of Man, when I heard a voice repeat the following:

"Joseph, my son, if thou livest until thou art eighty-five years old, thou shalt see the face of the Son of Man; therefore let this suffice, and trouble me no more on this matter.

"I was left thus, without being able to decide whether this coming referred to the beginning of the millennium or to some previous appearing, or whether I should die and thus see his face.

"I believe the coming of the Son of Man will not be any sooner than that time."

If the angels in heaven do not know, and the Prophet of the dispensation of the fulness of times could not find out, it is highly unlikely that any of the rest of us will successfully discover the time of the Lord's coming. But we are not left totally without some guidelines in the matter. First, we are told that this earth has a temporal existence of seven thousand years, the last one thousand of which will be the Millennium (see D&C 77:6–7; 29:11, 22; 88:101). Further, we learn that the Lord will come "in the beginning of the seventh thousand years" (D&C 77:12). Joseph Smith taught that "the world has had a fair trial for six thousand years; the Lord will try the seventh thousand Himself."[34] If we can rely upon biblical chronology and our calendar system, we are nearing the end of the sixth thousand years and thus approaching the seventh thousand-year period. That transition should take place sometime around the year A.D. 2000. What can we conclude from the statement that the Lord will come "in the beginning of the seventh thousand years?" Will he come right at the beginning? Not according to Doctrine and Covenants 77:13:

"Q. When are the things to be accomplished, which are written in the 9th chapter of Revelation?

"A. They are to be accomplished *after the opening of the seventh seal, before the coming of Christ*" (italics added).

This passage assures us there will be a space of time "after the opening of the seventh seal" wherein the events spoken of in Revelation 9 will be accomplished. And those events will take place "before the coming of Christ." How long will those events take? We are not told. We do know that the events include wars, plagues, idolatry, murders, sexual sin, and thefts. It will be a time when "a third part of men" are slain, and those who are left refuse to repent (Revelation 9:1–21). We are left to wonder whether this period of time will span a generation, or two, or three. But we are also cautioned not to procrastinate our preparation, for, from the Lord's perspective, his coming is "nigh at hand" (D&C 35:15), "near, even at the doors" (D&C 110:16).

CONCLUSION

The second coming of the Lord is a topic that captures the interest of many people, and rightly so, for in one way or another, it affects all of us. What should be our approach? I suggest that we prepare. We need not panic nor become obsessed with focusing upon the promised judgments. We do need to learn what the Lord and his servants have taught concerning it, and as covenant people of the Lord, we are to gather, to live the gospel and share it with others, to be a city on a hill, a candle on a candlestick, the salt of the earth, a royal priesthood, an holy nation. Those tasks should occupy our thoughts, our hearts, and our behavior. In that way we can effectively respond to the Lord's invitation to "awake and arise and go forth to meet the Bridegroom; behold and lo, the Bridegroom cometh; go ye out to meet him. Prepare yourselves for the great day of the Lord" (D&C 133:10).

NOTES

1. See the Topical Guide in the Latter-day Saint edition of the King James Version of the Bible, s.v. "Jesus Christ, Second Coming." In the Pearl of Great Price, see Moses 7 and Articles of Faith 1:10.

2. See, for example, D&C 1:13–17; 5:18–19; 45:31–33; 84:95–97; 86:4–7; 88:81–94; 112:23–26; 133:2, 10–15, 42–51, 62–74.

3. L. Tom Perry, in Brigham Young University *Daily Universe,* 13 Nov. 1989, 3.

4. LDS Bible Dictionary, s.v. "Gentile," 679.

5. See 2 Nephi 3:7; Brigham Young, in *Journal of Discourses,* 26 vols. (London: Latter-day Saints' Book Depot, 1854–86), 2:269.

6. Note that the revelation says "to" the Jewish nation, indicating that the two prophets could come from outside the Jewish nation.

   Elder Bruce R. McConkie has written of them: "Who will these witnesses be?

We do not know, except that they will be followers of Joseph Smith; they will hold the holy Melchizedek Priesthood; they will be members of The Church of Jesus Christ of Latter-day Saints. It is reasonable to suppose, knowing how the Lord has always dealt with his people in all ages, that they will be two members of the Council of the Twelve or of the First Presidency of the Church" *(The Millennial Messiah* [Salt Lake City: Deseret Book, 1982], 390).

At the very least we know that the two prophets will be "raised up" by God and will be authorized and commissioned by him to "prophesy a thousand two hundred and threescore days" and have "power to shut the heaven, that it rain not . . . power over the waters to turn them to blood, and to smite the earth with all plagues, as often as they will" (Revelation 11:3–6).

7. Joseph Smith, *Teachings of the Prophet Joseph Smith,* sel. Joseph Fielding Smith (Salt Lake City: Deseret Book, 1976), 365; italics added.

8. Brigham Young, in *Journal of Discourses,* 7:277.

9. Joseph F. Smith, *Gospel Doctrine* (Salt Lake City: Deseret Book, 1970), 6.

10. Joseph Smith, in Orson F. Whitney, *Life of Heber C. Kimball* (Salt Lake City: Stevens & Wallis, 1945), 132.

11. Smith, *Teachings of the Prophet Joseph Smith,* 161.

12. Passages of scripture affirming that the First Presidency and the Quorum of the Twelve share the keys of the kingdom include D&C 81:2; 90:6–7; 112:30–32.

13. Smith, *Teachings of the Prophet Joseph Smith,* 246.

14. Harold B. Lee, *Stand Ye in Holy Places* (Salt Lake City: Deseret Book, 1974), 138.

15. Smith, *Teachings of the Prophet Joseph Smith,* 328.

16. Joseph Fielding Smith, *Doctrines of Salvation,* comp. Bruce R. McConkie, 3 vols. (Salt Lake City: Bookcraft, 1954–56), 3:20.

17. Spencer W. Kimball, in Conference Report, Oct. 1975, 7.

18. See Joseph Smith–Matthew 1:23, 30; D&C 45:26–27, 68–69; 63:33; 88:91.

19. See D&C 29:15–20; 43:25; 45:31, 33.

20. See D&C 43:25; 45:33; 87:6; 88:87–90.

21. Smith, *Teachings of the Prophet Joseph Smith,* 162–63.

22. Ibid., 161.

23. See D&C 101:17–23; Smith, *Teachings of the Prophet Joseph Smith,* 71, 161.

24. Ezra Taft Benson, *Come unto Christ* (Salt Lake City: Deseret Book, 1983), 115–16.

25. Smith, *Teachings of the Prophet Joseph Smith,* 280.

26. Ibid., 286–87.

27. McConkie, *Millennial Messiah,* 418.

28. Ibid., 635.

29. Smith, *Teachings of the Prophet Joseph Smith,* 157.

30. Joseph Fielding Smith, *The Way to Perfection* (Salt Lake City: Deseret Book, 1966), 289–91.

31. Charles W. Penrose, "The Second Advent," *The Latter-day Saints' Millennial Star* 21, no. 37 (September 1859): 582–83.

32. Ezra Taft Benson, "Prepare Yourselves for the Great Day of the Lord," *BYU Fireside and Devotional Speeches, 1981* (Provo, Utah: Brigham Young University Press, 1982), 67.

33. Smith, *Teachings of the Prophet Joseph Smith,* 341.

34. Ibid., 252.

CHAPTER SEVEN

LIFE IN THE MILLENNIUM

ROBERT L. MILLET

It is easy in our busy and complex world to become ensnared by programs, points of view, and ways of life that have no lasting value, no everlasting import. We are eternal beings involved in a mortal experience, and one of the tasks of this estate is to see to it that we do not become preoccupied with the ephemeral, that which is wholly temporal, that which will eventually pass away. We live in a day of wickedness and vengeance, an era in this world's temporal continuance when Satan, the god of the worldly, rages in the hearts of men and women. But we look upon the present distress with an eye of faith, with an eye to the future, with the certain assurance that one day soon the God of gods shall bring an abrupt end to all unholiness and inaugurate an age of peace and happiness. In a not too distant day, the light of the great Millennium will dawn, and things will be very different on this earth.

THE END OF THE WORLD

When the Lord of Sabaoth, the Lord of Hosts, literally the Lord of armies, returns in glory, every corruptible thing will be destroyed. "The presence of the Lord shall be as the melting fire that burneth, and as the fire which causeth the waters to boil. . . . And so great shall be the glory of his presence that the sun shall hide his face in shame, and the moon shall withhold its light, and the stars shall be hurled from their places" (D&C 133:41, 49). It will be a selective burning, for those who are of a celestial or a terrestrial state or order shall abide the day; all else will be cleansed from the surface of this planet. Those who lie and cheat and steal, those who revel in

---

Robert L. Millet is dean of Religious Education at Brigham Young University.

immorality and pervert the ways of righteousness, those who mock and point the finger of scorn at the Saints of the Most High—all these shall be burned at his coming, shall die the death with which we are familiar, and their spirits shall take up residence in the spirit world, there to await the last resurrection at the end of a thousand years. The Second Coming in glory is "the end of the world," meaning the worldly, the destruction of the wicked (Joseph Smith–Matthew 1:4).

The prophet Zenos said: "The time cometh speedily that Satan shall have no more power over the hearts of the children of men; for the day soon cometh that all the proud and they who do wickedly shall be as stubble; and the day cometh that they must be burned. For the time soon cometh that the fulness of the wrath of God shall be poured out upon all the children of men; for he will not suffer that the wicked shall destroy the righteous. Wherefore, *he will preserve the righteous by his power, even if it so be that the fulness of his wrath must come, and the righteous be preserved, even unto the destruction of their enemies by fire.* Wherefore, the righteous need not fear; for thus saith the prophet, they shall be saved, even if it so be as by fire" (1 Nephi 22:15–17; italics added; compare Malachi 4:1). Nephi added that "the time speedily shall come that all churches which are built up to get gain, and all those who are built up to get power over the flesh, and those who are built up to become popular in the eyes of the world, and those who seek the lusts of the flesh and the things of the world, and to do all manner of iniquity; yea, in fine, all those who belong to the kingdom of the devil are they who need fear, and tremble, and quake; they are those who must be brought low in the dust; they are those who must be consumed as stubble" (1 Nephi 22:23). Moroni explained that "they that come"—meaning the Lord and his destroying angels— "shall burn them, saith the Lord of Hosts, that it shall leave them neither root nor branch" (Joseph Smith–History 1:37).

Thus it is that the great day of division comes at the time of our Lord's second advent, "for the time speedily cometh that the Lord

God shall cause a great division among the people, and the wicked will he destroy; and he will spare his people, yea, even if it so be that he must destroy the wicked by fire" (2 Nephi 30:10). Indeed, as a modern revelation attests, "at that hour cometh an entire separation of the righteous and the wicked; and in that day will I send mine angels to pluck out the wicked and cast them into unquenchable fire" (D&C 63:54). This is a day of power. Just as the power of the Almighty was felt in the cleansing of the earth in the days of Noah—wherein the earth received its baptism—so also shall that same power be manifest in the last times when the earth is cleansed by fire and receives its confirmation. "After you have been immersed," Elder Orson Pratt observed, "as this earth was, in the water, and been cleansed and received the remission of your sins, you also have the promise of baptism of fire and of the Holy Ghost, by which you are purified, as well justified and sanctified from all your evil affections, and you feel to love God and that which is just and true, and to hate that which is sinful and evil. Why? Because of this sanctifying, purifying principle that comes upon you, by the baptism of fire and the Holy Ghost. So must this earth be baptised by fire, it must be cleansed from all sin and impurity. Will it be filled with the Holy Ghost? Yes."[1]

The second coming in glory of our Lord and Savior initiates the Millennium. The Millennium does not begin when Christ comes to Adam-ondi-Ahman, when he appears at his temple in Independence, Missouri, or when he stands upon the Mount of Olives in the midst of Armageddon. The Millennium will not come because men and women on earth have become noble and good, because Christian charity will have spread across the globe and goodwill is the order of the day. The Millennium will not come because technological advancements and medical miracles will have extended human life or because peace treaties among warring nations will have soothed injured feelings and eased political tensions for a time. The Millennium will be brought in by power, by the power of Him who is the King of kings and Lord of lords. Satan will be bound by power, and the glory of the Millennium will be maintained by the righteousness of those who are permitted to live on earth (1 Nephi 22:15, 26).

At the beginning of the Millennium the earth and all things upon it will be quickened, made alive, and transfigured—lifted spiritually to a higher plane for a season. The earth will be transformed from a telestial to a terrestrial glory, to that paradisiacal condition of which the scriptures and the prophets speak, that glorious condition that prevailed in Eden before the Fall (Articles of Faith 1:10). There will indeed be a new heaven and a new earth (Isaiah 65:17; Revelation 21:1).

THE FIRST RESURRECTION RESUMES

When "the face of the Lord shall be unveiled," then, in that day, "the saints that are upon the earth, who are alive, shall be quickened and be caught up to meet him" (D&C 88:95–96). That quickening would seem to entail the accentuation of man's spiritual nature and the subduing of his fallen nature. Elder Orson Pratt explained that "all the inhabitants who are spared from this fire—those who are not proud, and who do not do wickedly, will be cleansed more fully and filled with the glory of God. A partial change will be wrought upon them"—a type of translation—"not a change to immortality, like that which all the Saints will undergo when they are changed in the twinkling of an eye, from mortality to immortality; but so great will be the change then wrought that the children who are born into the world will grow up without sin unto salvation [see D&C 45:58]. Why will this be so? Because *that fallen nature, introduced by the fall, and transferred from parents to children, from generation to generation, will be, in a measure, eradicated by this change.*"[2]

The first resurrection began with the resurrection of Christ in the meridian of time. All of the prophets and those who gave heed to the words of the prophets, from the days of Adam to Christ— and, we would presume, all those who never had an opportunity to receive the gospel but would have received it if they had been given the privilege (D&C 137:7–9)—came forth from the grave some time after the rise of the Savior to immortal glory (see Mosiah 15:21–25; Alma 40:20). We have no indication that there has been a wholesale resurrection of Saints since the resurrection of the Savior. "There are some who feel," President Ezra Taft Benson pointed out, "that the resurrection is going on continually and has been since that time. This is not scripturally true, but we do know that it is possible for our Father to call from the graves those whom He needs to perform special missions and special service. For example, we know of at least three [Peter, James, and Moroni] who have been called up since the resurrection of the Master and since that first mass resurrection when the graves were opened and many of the Saints arose."[3]

When the Master returns in glory to take charge of affairs on this earth, with him will come a host of the righteous dead. The first resurrection will thereby resume. Those who have died true to the faith, those who were valiant in the testimony of Jesus, who have kept the celestial law, shall return to earth with resurrected, immortal bodies. "They who have slept in their graves shall come forth, for their graves shall be opened; and they also shall be caught up to meet him in the midst of the pillar of heaven—they are Christ's, the first fruits, they who shall descend with him first, and they who are on the earth and in their graves, who are first caught up to meet him" (D&C 88:97–98). Or, according to the testimony of the apostle Paul, "they who are alive"—meaning, presumably, physically alive when the Lord comes—"shall be caught up together into the clouds with them who remain, to meet the Lord in the air; and so shall we be ever with the Lord" (JST 1 Thessalonians 4:17). The Lord of the living and the dead "will come with ten thousands of his saints, all of them resurrected persons from ages past. He will call forth from their graves and from the watery deep ten thousands of his other saints, all of them righteous persons who have lived since his mortal ministry. Those among his saints on earth who are faithful will be caught up to meet him in the clouds of glory, and they will then return to earth with him to live out their appointed days on the new earth with its new heavens."⁴ That is the first resurrection, or, as we have come to call it, the morning of the first resurrection, the resurrection of the celestial.

With Christ will come the hosts of persons who were translated before the resurrection of Christ, those who were taken into terrestrial glory without tasting death. Enoch and Melchizedek with their cities, Elijah and Moses and Alma and Nephi, and, surely, congregations and communities of the pure in heart of which we have no knowledge, shall return as resurrected personages. These were with Christ in his resurrection (see D&C 133:54–55).⁵ Those who have been translated since the resurrection of Christ—John the Beloved, the three Nephites, and other holy men or women that we know not of (D&C 49:8)—shall undergo the change equivalent to death and be transformed instantaneously from their translated mortal state to resurrected immortality at the time of our Savior's return in glory (see 3 Nephi 28:8).⁶

Although men and women who are alive at the time of Christ's second coming will be changed and quickened, they will yet continue to live as mortals. That is, for them death and immortality lie ahead. The mortal Saints shall live to "the age of man" (D&C 63:50) during the Millennium, what Isaiah explained to be one hundred years (Isaiah 65:20). At that point they will pass from mortality through death into resurrected immortality instantly, "in the twinkling of an eye." For these there will be no time for the body in the grave, no sojourn in the postmortal world of spirits, for they will be received into glory immediately after their death: "Wherefore, children shall grow up until they become old; old men shall die; but they shall not sleep in the dust, but they shall be changed in the twinkling of an eye" (D&C 63:51).

"During the Millennium," Elder Bruce R. McConkie has written, "there will, of course, be two kinds of people on earth. There will be those who are mortal, and those who are immortal. There will be those who have been changed or quickened or transfigured or translated (words fail us to describe their state), and those who have gone through a second change, in the twinkling of an eye, so as to become eternal in nature. There will be those who are on probation, for whom earth life is a probationary estate, and who are thus working out their own salvation, and those who have already overcome the world and have entered into a fulness of eternal joy. There will be those who will yet die in the sense of being changed from their quickened state to a state of immortality, and those who, having previously died, are then living in a resurrected state. There will be those who are subject to the kings and priests who rule forever in the house of Israel, and those who, as kings and priests, exercise power and dominion in the everlasting kingdom of Him whose we are. There will be those who, as mortals, provide bodies for the spirit children of the Father, for the spirits whose right it is to come to earth and gain houses for their eternal spirits, and those who, as immortals (Abraham is one), are already begetting spirit children of their own. There will be those for whom the fulness of eternal glory is ahead, and those who, again like Abraham, have already entered into their exaltation and sit upon their thrones and are not angels but are gods forever and ever."[7]

Why it is that certain persons, surely billions of our brothers and sisters, will be sent to earth to gain their mortal and then immortal bodies during this glorious era—an era during which they will not be tested, at least in the same ways we are now—is not known. This we do know: our God is perfectly just. He is perfectly merciful. And he is impartial. He is no respecter of persons and delights in the development and ultimate salvation of all his sons and daughters. He is all-wise and all-knowing, and thus we would assume that he would arrange and orchestrate the times and seasons and events of our lives in such a way as to maximize our growth and further our spirituality. The Saints of the Most High ought to glory in the knowledge that so many could come to the earth and be born, nurtured in an Edenic atmosphere, and grow up without sin unto salvation.

THE GROWING GLORY OF THE MILLENNIUM

When the telestial elements are stripped away from this orb, when sin and iniquity are burned away by the brightness of the coming of the King of Zion, the wickedness that befouls the planet will be no more and earth shall rest. No longer shall mother earth cry out in painful weariness because of the pollutions upon her surface (Moses 7:48; compare Romans 8:22), for the stains of wilful sin will have been purged out, and the glory of heaven will be felt by every person. The Savior will be in our midst (3 Nephi 20:22; 21:25). He shall reign over Zion and minister among his chosen people in both the Old and the New Jerusalem. He shall dwell among his Saints, teach them in their congregations, and see to it that his doctrine is declared from one end of this earth to the other.

But not all who inhabit the earth during the beginning of the Millennium will be of one faith and one baptism. In that early hour of millennial splendor not all will be converted to The Church of Jesus Christ of Latter-day Saints. Inasmuch as the terrestrial of the earth, those who are honorable and good, who are kindly and well-disposed, will be spared the burning, they shall live and move and have their being on the same earth as the members of the household of faith. Seeing is often not believing. Just as men and women are actuated and driven in this life by their quest for the fulness of truth, so also will men and women of a millennial kind be likewise driven and motivated. And just as noble and upright souls in all nations and climes hesitate in our day to partake of the glories of the new and everlasting covenant, so also will many refuse the fulness of gospel light in that day when the Mediator of the new covenant presides among his Saints.

President Brigham Young stated: "If the Latter-day Saints think, when the kingdom of God is established on the earth, that all the inhabitants of the earth will join the church called Latter-day

Saints, they are egregiously mistaken. I presume there will be as many sects and parties then as now."[8] On another occasion President Young said: "When Jesus comes to rule and reign King of Nations as he now does King of Saints, the veil of the covering will be taken from all nations, that *all flesh may see his glory together, but that will not make them all Saints.* Seeing the Lord does not make a man a Saint, seeing an Angel does not make a man a Saint by any means." President Young then added that the leaders of nations in that day, "kings and potentates of the nations will come up to Zion to inquire after the ways of the Lord, and to seek out the great knowledge, wisdom, and understanding manifested through the Saints of the Most High. They will inform the people of God that they belong to such and such a Church, and do not wish to change their religion."[9] In short, "in the millennium men will have the privilege of being Presbyterians, Methodists or Infidels, but they will not have the privilege of treating the name and character of Deity as they have done heretofore. No, but every knee shall bow and every tongue confess to the glory of God the Father that Jesus is the Christ."[10]

And yet the testimony of the scriptures and the prophets is consistent that as the power of God's Spirit continues to spread, eventually "the earth shall be full of the knowledge of the Lord, as the waters cover the sea" (Isaiah 11:9; see also Habakkuk 2:14). Truly "in that day when the Lord shall come, he shall reveal all things—things which have passed, and hidden things which no man knew, things of the earth, by which it was made, and the purpose and the end thereof—things most precious, things that are above, and things that are beneath, things that are in the earth, and upon the earth, and in heaven" (D&C 101:32–34). "The gospel will be taught," President Joseph Fielding Smith observed, "far more intensely and with greater power during the millennium, *until all the inhabitants of the earth shall embrace it.* . . . Through the revelations given to the prophets, we learn that during the reign of

Jesus Christ for a thousand years *eventually all people will embrace the truth.*"[11]

The Prophet Joseph Smith, drawing upon the prophecies of Zechariah 14:16–18, said: "There will be wicked men on the earth during the thousand years." By *wicked* he presumably meant those of a terrestrial order, those who refused to come unto the Father through receiving the fulness of his gospel (see D&C 84:48–53; see also 35:12).[12] The Prophet's statement continues: "The heathen nations who will not come up to worship will be visited with the judgments of God, and must eventually be destroyed from the earth."[13] Isaiah testified: "In those days there shall be no more thence an infant of days, nor an old man that hath not filled his days; for the child shall not die, but shall live to be an hundred years old; but *the sinner, living to be an hundred years old, shall be accursed*" (JST Isaiah 65:20; italics added). Elder McConkie similarly explained that "there will be many churches on earth when the Millennium begins. False worship will continue among those whose desires are good, 'who are honorable men of the earth,' but who have been 'blinded by the craftiness of men.' (D&C 76:75.) Plagues will rest upon them until they repent and believe the gospel or are destroyed, as the Prophet said. It follows that missionary work will continue into the Millennium until all who remain are converted. . . . Then every living soul on earth will belong to The Church of Jesus Christ of Latter-day Saints."[14]

DAILY LIFE

We can only imagine such an existence—a life without physical pain, premature death, an existence without the sorrow that accompanies sin and waywardness, without the disappointment associated with dishonesty and greed. Isaiah proclaimed that in that day "the wolf also shall dwell with the lamb, and the leopard shall lie down with the kid; and the calf and the young lion and the fatling together; and a little child shall lead them. And the cow and the bear shall feed; their little ones shall lie down together: and the lion shall eat straw like the ox. And the sucking child shall play on the hole of the asp, and the weaned child shall put his hand on the cockatrice' den. They shall not hurt nor destroy in all my holy mountain" (Isaiah 11:6–9; compare 65:25). That is, "in that day the enmity of man, and the enmity of beasts, yea, the enmity of all flesh"—an animosity, a natural tension and unrest that came as a result of the Fall—"shall cease from before my face" (D&C 101:26). And so it is that "violence shall no more be heard in thy land, wasting nor destruction within thy borders; but thou shalt call thy walls Salvation, and thy gates Praise" (Isaiah 60:18).

Mortals shall inhabit the earth, alongside immortals, during the entirety of the thousand years. Men and women who abide the day of the Lord's coming in glory shall continue to live on this earth in an Edenic state. They shall labor and study and grow and interact and love and socialize as before, but such things shall be undertaken in a totally moral environment. "When the Savior shall appear," the Prophet Joseph Smith taught in Nauvoo, "we shall see him as he is. We shall see that he is a man like ourselves. And *that same sociality which exists among us here will exist among us there, only it will be coupled with eternal glory, which glory we do not now enjoy*" (D&C 130:1–2; italics added). "And they shall build houses, and inhabit them; and they shall plant vineyards, and eat the fruit of them. They shall not build, and another inhabit; they shall not plant, and another eat" (Isaiah 65:21–22). That is to say, in the Millennium men and women shall enjoy the fruits of their labors. In a world where there is no extortion, no bribery, no organized crime, where there are no unjust laws, no class distinctions of men and women according to income or chances for learning, people shall no longer be preyed upon by the perverse or the malicious or forced to relocate because of financial demands or pressures. Our longings for stability, for longevity, and for permanence shall be largely satisfied, for the father of lies and those who have spread his influence will have no place on the earth during the thousand years.

"Now, how will it be on this earth when Christ reigns?" President George Q. Cannon inquired. "When the Millennium dawns," he answered his own question, "Satan bound and the elements of the earth at our disposal and under our control, there will be no hunger, no thirst, no nakedness, no vagrants, no houseless people; *all will have that which is necessary to supply their physical wants. But there will be no waste.* One man will not be allowed to lord it over another and take possession of more than he needs; but *all will have a fulness,* Satan will be bound. He will not have power to inflict the misery he has done and is doing."[15]

THE GREAT DAY OF TEMPLE WORK

The work of gathering people into the fold is not complete when they are baptized and confirmed members of The Church of Jesus Christ of Latter-day Saints. The final phase of this divine process consists of gathering to holy temples to be endowed with power from on high and receiving therein the ordinances of exaltation.[16] It follows that because millions upon millions of souls will join themselves to the Saints in the Millennium, the work of temples will be among the most significant labor performed. "I think there is a work to be done [in the Millennium]," President Brigham Young said, "which the whole world seems determined we shall not do. What is it? To build temples."[17]

President Wilford Woodruff taught that "this work of administering the ordinances of the house of God to the dead . . . will require the whole of the Millennium, with Jesus at the head of the resurrected dead to attend to it."[18] President Joseph F. Smith likewise observed that "the great work of the Millennium shall be the work in the temples for the redemption of the dead; and then, we hope to enjoy the benefits of revelation through the Urim and Thummim, or by such means as the Lord may reveal concerning those for whom the work shall be done."[19] The scriptures attest that there will be kings and priests in every land and among every kindred, tongue, and people before the Lord Jesus comes in glory

(Revelation 5:9–10). That implies that temples will dot the earth, that the fulness of priesthood blessings will be available to men and women everywhere, even before the ushering in of the Millennium. Such sacred labor will be intensified during the thousand-year era of peace and righteousness, for "*to accomplish this work there will have to be not only one temple but thousands of them,* and thousands and tens of thousands of men and women will go into those temples and officiate for people who have lived as far back as the Lord shall reveal."[20]

We suppose that the work of the Church and kingdom of God—the establishment of men, women, and children in eternal family units through the powers of the Holy Priesthood—will come to complete fruition by the end of the Millennium. When, by the end of the thousand years, people of the Church will have achieved a unity of the faith, the Church of Jesus Christ, as we know it now, will have served its function (see Ephesians 4:11–14). What church, what ecclesiastical system of organization, will exist in eternity, beyond the patriarchal order, has not been made known. As to the ordinances and work of the Church during the thousand years, Elder McConkie has suggested: "During the Millennium children will be named and blessed by the elders of the kingdom. When those of the rising generation arrive at the years of accountability, they will be baptized in water and of the Spirit by legal administrators appointed so to act. Priesthood will be conferred upon young and old, and they will be ordained to offices therein as the needs of the ministry and their own salvation require. At the appropriate time each person will receive his patriarchal blessing, we suppose from the natural patriarch who presides in his family, as it was in Adamic days and as it was when Jacob blessed his sons. The saints will receive their endowments in the temples of the Lord, and they will receive the blessings of celestial marriage at their holy altars. And all of the faithful will have their callings and elections made sure and will be sealed up unto that eternal life which will come to them when they reach the age of a tree. We see no reasons why the ordinances of administering to the sick or the dedication of graves should continue, for disease and death shall be no more."[21]

We sing an anthem of praise and anticipation, a hymn that points our minds toward the glorious days ahead:

> *The day dawn is breaking, the world is awaking,*
> *The clouds of night's darkness are fleeing away.*
> *The worldwide commotion, from ocean to ocean,*
> *Now heralds the time of the beautiful day.*
>
> *In many a temple the Saints will assemble*
> *And labor as saviors of dear ones away.*
> *Then happy reunion and sweetest communion*
> *We'll have with our friends in the beautiful day.*
>
> *Still let us be doing, our lessons reviewing,*
> *Which God has revealed for our walk in his way;*
> *And then, wondrous story, the Lord in his glory*
> *Will come in his pow'r in the beautiful day.*
>
> *Then pure and supernal, our friendship eternal,*
> *With Jesus we'll live, and his counsels obey*
> *Until ev'ry nation will join in salvation*
> *And worship the God of the beautiful day.*
>
> *Beautiful day of peace and rest,*
> *Bright be thy dawn from east to west.*
> *Hail to thine earliest welcome ray,*
> *Beautiful, bright, millennial day.*[22]

GATHERING ALL THINGS IN ONE

Ancient and modern scripture affirms that a significant part of the drama we know as the gathering of Israel will be millennial. We have witnessed miracles as the gospel has made its way into many parts of the earth, but the greatest miracles lie ahead. A major conversion of the Jews—the birth of a nation under their Head, Jesus the Messiah—will take place when he appears on the Mount of Olives (see Zechariah 12:9–10; 13:6; D&C 45:48–53). Elders and sisters and righteous couples shall, in addition, be the means of delivering the message of salvation to men and women throughout the globe. We would expect that very soon our missionaries will enter into lands wherein pockets of Israelites will be baptized and confirmed and where patriarchs will declare their lineage through such tribes as Issachar, Zebulun, Gad, Asher, and Naphtali. Further, during the time preceding and following our Lord's return in glory, we anticipate that millions of those not of the lineal descent of Jacob shall receive the glad tidings of the Restoration, come unto Christ through the saving ordinances, and be counted by adoption as sons and daughters of Abraham, Isaac, and Jacob (see Abraham 2:10).[23] Leaning heavily upon the words of an ancient prophet, presumably Zenos, Nephi recorded: "And the time cometh speedily that the righteous must be led up as calves of the stall, and *the Holy One of Israel must reign in dominion, and might, and power, and great glory. And he gathereth his children from the four quarters of the earth;* and he numbereth his sheep, and they know him; and there shall be one fold and one shepherd; and he shall feed his sheep, and in him they shall find pasture" (1 Nephi 22:24–25; italics added; see also 2 Nephi 30:6–18).

The Savior himself explained to the Nephites that in the Millennium the "work of the Father"—the work of gathering, the work of inviting people to come unto Christ through missionary work—shall "commence at that day" (3 Nephi 21:26). How is it that the work of the gathering of Israel will *commence* during the Millennium, when we have been gathering the people of the Lord since the inception of this latter-day work? Simply stated, the magnitude and magnificence and breadth and depth of the gathering in that glorious day will be such as to cause all previous efforts at gathering to pale into insignificance. It will be as though the work had just begun.

"Therefore, behold, the days come, saith the Lord, that it shall no more be said, The Lord liveth, that brought up the children of Israel out of the land of Egypt; but, The Lord liveth, that brought up the children of Israel from the land of the north, and from all the lands whither he had driven them: and I will bring them into their land that I gave unto their fathers." And how is this great gathering to be accomplished? "Behold, I will send for many fishers, saith the Lord, and they shall fish them; and after will I send for many hunters, and they shall hunt them from every mountain, and from every hill, and out of the holes of the rocks. For mine eyes are upon all their ways" (Jeremiah 16:14–17).

Our Lord and God shall govern his people from two world capitals, "for out of Zion shall go forth the law, and the word of the Lord from Jerusalem" (Isaiah 2:3). "And he shall utter his voice out of Zion"—meaning, Independence, Missouri—"and he shall speak from Jerusalem, and his voice shall be heard among all people; and it shall be a voice as the voice of many waters, and as the voice of a great thunder, which shall break down the mountains, and the valleys shall not be found" (D&C 133:21–22). In that day the latter-day David, even Jesus Christ, the true son of David, shall unite Ephraim and Judah, and shall preside over all Israel, from one end of the earth to the other.[24] Thus will be fulfilled the divine decree: "Be subject to the powers that be, *until he reigns whose right it is to reign, and subdues all enemies under his feet*" (D&C 58:22; italics added).

"How long can rolling waters remain impure?" the Prophet Joseph Smith wrote by inspiration from Liberty Jail. "What power shall stay the heavens? As well might man stretch forth his puny arm to stop the Missouri river in its decreed course, or to turn it up stream, as to hinder the Almighty from pouring down knowledge from heaven upon the heads of the Latter-day Saints" (D&C 121:33). The Saints have been blessed beyond measure with light and truth and sacred insights; the scriptures of the Restoration now shed forth their resplendent rays upon a darkened and benighted world. But there is more to come, more light, more knowledge, more doctrine, more precepts. Nothing is more set and established than the eternal fact that the canon of scripture is open, flexible, and expanding.

We shall yet read the sealed portion of the Book of Mormon, that panoramic vision vouchsafed to the brother of Jared in which is to be found "a revelation from God, from the beginning of the world to the ending thereof," even "all things from the foundation of the world unto the end thereof" (2 Nephi 27:7, 10). Truly in that millennial day when men and women exercise dynamic faith like unto that of the brother of Jared, the damning veil of unbelief shall be rent and we shall have a complete Book of Mormon (Ether 4:7, 15). Further, we shall be privileged to search, as did Lehi, the brass plates (see 1 Nephi 5:17–19; Alma 37:4) and to become privy to details of history and doctrine found only on the large plates of Nephi. In addition to that portion of the record of the ten tribes in our possession that we know now as the Doctrine and Covenants—the record of God's dealings with modern Ephraim—we delight in the assurance that other sacred volumes chronicling our Redeemer's ministry to the lost tribes shall come forth during the Millennium (2 Nephi 29:13). In short, in that glorious day we shall exult in truths without number found on the myriad of records kept chiefly by the Nephites (Helaman 3:13–16) as well as by other scattered branches of Israel of whom we have no knowledge. Elder Neal A. Maxwell thus observed: "Today we carry convenient quadruple combinations of the scriptures, but one day, since more scriptures are coming, we may need to pull little red wagons brimful with books."[25]

The apostle Paul taught that "in the dispensation of the fulness of times [the Lord would] gather together in one all things in Christ, both which are in heaven, and which are on earth; even in him" (Ephesians 1:10). And surely what begins as a flowing stream in our day shall become a mighty river during the thousand years of peace. In that day the heavens will be opened, pure and sweet communion with God and angels will be enjoyed by the Saints of the Most High, and eternal verities will be made known constantly, without let or hindrance. The Saints shall have been cleansed of sin, and their motives will have been purified; they will no longer ask amiss for that which they ought not. Thus, "in that day whatsoever any man shall ask, it shall be given unto him" (D&C 101:27). "And it shall come to pass, that before they call, I will answer; and while they are yet speaking, I will hear" (Isaiah 65:24). During the thousand years the covenant people from Christ's church on earth will have internalized the principles of his gospel and incorporated the law of the Lord into their very being. They will then see "eye to eye" with one another and with their Lord and Master (D&C 84:98). Jeremiah recorded the words of Jehovah: "Behold, the days come, saith the Lord, that I will make a new covenant with the house of Israel, and with the house of Judah: not according to the covenant that I made with their fathers in the day that I took them by the hand to bring them out of the land of Egypt; which my covenant they brake, although I was an husband unto them, saith the Lord: but this shall be the covenant that I will make with the house of Israel; after those days, saith the Lord, *I will put my law in their inward parts, and write it in their hearts;* and will be their God, and they shall be my people" (Jeremiah 31:31–33; italics added).

The people who have accepted the fulness of the gospel in that day will know their God and be constrained to obey his will and keep his commandments. "And they shall teach no more every man his neighbour, and every man his brother, saying, Know the Lord: for *they shall all know me, from the least of them unto the greatest of them,* saith the Lord: for I will forgive their iniquity, and I will remember their sin no more" (Jeremiah 31:34; italics added). "How is this to be done?" Joseph Smith asked. "It is to be done by this sealing power, and the other Comforter spoken of, which will be manifest by revelation."[26]

It is a day when Christ and the resurrected Saints will dwell on earth—not permanently, but periodically, "when they please, or when it is necessary to govern it."[27] It is a time wherein men and women will have grown up in the Lord (Helaman 3:21), will have cultivated the gifts of the Spirit, and will have received a fulness of the Holy Ghost (D&C 109:15). The Holy Ghost will have taught and sanctified them until they are prepared to come into the presence of Christ, and even unto the Father.[28] It is the day of the Second Comforter, the day when the Saints whose eyes are single to the glory of God shall see him (D&C 88:67–68). Elder Bruce R. McConkie has written: "Men will know God in the millennial day because they see him. He will teach them face to face. They will know the mysteries of his kingdom because they are caught up to the third heaven, as was Paul. They will receive the Second Comforter. The millennial day is the day of the Second Comforter, and whereas but few have been blessed with this divine association in times past, great hosts will be so blessed in times to come."[29]

THE FINAL BATTLE AND THE END OF THE EARTH

For a thousand years men and women on earth will live lives of quiet nobility, will bow the knee and acknowledge Jesus the Messiah as the King of Zion and the Redeemer of all mankind. As we have noted, at the beginning of the Millennium not all of earth's inhabitants will join the true church, but by the end of the thousand years all will be of one faith. Though Satan will have been dismissed from the earth by the true King of kings, and though he will have been bound by the righteousness of the people, men and women will have their moral agency. They will exercise the power of choice. The Prophet Joseph Smith observed that "Satan was generally blamed for the evils which we did, but if he was the cause of all our wickedness, men could not be condemned. The devil could not compel mankind to do evil; all was voluntary."[30]

For reasons that have not been fully revealed, there will come a time at the end of the thousand years when "men again begin to deny their God" (D&C 29:22). That is, they will choose, despite the light and truth that surround them, to come out in open rebellion against our Father, his Beloved Son, and the great plan of happiness. Satan will be loosed again "for a little season" that he might "gather together his armies" (D&C 88:111; see also 43:31). Perhaps we can gain some insight into why such a turn of events should take place by searching the Book of Mormon. We remember during the almost two hundred years after the risen Lord's visit to America that all were converted to Christ, dealt justly with one another, had all things in common, and were united in that order of priesthood society we know as Zion. "And it came to pass that there was no contention in the land, because of the love of God which did dwell in the hearts of the people" (4 Nephi 1:15; see also vv. 1–17). And what was it that changed things? It was *pride,* pride in what one was called, pride in what one earned, pride in one's dress and appearance, pride in one's place and station in society. "And from that time forth they did have their goods and their substance no more common among them. And they began to be divided into classes; and they began to build up churches unto themselves to get gain, and began to deny the true church of Christ" (4 Nephi 1:25–26; see also vv. 20–24).

President George Q. Cannon taught: "After the thousand years [Satan] will regain some of his present power. It will be as it was among the Nephites. . . . Men will arise who will object to working for the benefit of others; class distinctions will once more make themselves apparent."[31] On another occasion he explained "that when Satan is loosed again for a little while, when the thousand years shall be ended, it will be through mankind departing from the practice of those principles which God has revealed, and this Order of Enoch probably among the rest. He can, in no better way, obtain power over the hearts of the children of men, than by appealing to their cupidity, avarice, and low, selfish desires."[32]

It should be obvious that Satan's final conquest over the souls of men at the end of the Millennium will be limited to mortals. Exalted, immortal beings—those who have been changed in the twinkling of an eye, or resurrected personages who minister on earth from time to time—cannot fall, cannot apostatize. Their salvation is secure. The father of lies will thus have his way only among those living during the final years of the Millennium, those who have not arrived at the age of one hundred.[33] Those who choose to reject the Lord and his plan at this late date do so against the light of heaven; they in essence say that the sun does not shine while they see it. They are thus consigned hereafter to a kingdom of no glory as sons of perdition.[34] "Michael, the seventh angel, even the archangel, shall gather together his armies, even the hosts of heaven. And the devil shall gather together his armies; even the hosts of hell, and shall come up to battle against Michael and his armies. And then cometh the battle of the great God"—known also as the battle of Gog and Magog[35]—"and the devil and his armies shall be cast away into their own place, that they shall not have power over the saints any more at all" (D&C 88:112–14).

At the end of the thousand years, after the battle of Gog and Magog, we come to that time known as "the end of the earth" (D&C 88:101; Joseph Smith–Matthew 1:55), the final cleansing and celestialization of the planet. Having been baptized by water in the days of Noah and confirmed, or baptized by fire, at the time of the Second Coming, the earth will pass through the equivalent of a death and a resurrection. It will become a glorified celestial orb, inasmuch as it will have filled the measure of its creation (D&C 88:25). The earth will then be a fit abode for the true and faithful, "that bodies who are of the celestial kingdom may possess it forever and ever; for, for this intent was it made and created, and for this intent are they sanctified" (D&C 88:20). The revelations attest of those who qualify for exaltation in eternity: "They are they who are the church of the Firstborn"—meaning, those who qualify for the blessings of the Firstborn, the right to inherit, possess, and receive equally as joint heirs with Christ all the Father has. "They are they into whose hands the Father has given all things—they are they who are priests and kings"—and we would add, queens and priestesses—"who have received of his fulness, and of his glory. . . . Wherefore, as it is written, they are gods, even the sons of God" (D&C 76:54–56, 58).

Unlike so many in the religious world, the Latter-day Saints anticipate celestial life on a material world. Elder Orson Pratt eloquently and powerfully made this point as follows: "A Saint who is one in deed and truth, does not look for an immaterial heaven, but he expects a heaven with lands, houses, cities, vegetation, rivers, and animals; with thrones, temples, palaces, kings, princes, priests, and angels; with food, raiment, musical instruments, etc., all of which are material. Indeed, *the Saints' heaven is a redeemed, glorified, celestial material creation, inhabited by glorified material beings, male and female, organized into families,* embracing all the relationships of husbands and wives, parents and children, where sorrow, crying, pain, and death will be known no more. Or to speak still more definitely, *this earth, when glorified, is the Saints' eternal heaven. On it they expect to live, with body, parts, and holy passions; on it they expect to move and have their being;* to eat, drink, converse, worship, sing, play on musical instruments, engage in joyful, innocent, social amusements, visit neighboring towns and neighboring worlds; *indeed, matter and its qualities and properties are the only beings or things with which they expect to associate.* . . .

"Materiality is indelibly stamped upon the very heaven of heavens, upon all the eternal creations; it is the very essence of all existence."[36]

CONCLUSION

Those who seek to prepare themselves for what lies ahead, who have taken the Holy Spirit for their guide, attempt to view things as they are now in terms of things as they shall be. One day things will change. Goodness and honesty and integrity will be the order of the day; morality and decency will characterize men and women across the globe. In that sense, we look forward to the great millennial day. Though there are many tight places through which the Saints will be required to pass, though trials and difficulties will abound on every side, though disease and death and despair will be rampant prior to the Lord's coming in glory, yet we glory in the fact that one day the King of kings and Lord of lords will take control of things, and a new day will dawn. "For I, the Almighty, have laid my hands upon the nations, to scourge them for their wickedness. And plagues shall go forth, and they shall not be taken from the earth until I have completed my work, which shall be cut short in righteousness—until all shall know me, who remain, even from the least unto the greatest, and shall be filled with the knowledge of the Lord, and shall see eye to eye, and shall lift up their voice, and with the voice together sing this new song, saying:

> *The Lord hath brought again Zion;*
> *The Lord hath redeemed his people, Israel,*
> *According to the election of grace,*
> *Which was brought to pass by the faith*
> *And covenant of their fathers.*
> *The Lord hath redeemed his people;*
> *And Satan is bound and time is no longer.*
> *The Lord hath gathered all things in one.*
> *The Lord hath brought down Zion from above.*
> *The Lord hath brought up Zion from beneath.*
> *The earth hath travailed and brought forth her*
>   *strength;*
> *And truth is established in her bowels;*
> *And the heavens have smiled upon her;*
> *And she is clothed with the glory of her God;*
> *For he stands in the midst of his people.*
> *Glory, and honor, and power, and might,*
> *Be ascribed to our God; for he is full of mercy,*
> *Justice, grace and truth, and peace,*
> *Forever and ever, Amen.*
> (D&C 84:96–102)

"And again, verily I say unto you, the coming of the Lord draweth nigh, and it overtaketh the world as a thief in the night—therefore, gird up your loins, that you may be the children of light, and that day shall not overtake you as a thief" (D&C 106:4–5). The faithful shall not be surprised. The children of light, those who honor their covenants and are true to their trusts, who seek for and cultivate the spirit of revelation, these shall be in a position to read the signs of the times and be prepared for the great and terrible day of the Lord. They shall abide the day, be caught up to meet their Master, and feel peace and confidence in his presence. In harmony with the soul-cry of the beloved Revelator (Revelation 22:20), they exclaim: "Even so, come, Lord Jesus."

NOTES

1. Orson Pratt, in *Journal of Discourses* (London: Latter-day Saints' Book Depot, 1854–86), 16:319.

2. Ibid.; italics added.

3. Ezra Taft Benson, *The Teachings of Ezra Taft Benson* (Salt Lake City: Bookcraft, 1988), 18.

4. Bruce R. McConkie, *The Millennial Messiah* (Salt Lake City: Deseret Book, 1982), 627.

5. See Bruce R. McConkie, *Mormon Doctrine,* 2d ed. (Salt Lake City: Bookcraft, 1966), 807–8; *Millennial Messiah,* 628, 636, 647; *A New Witness for the Articles of Faith* (Salt Lake City: Deseret Book, 1985), 588.

6. See Joseph Smith, *Teachings of the Prophet Joseph Smith,* sel. Joseph Fielding Smith (Salt Lake City: Deseret Book, 1938), 191.

7. McConkie, *Millennial Messiah,* 644–45.

8. Brigham Young, in *Journal of Discourses,* 11:275.

9. Brigham Young, in *Journal of Discourses,* 2:316; italics added.

10. Brigham Young, in *Journal of Discourses,* 12:274.

11. Joseph Fielding Smith, *Doctrines of Salvation,* comp. Bruce R. McConkie, 3 vols. (Salt Lake City: Bookcraft, 1954–56), 3:64.

12. Smith, *Doctrines of Salvation,* 3:63–64.

13. Smith, *Teachings of the Prophet Joseph Smith,* 268–69; compare Isaiah 60:12.

14. McConkie, *Millennial Messiah,* 652.

15. George Q. Cannon, *Gospel Truth,* comp. Jerreld L. Newquist, 2 vols. in 1 (Salt Lake City: Deseret Book, 1987), 70; italics added.

16. See Smith, *Teachings of the Prophet Joseph Smith,* 308.

17. Brigham Young, in *Journal of Discourses,* 13:329.

18. Wilford Woodruff, in *Journal of Discourses,* 13:327.

19. *Improvement Era* 5 (December 1901): 146–47.

20. Brigham Young, in *Journal of Discourses,* 3:372; italics added.

21. McConkie, *Millennial Messiah,* 673–74.

22. *Hymns of The Church of Jesus Christ of Latter-day Saints* (Salt Lake City: The Church of Jesus Christ of Latter-day Saints, 1985), no. 52.

23. See also Smith, *Teachings of the Prophet Joseph Smith*, 149–50.

24. See McConkie, *Millennial Messiah*, 602–11; *New Witness for the Articles of Faith*, 518.

25. Neal A. Maxwell, *A Wonderful Flood of Light* (Salt Lake City: Bookcraft, 1990), 18.

26. Smith, *Teachings of the Prophet Joseph Smith*, 149.

27. Ibid., 268.

28. See *Words of Joseph Smith*, ed. Andrew F. Ehat and Lyndon W. Cook (Provo, Utah: Religious Studies Center, Brigham Young University, 1980), 14–15.

29. McConkie, *Millennial Messiah*, 682.

30. Smith, *Teachings of the Prophet Joseph Smith*, 187.

31. Cannon, *Gospel Truth*, 71.

32. George Q. Cannon, in *Journal of Discourses*, 16:120.

33. See Pratt, in *Journal of Discourses*, 16:322; Smith, *Doctrines of Salvation*, 2:56–57.

34. See McConkie, *New Witness for the Articles of Faith*, 652.

35. See Smith, *Teachings of the Prophet Joseph Smith*, 280.

36. *Masterful Discourses and Writings of Orson Pratt* (Salt Lake City: Bookcraft, 1962), 62–63; italics added.

CHAPTER EIGHT

"IF YE ARE PREPARED
YE SHALL NOT FEAR"

GERALD N. LUND

When a group of Latter-day Saints were asked what one question they would most like to ask of the Savior about his second coming, three came up again and again. Not surprisingly, When will it be? was the most-asked question. The second took various forms but had essentially the same intent: What is life going to be like before he comes and then when he comes? The third most-asked question was, How do I prepare myself so I will be ready? Although the answers to the first two questions are of great interest, the answer to the third question is probably of greatest immediate importance. The nature of Christ's coming is described with the paradoxical phrase "the great and dreadful day of the Lord" (D&C 110:14; italics added; see also v. 16).

How can something be both great and dreadful at the same time? Yet that is part of the reality of Christ's return to the earth and the judgments that usher it in. In many respects, the future holds things that are horrible and dreadful—war, wickedness, earthquakes, storms, famine, disease. On the other hand, the future also holds many things that will make it a great day—the establishment of Zion, the return of the lost tribes, the great council at Adam-ondi-Ahman, the return of Christ to the earth, a thousand years of peace and prosperity.

So what determines whether it will be a great day or a dreadful day for us as a people and as individuals? What makes the difference of whether we look forward to the future with fear and anxiety or faith and anticipation? There may be several answers to those

---

Gerald N. Lund is a zone administrator in the Church Educational System.

questions, but one thing is clear. Whether the Lord's return will be
great or dreadful for us will depend largely on whether or not we
are prepared. The Lord has specifically commanded us, "Prepare
yourselves for the great day of the Lord" (D&C 133:10). And in
another revelation he gave this wonderful promise: "If ye are prepared ye shall not fear" (D&C 38:30). That promise may apply in
many situations, but it certainly has particular relevance when we
talk about the Second Coming.

Many people, especially those along in years, are certain that
they will not live long enough to see the Second Coming. Does
preparation really matter that much for them? Of course it does.
Taking the broader perspective, remember that every one of us will
be alive when Christ comes again to the earth. In many cases, our
bodies will have died and will lie waiting in the grave, but the
spirit part of us, the part that gives us personality, character, individuality, will still be living. Thus the Lord's admonition that if we
are prepared we shall not fear applies to everyone. If we are to be
properly prepared for what the future holds, we must gain knowledge and understanding and prepare both temporally and spiritually.

GAIN KNOWLEDGE AND UNDERSTANDING

President Jedediah M. Grant of the First Presidency asked the
following question and then gave the answer: "Why is it that the
Latter-day Saints are perfectly calm and serene among all the con-
vulsions of the earth—the turmoils, strife, war, pestilence, famine
and distress of nations? It is because the spirit of prophecy has
made *known* to us that such things would actually transpire upon
the earth. We *understand* it, and view it in its true light. We have
learned it by the visions of the Almighty."[1] It is knowledge and
understanding that make the difference in whether we view the
future with anxiety or anticipation.

Just before his death, the Savior was on the Temple Mount in
Jerusalem with his disciples. The temple built by Herod was one of
the wonders of the ancient world—great walls, massive stones,

beautiful gates. It was a marvel of engineering and architecture. As they walked along, the disciples commented on what a wonderful building it was. Then the Savior turned to them and said, "See ye not all these things? verily I say unto you, There shall not be left here one stone upon another, that shall not be thrown down" (Matthew 24:2). They left the Temple Mount, crossed through the Kidron Valley, and went up on the Mount of Olives. The temple and all of Jerusalem lay before them. The disciples, troubled by the Savior's stunning declaration, said, "Tell us, when shall these things be? and what shall be the sign of thy coming, and of the end of the world?" (Matthew 24:3).

The Savior's reply, because it was given on the Mount of Olives, has come to be known as the Olivet Discourse. It is one of the most complete discussions of the Second Coming that Jesus himself gave. In the Doctrine and Covenants version of the Olivet Discourse, the Savior said that after the disciples had heard about all the signs of the times, "they were troubled" (D&C 45:34). That should be of interest to us today. Just hearing about those events that were still centuries away troubled them. It is not surprising that we who live in the day when those signs are being fulfilled should also be troubled. But the Lord specifically commanded his disciples, "Be not troubled" (D&C 45:35). And then he told them why. "And I said unto them: Be not troubled, for, when all these things shall come to pass, ye may know that the promises which have been made unto you shall be fulfilled" (D&C 45:35).

President Marion G. Romney noted the importance of knowledge in that scriptural admonition: "It was in the light of Christ's foreknowledge of this glorious consummation that he said to his disciples, 'be not troubled.' . . .

"I hope we are all familiar with these words of the Lord and with his predictions concerning other coming events, such as the building of the new Jerusalem and the redemption of the old, the return of Enoch's Zion, and Christ's millennial reign.

"Not only do I hope that we are familiar with these coming

events; I hope also that we keep the vision of them continually before our minds. This I do because upon a *knowledge* of them, and an assurance of their reality and a witness that each of us may have part therein, rests the efficacy of Christ's admonition, 'be not troubled.'"[2]

At least two kinds of knowledge and understanding will be particularly valuable to us as we prepare ourselves for what is to come.

UNDERSTANDING THE PROPHETIC VIEW OF THE FUTURE

After telling the disciples that they were not to be troubled, the Lord referred to a proverb common in the Holy Land in his day: "It shall be with them like unto a parable which I will show you—Ye look and behold the fig trees, and ye see them with your eyes, and ye say when they begin to shoot forth, and their leaves are yet tender, that summer is nigh at hand" (D&C 45:36–37).

It is an interesting fact of nature that the fig tree is one of the last of all the trees to come into leaf. That part of its nature is so dependable that it became a common thing in the Middle East to say that if the fig tree was in leaf, then summer was now come, or in other words, the cold weather was over.

The Lord continued by comparing the leaves of the fig tree to the signs of the times: "Even so it shall be in that day when they shall see all these things, then shall they know that the hour is nigh. And it shall come to pass that he that feareth me shall be looking forth for the great day of the Lord to come, even for the signs of the coming of the Son of Man" (D&C 45:38–39). Thus the Lord himself has specifically counseled us to watch for the signs of the times. Like the leaves of the fig tree, these prophetic signs will signal that his coming is approaching.

Many of the events that are prophesied for that time are not pleasant. Some of what the world will bring upon itself through its own wickedness is terrible and depressing. If that were all we could look forward to, we could honestly say, "I hope I die before those things happen." But the Lord has given us considerable detail about future events—even about the terrible things—so that when they come to pass, those who understand and know the prophecies will see them as the fulfillment of God's word. They will see them as proof that his great plan is rolling forward.

Joseph Fielding Smith, then a member of the Quorum of the Twelve Apostles, gave a series of lectures in Salt Lake City shortly after World War II began. After describing some of the terrible things associated with the battle of Armageddon, Elder Smith said: "I know these are unpleasant things. It is not a pleasant thing even for me to stand here and tell you that this is written in the Scriptures. If the Lord has a controversy with the nations, He will put them to the sword. Their bodies shall lie unburied like dung upon the earth. That is not nice, is it, but should we not *know* it? Is it not our duty to read these things and *understand* them? Don't you think the Lord has given us these things that we might know and we might prepare ourselves through humility, through repentance, through faith, that we might escape from these dreadful conditions that are portrayed by these ancient prophets?"[3]

Unpleasant or not, however, those who are watching and waiting for the signs can better prepare for what is to come. How can we watch for those signs unless we have studied the scriptures and listened to the modern prophets carefully? Through them the Lord has told us about what is going to happen. We should know what they say. We should understand their words so that we can prepare for and live through those times without a loss of faith. It is upon our knowledge and understanding of those prophetic events that a large part of our personal preparation rests. In a proclamation made to the world shortly after the Saints arrived in Utah, the First Presidency stated: "Of the day and the hour of the coming of Christ no man knoweth. It is not yet, neither is it far off; there are prophecies yet to be fulfilled before that event takes place; therefore let no man deceive the Saints with vain philosophy and false prophecy; for false prophets will arise, and deceive the wicked, and, if possible, the good; but while the wicked fear and tremble at surrounding judgments, the Saints will watch and pray; and, waiting the final event in patience, will look calmly on the passing scenery of a corrupted world, and view transpiring events as confirmation of their faith in the holy gospel which they profess, and rejoice more and more, as multiplied signs shall confirm the approach of the millennial day."[4]

UNDERSTANDING THE WORLD AROUND US

In Doctrine and Covenants 88, a revelation directed to those in the School of the Prophets, the Lord gave a very specific and direct commandment to study and learn about "things that pertain unto the kingdom of God, that are expedient for you to understand; of things both in heaven and in the earth, and under the earth; things which have been, things which are, things which must shortly come to pass; things which are at home, things which are abroad; the wars and the perplexities of the nations, and the judgments which are on the land; and a knowledge also of countries and of kingdoms" (D&C 88:78–79).

The judgments that will precede the coming of Christ and prepare the world for the millennial reign will have a profound effect upon the nations of the world. Eventually, there will even be an end to "all nations" (D&C 87:6). Can such things come to pass without a profound change in the political situation as we know it today? Already great changes are taking place around the world. For those watching with eyes of faith, things that make daily headlines or the evening television news are seen as at least partial fulfillment of things prophesied centuries ago. But how can we see the hand of the Lord in these things if we do not keep abreast of world events and know what is going on around us? For example, in recent years we have seen dramatic changes in what used to be the Soviet Union. Is the hand of God in such events? More than sixty years ago, Elder Melvin J. Ballard of the Quorum of the Twelve Apostles made a most remarkable statement about Russia: "I am sure also that God is moving in Russia. . . . I can see God moving also in preparing the way for other events that are to come. The field that has gone to wild oats needs to be plowed up and harrowed and prepared for a new seed. So in Russia. It may seem appalling to us, but it is God breaking up and destroying an older order of things, and *the process will be the accomplishment of God's purposes within a very short period of time,* which normally may have taken generations. But that people will come back, for I bear witness that there are thousands of the blood of Israel in that land, and God is preparing the way for them."[5]

More recently, President Thomas S. Monson also spoke of what has been happening in that part of the world: "In the month of May, my wife and I were in the historic city of Berlin. We boarded a taxi and asked that the driver take us to the Berlin Wall. When the driver failed to respond to the direction provided, again the desired destination was given. Still no movement. Then he turned toward us and, in halting English, explained, 'I can't. The wall is *kaput—* gone!' We drove to the Brandenburg Gate. We viewed its restoration. We gazed from West Berlin to East Berlin, now one Berlin, and reflected on the events which followed the wall's demise: a new mission of the Church established in Poland, another in Hungary, yet another in Greece, and a mission reestablished in Czechoslovakia. And now, official recognition of our Leningrad Branch in the Soviet Union. Who, except the Lord Himself, could have foreseen these historic events? It was He who declared, 'This gospel of the kingdom shall be preached in all the world for a witness unto all nations.' (Matt. 24:14.) Surely the purposes of the Lord continue to unfold to our view if we but have eyes that truly see and hearts that know and feel."[6]

In summary, then, one important thing that we can do to prepare ourselves for the Second Coming is to gain greater knowledge and understanding. Part of that knowledge will come directly from the scriptures and what the modern prophets have said and are saying to us. But the Lord has also commanded us to be knowledgeable about the world around us and the unfolding events that are all part of his great plan, leading up to the return of his Son to earth to reign as King of kings.

PREPARE TEMPORALLY

Get together with a group of Latter-day Saints, mention getting oneself prepared for the Second Coming, and it is almost certain that talk will quickly turn to food storage. That is not wrong, of course, but if the discussion stays focused only upon home storage, it will be woefully inadequate, even if the discussion is limited to preparing oneself temporally for Christ's return.

Natural disasters have struck with increasing frequency in recent years—the great earthquakes in Armenia, California, China, and other parts of the world; great storms, such as Hurricane Andrew in Florida and Hurricane Iniki in Hawaii; devastating floods in Europe and Asia and the midwestern United States. We see long lines at grocery stores as people try to purchase food and safe water. It is not surprising that when such disasters hit, our minds immediately jump to the importance of having a year's supply of food and clothing and fuel. And one can hardly say enough about the importance of this principle. For example, President Ezra Taft Benson declared: "The revelation to produce and store food may be as essential to our temporal welfare today as boarding the ark was to the people in the days of Noah."[7]

But the signs of the times include political, social, and economic events that will try the preparedness of individuals and families in different ways. Economic turmoil is common in our day. Recession, depression, widespread unemployment, runaway inflation—any one of these can be as disastrous for an individual or a family as a major earthquake. War and widespread social upheaval are becoming the norm in some countries. Major storms can seriously affect food supplies or transportation. Even normal life has a way of testing the limits of our physical, mental, emotional, and spiritual health from time to time.

When we speak of being prepared temporally, food storage is

an important part of that preparation, but it is only a part, one aspect of the greater principle of self-reliance. President Spencer W. Kimball explained that principle clearly: "The responsibility for each person's social, emotional, spiritual, physical, or economic well-being rests first upon himself, second upon his family, and third upon the Church if he is a faithful member thereof.

"No true Latter-day Saint, while physically or emotionally able will voluntarily shift the burden of his own or his family's well-being to someone else. So long as he can, under the inspiration of the Lord and with his own labors, he will supply himself and his family with the spiritual and temporal necessities of life."[8]

The Church has defined six areas in which we need to develop self-reliance: education, health, employment, home storage, resource management, and social, emotional, and spiritual strength (these six areas are detailed in materials published by the Welfare Services Department of the Church). When some of the future judgments strike, our self-reliance in these areas may be sorely tested. If we have properly prepared ourselves in such balanced and well-rounded ways as outlined by the Church, then surely we shall be able to claim the promise, "If ye are prepared ye shall not fear."

There are at least three reasons why temporal preparation will be so important in the days that lie ahead:

1. *The Church may be cut off from normal avenues of transportation, commerce, and social interaction.* Recent natural disasters have shown us how fragile and complex are the infrastructures that support our day-to-day living. When an earthquake strikes and freeway overpasses collapse, the traffic flow, the ability to get to work or school, the flow of food and goods into a city, can be seriously disrupted if not stopped altogether. That can put a whole city into immediate crisis. Widespread social disruption, such as a riot or civil war, can cut a whole people off from the normal avenues of supply, security, and protection.

Both as a church and as individual members of the Church, we are heavily dependent on current social structure for the normal functioning of our lives. Yet in a revelation given in March 1832, the Lord made this statement: "Behold, *this is the preparation wherewith I prepare you,* and the foundation, and the ensample which I give unto you, whereby you may accomplish the commandments which are given unto you; that through my providence, notwithstanding the tribulation which shall descend upon you, *that the church may stand independent* above all other creatures beneath the celestial world" (D&C 78:13–14; italics added).

That seems to be one main reason why the welfare program of the Church was organized: not only to meet the needs of those who are poor but also to move the Church toward greater independence. Harold B. Lee, when he was president of the Church, recounted an experience he had had in the earliest days of the Welfare Program. He had been asked by the General Authorities to go to the various stakes and talk about the importance of getting the program in place. "In one of those meetings, the thought came to me, 'I wonder what this [the welfare program] is all about?' And there came to me something that has stayed with me to this day, 'There is no person who knows the real purpose for which this Welfare Program is being instituted. But hardly before sufficient preparation has been made, the real purpose will be revealed, and *when that time comes it will challenge every resource of the Church to meet it.*'"[9]

In the welfare session of the April 1975 general conference, Marion G. Romney of the First Presidency made a similar statement: "I do not want to be a calamity howler. I don't know in detail what's going to happen in the future. I know what the prophets have predicted. But I tell you that the welfare program, organized to enable us to take care of our own needs, has not yet performed the function that it was set up to perform. *We will see the day when we will live on what we produce.*"[10]

A year earlier, also in a welfare session of general conference, President Spencer W, Kimball said: "I remember when the sisters used to say, 'Well, but we could buy it at the store a lot cheaper than

we can put it up.' But that isn't quite the answer, is it, Sister
Spafford [Relief Society General President]? Because *there will
come a time when there isn't a store.*"[11]

Therefore, one of the important reasons for being temporally
prepared—and this is in all aspects of self-reliance, not just food
storage—is that in the coming calamities we may see groups of
Church members cut off from the normal structure of society which
provides so many of their daily needs. We may also see the day
when as a Church we must be independent of the world and be able
to carry on with nothing but our own resources.

2. *We shall have to help others in the coming calamities.* A second reason why our personal and family preparedness will be especially critical has to do with another effect that is prophesied to
happen. As wickedness increases and iniquity abounds (see D&C
45:27), or when the predicted judgments descend upon the world,
many people will look to the Church for peace and security. And
when they do, many will come with few or no resources. That
means that they will need help and could become a severe demand
on the resources of the Church and its members.

In the scriptures, the city of Zion and the stakes of Zion are
described in terms that should give the Saints some consolation.
The New Jerusalem, for example, will be "a land of peace, a city of
refuge, a place of safety for the saints of the Most High God" (D&C
45:66). The Lord also said that the Saints would gather to the stakes
of Zion "for a defense, and for a refuge from the storm, and from
wrath when it shall be poured out without mixture upon the whole
earth" (D&C 115:6).

Such conditions—peace, safety, refuge, defense—clearly will
attract others who are not members of the Church. Good people
will seek those conditions. The Lord specifically noted that in coming years, people will flock to the Saints for safety. Speaking of the
city of Zion, he said: "And it shall come to pass among the wicked,
that every man that will not take his sword against his neighbor
must needs flee unto Zion for safety. And there shall be gathered

unto it out of every nation under heaven; and it shall be the only people that shall not be at war one with another" (D&C 45:68–69).

Obviously, this scripture suggests a state of widespread and probably lasting social chaos. In such conditions, thousands, perhaps tens of thousands, of people will join with the Saints in an attempt to escape the horrible things going on around them. The modern prophets have also talked about such possibilities. In 1856, President Heber C. Kimball, speaking of the handcart companies, asked: "Is this the end of it? No; there will be millions on millions that will come much in the same way, only they will not have hand carts, for they will take their bundles under their arms, and their children on their backs, and under their arms, and flee; and Zion's people will have to send out relief to them, *for they will come when the judgments come on the nations.*" About a year later, he returned to that same theme and said: "It behooves us to be saving and to prepare for the time to come. The day will come when the people of the United States will come lugging their bundles under their arms, *coming to us for bread to eat.*"[12]

Orson Pratt, of the Quorum of the Twelve Apostles, who was told in a specific revelation that he was to prophesy and it would be given him by the power of the Holy Ghost what he should say (see D&C 34:10), also saw a time when there would be thousands of people coming to the Church for help: "They [the world] will read her laws, and say, 'Our laws are as nothing, our wisdom as foolishness, our words like the tow that is exposed to the devouring flame; we are broken asunder, torn into fragments, and ready to crush under our own weight; but your laws, government, and officers are all good, righteous, just, and true; surely the God of Israel is in your midst. Come, let us go up to Zion, let us hear from the wise legislators of Zion, and let us hear the laws proclaimed therein; let us learn of the wisdom that dwells in the servants of the Most High.' And they will come up with their armies, and their mighty men, and their judges, and their rulers, and kings will come to the brightness of her rising, and *the Gentiles will come like a flowing stream,* and the gates of Zion will be open day and night, and never be shut."[13]

Elder Pratt said later: "A flowing stream is one that runs continually; and the Gentiles will, in that day, come to us as a flowing stream, and we shall have to set our gates open continually, they will come as clouds and as doves in large flocks. . . .

"The people will see that the hand of God is over this people; they will see that He is in our midst, and that He is our watchtower, that He is our shield and our defence, and therefore, they will say, 'Let us go up and put our riches in Zion, for there is no safety in our own nations.' Those nations are trembling and tottering and will eventually crumble to ruin, and those men of wealth will come here, not to be baptized, but many of them will come that have never heard the servants of God; but they will hear that peace and health dwell among us, and that our officers are all peace officers, and our tax-gatherers men of righteousness."[14]

If large numbers of people come in who have not made the proper temporal preparation—or who have had to abandon whatever temporal preparation they had—that will be a great drain on the resources of the Church. They will need to be fed and clothed and housed. The clear implication is that if we as individual members of the Church have prepared ourselves temporally and properly, we will be able to help those in need rather than ourselves being a drain on the resources of the Church.

3. *The Church cannot meet the needs of everyone who is unprepared.* A third reason why our temporal preparation will be important is that it is not possible for the Church, as an organization, to care for everyone's needs if there is widespread social disruption. The Welfare Program was not created for that purpose. Two of its foundational principles are self-reliance and personal and family preparedness. Occasionally we will hear comments like, "Well, if things get really bad, I can always turn to the Church for help." Such misplaced hope not only is contrary to gospel principles but it will likely be impossible in every case. In the welfare session of the

April 1976 general conference, Victor L. Brown, then Presiding Bishop of the Church, summarized possible conditions the Church might face and described the Church's ability to handle the needs of people in those conditions:

"Let me share the panorama of conditions that could befall each of us individually and the Church collectively. I would like you to see what might happen under three hypothetical but potentially real conditions.

"Condition One is characterized by a relatively stable economy, modest unemployment, and only limited natural disasters—a condition much like that which we now experience in this and many other countries. Only a small number of families or individuals in the Church would need to call upon their bishops for temporary health, emotional, or economic assistance. For those families or individuals unable to fully care for themselves, we would use our production projects, storehouses, employment efforts, and fast offering funds to help meet their needs. Appropriate health and social services capabilities of the Church would support the priesthood in administering to these special needs. Our present state of Church preparedness allows us to meet the claims on the Church which Condition One seems to imply.

"Condition Two is characterized by more serious health, social, and economic stress. This could include a depressed economy with serious unemployment, or perhaps localized natural disasters. Society would be unstable and disunited. In order for the Church to meet the needs of those who could not care for themselves, we would be required to produce the maximum from our production projects, reduce the variety of items produced and distributed, provide broad-scale work opportunities, and organize special quorum relief efforts. Health and social services would be needed in many places. Clearly, the material resources of the Church would be taxed heavily to meet this burden, particularly if Condition Two lasted very long or were very widespread.

"Under Condition Three, circumstances would be very serious.

The economy would be very depressed, perhaps even suffering a near breakdown. Unemployment would be widespread. There would probably be widespread social disunity. This condition could be the result of either economic problems such as severe crop loss, broad-scale natural disasters, or possibly international conflict. *Under such circumstances, the Church, relying on its present resources, would very likely not be able to provide any more assistance than that rendered under Condition Two, and therefore could not meet the total welfare needs of the people. . . .*

"Therefore, if the time comes that we move out of Condition One into a widespread Condition-Two situation, we are well beyond the current capacity of the Church alone to meet the temporal needs of the Saints.

"I would like to stress that this preparedness includes more than temporal preparedness. Particularly in Conditions Two and Three we would encounter social disunity, worry, fear, depression, and all the emotional stresses that accompany such economic and social conditions. Health conditions would be precarious. Families and individuals would need to be prepared emotionally and physically to weather this condition. Members would have greater need than ever to rely on each other for strength and support.

"Our temporal salvation will come only in following the counsel of the Brethren to be prepared as families and individuals, as wards and as stakes. As we apply their counsel, we make of Zion a refuge and a standard of righteous living as commanded by the Lord."[15]

If faithful members of the Church who have prepared themselves and their families for whatever calamities, setbacks, or disasters may strike, whether widespread or individually, are able to cope with those challenges and problems without having to draw upon the resources of the Church, the capability of the Church to help those in need would be greatly expanded. Thus, not only are we fulfilling a commandment of the Lord to be self-reliant ourselves, but we could also become a great blessing to our fellowmen.

Preparing ourselves in all six areas of temporal self-reliance is one important thing we can do so that we can claim the Lord's promise, "If ye are prepared ye shall not fear."

PREPARE SPIRITUALLY

In the closing chapter of the first book of Nephi, Nephi detailed some marvelous prophecies about the events of the last days. He talked about terrible conditions in Babylon, or the world, in which the people will be warring among themselves, every nation will be warring against the house of Israel, and the fulness of the wrath of God will be poured out upon the children of men (see 1 Nephi 22:13–16). But in the midst of that terrible picture are some marvelous promises. Note what Nephi said: "Wherefore, he will *preserve the righteous* by his power, even if it so be that the fulness of his wrath must come, and the *righteous be preserved,* even unto the destruction of their enemies by fire. Wherefore, *the righteous need not fear;* for thus saith the prophet, they shall be saved, even if it so be as by fire. . . . For behold, *the righteous shall not perish;* for the time surely must come that all they who fight against Zion shall be cut off. And *the Lord will surely prepare a way for his people. . . .* And *the righteous need not fear*" (1 Nephi 22:17–22; italics added).

The key word Nephi used here is *righteous.* The promises of deliverance and protection are for the righteous.

The scriptures and the modern prophets make it clear that of the three areas of personal preparation—knowledge and understanding, temporal preparation, and spiritual preparation—spiritual preparation is the most critical. President Ezra Taft Benson said in 1981: "We will live in the midst of economic, political, and spiritual instability. When these signs are observed—unmistakable evidences that His coming is nigh—we need not be troubled, but 'stand in holy places, and be not moved, until the day of the Lord come' (D&C 87:8). *Holy men and women stand in holy places,* and these holy places consist of our temples, our chapels, our homes, and stakes of Zion."[16]

Unfortunately, in some cases, spiritual preparedness is the most neglected area of preparation. During the winter of 1976–77, a severe drought had set in in the western United States. Scarcely any snow had fallen through December. In the news was constant talk of a severe water shortage if things did not change. The reaction in Utah and surrounding states with high concentrations of Latter-day Saints was an interesting one. One news report indicated that wheat—primarily for home storage—was normally trucked from Idaho into Utah at the rate of one semi-truck load per week. Suddenly the rate jumped to three semi-truck loads per day! Another television news broadcast reported that purchase of food storage items jumped 800 percent in January 1977. Newspapers reported that people were taking out loans and mortgages on property to add to their food supplies.

It would be interesting to know if at that same time there was a resulting rise in the concern about one's spiritual readiness. Did family prayer jump 800 percent during that same period? Was there a significant increase in the holding of family home evening or personal scripture study? Did temple attendance go up sharply? In short, as we rushed to beef up our food storage, was there also a great turning to the Lord and an increased desire to put one's spiritual life in order?

Remember the question people would most like to ask the Savior about his second coming? Most would ask, How do I prepare myself for what is coming? In a way, we already have the Savior's answer to that question—the Olivet Discourse, found in Matthew and other places. Some may think Matthew 24 contains the full discourse, but a careful reading of chapter 25 shows that Jesus continued his teaching to the disciples through chapter 25, ending with three parables whose very context was Christ's second coming. That assertion is borne out by the opening words of chapter 25: "And then, at that day, before the Son of man comes, the kingdom of Heaven shall be likened unto . . . " (JST Matthew 25:1). Then follow the three parables: the parable of the ten virgins, the parable of the talents, and the parable of the sheep and the goats. These parables do not discuss the signs of the times per se but rather relate to our spiritual condition. In that sense, they could be thought of as parables of spiritual preparation. So, in a way, we already have the Lord's answer to the question, How do I prepare myself for what is to come?

THE PARABLE OF THE TEN VIRGINS (MATTHEW 25:1–13)

The well-known parable of the ten virgins draws on the wonderful imagery of a wedding celebration in the Middle East. George Mackie, a Christian minister who spent much of his life in the Holy Land, described what a wedding ceremony was like in Palestine in the nineteenth century. In it we see the rich imagery of the parable of the ten virgins.

"Oriental [Near Eastern] marriages usually take place in the evening. . . . The whole attention is turned to the public arrival of the bridegroom to receive the bride prepared for him and waiting in the house among her female attendants. . . .

"As the hours drag on their topics of conversation become exhausted, and some of them grow tired and fall asleep. There is nothing more to be done, and everything is in readiness for the reception of the bridegroom, when the cry is heard outside announcing his approach.

"The bridegroom meanwhile is absent, spending the day at the house of one of his relatives. There, soon after sunset, that is between seven and eight o'clock, his male friends begin to assemble. . . . The time is occupied with light refreshments, general conversation and the recitation of poetry in praise of the two families chiefly concerned and of the bridegroom in particular. After all have been courteously welcomed and their congratulations received, the bridegroom, about eleven o'clock, intimates his wish to set out. Flaming torches are then held aloft by special bearers, lit candles are handed at the door to each visitor as he goes out, and the procession sweeps slowly along toward the house where the bride and her female attendants are waiting. A great crowd has meanwhile assembled on the balconies, garden-walls, and flat roofs of the houses on each side of the road. . . . The bridegroom is the centre of interest. Voices are heard whispering, 'There he is! there he is!' From time to time women raise their voices in the peculiar shrill, wavering shriek by which joy is expressed at marriages and other times of family and public rejoicing. The sound is heard at a great distance, and is repeated by other voices in advance of the procession, and thus intimation is given of the approach half an hour or more before the marriage escort arrives. . . . As the house is approached the excitement increases, the bridegroom's pace is quickened, and the alarm is raised in louder tones and more repeatedly, *'He is coming, he is coming!'*

"Before he arrives, the maidens in waiting come forth with lamps and candles a short distance to light up the entrance, and do honour to the bridegroom and the group of relatives and intimate friends around him. These pass into the final rejoicing and the marriage supper; the others who have discharged their duty in accompanying him to the door, immediately disperse, and the door is shut."[17]

In the time of Christ, olive oil was used as the fuel for lamps. Some of those lamps, particularly those carried outside at night, were small. Made of clay or brass, they were filled with olive oil, in which a wick was laid and then lit to provide light. Because these lamps were small enough to fit in the palm of the hand, they obviously contained only a small amount of oil. They would generally burn for about an hour without resupply.

A careful study of the parable shows that the key element is the oil for the lamps. All of the ten were virgins. All of the ten had lamps. What distinguished the five wise virgins from the five foolish ones was the extra supply of oil they carried. In the Doctrine and Covenants, the Lord gives us the key for understanding what the oil symbolized: "At that day, when I shall come in my glory, shall the parable be fulfilled which I spake concerning the ten virgins. For they that are wise and have received the truth, *and have taken the Holy Spirit for their guide,* and have not been deceived— verily I say unto you, they shall not be hewn down and cast into the fire, but shall abide the day" (D&C 45:56–57; italics added).

Olive oil is a wonderful symbol for the power of the Holy Ghost. He is a source of light and truth. His influence is sometimes described in terms of burning and fire. For example, we speak of the burning of the bosom that sometimes accompanies his presence (see D&C 9:8). The scriptures also refer to the "baptism of fire" or of the Holy Ghost (D&C 33:11). So the oil in the parable symbolizes having the light, or the power, of the Holy Ghost in our lives.

Once we understand that symbolism, the message of the parable is clear. We must have the influence of the Spirit with us if we are to be prepared for the Bridegroom's coming. President Spencer W. Kimball commented at some length on the meaning of this parable for our day: "I believe that the Ten Virgins represent the people of the Church of Jesus Christ and not the rank and file of the world. All of the virgins, wise and foolish, had accepted the invitation to the wedding supper; they had knowledge of the program and had been warned of the important day to come. They were not the gentiles or the heathens or the pagans, nor were they necessarily corrupt and reprobate, but *they were knowing people who were foolishly unprepared* for the vital happenings that were to affect their eternal lives. . . .

"Hundreds of thousands of us today are in this position. Confidence has been dulled and patience worn thin. It is so hard to wait and be prepared always. But we cannot allow ourselves to slumber. The Lord has given us this parable as a special warning.

"At midnight, the vital cry was made. . . . At midnight! Precisely at the darkest hour, when least expected, the bridegroom came. When the world is full of tribulation and help is needed, but it seems the time must be past and hope is vain, then Christ will come. The midnights of life are the times when heaven comes to offer its joy for man's weariness. But when the cry sounds, there is no time for preparation. . . . In the daytime, wise and unwise seemed alike; midnight is the time of test and judgment. . . .

"The foolish asked the others to share their oil, but spiritual preparedness cannot be shared in an instant. . . .

"The kind of oil that is needed to illuminate the way and light up the darkness is not shareable. How can one share obedience to the principle of tithing; a mind at peace from righteous living; an accumulation of knowledge? How can one share faith or testimony? How can one share attitudes or chastity, or the experience of a mission? How can one share temple privileges? Each must obtain that kind of oil for himself. . . .

"In the parable, oil can be purchased at the market. In our lives the oil of preparedness is accumulated drop by drop in righteous living. Attendance at sacrament meetings adds oil to our lamps, drop by drop over the years. Fasting, family prayer, home teaching, control of bodily appetites, preaching the gospel, studying the scriptures—each act of dedication and obedience is a drop added to our store. Deeds of kindness, payment of offerings and tithes, chaste thoughts and actions, marriage in the covenant for eternity—these, too, contribute importantly to the oil with which we can at midnight refuel our exhausted lamps."[18]

That is the real oil crisis of our generation, not the one that we sometimes see at the gas pumps. And *crisis* may not be too strong a word, considering how important it will be to have the Spirit with us in the days that lie ahead.

President Harold B. Lee quoted extensively from a statement by President Heber C. Kimball that directly referred to the imagery of the parable of the ten virgins: "I want to say to you, my brethren, the time is coming when we will be mixed up in these now peaceful valleys to that extent that it will be difficult to tell the face of a Saint from the face of an enemy to the people of God. Then, brethren, look out for the great sieve, for there will be a great sifting time, and many will fall—for I say unto you there is a *test,* a TEST, a TEST coming, and who will be able to stand? . . .

"Let me say to you, that many of you will see the time when you will have all the trouble, trial and persecution that you can stand, and plenty of opportunities to show that you are true to God and his work. This Church has before it many close places through which it will have to pass before the work of God is crowned with victory. To meet the difficulties that are coming, it will be necessary for you to have a knowledge of the truth of this work for yourselves. The difficulties will be of such a character that the man or woman who does not possess this personal knowledge or witness will fall. If you have not got the testimony, live right and call upon the Lord and cease not till you obtain it. If you do not you will not stand.

"Remember these sayings, for many of you will live to see them fulfilled. The time will come when no man nor woman will be able to endure on borrowed light. Each will have to be guided by the light within himself. If you do not have it, how can you stand?"[19]

From this we can conclude that perhaps the single most important thing that we can do in preparing ourselves for the Second Coming is to live so that we can have the power of the Holy Ghost in our lives to guide us, to help us to avoid deception, to give us testimony, and to prepare us for whatever is to come.

THE PARABLE OF THE TALENTS (MATTHEW 25:14–30)

The parable of the talents, the second parable given by the Savior in Matthew 25, is well known, although not often associated with preparing ourselves for the Second Coming. It has an important lesson for anyone seeking to live the gospel, but the context in which it was given—the Olivet Discourse—gives it special meaning in relation to preparing spiritually for the Savior's return.

In the parable, a man about to take a journey into a far country calls three servants together and delivers to them some of his goods. To one he gives five talents; to another, two; and to another, one. That is done "according to [their] several ability." Then the master takes his journey, leaving the servants to carry on. The first servant through diligent effort doubles the investment given him. When the master returns and learns that this servant now has ten talents, the master is greatly pleased and says to him, "Well done, thou good and faithful servant: thou hast been faithful over a few things. I will make thee ruler over many things: enter thou into the joy of thy lord" (Matthew 25:21). When the second servant reports that he too, through his diligent effort, has doubled the investment given to him, the master says exactly the same thing to him. That clearly indicates it was not the original amount that mattered but the effort to magnify it. We can assume, then, that if the servant to whom one talent had been given had also been diligent in the use of what the Lord had given him, the Lord would have said exactly the same thing to him as well. Only when the servant makes excuses is the master angry with him, calling him a "wicked and slothful servant" (Matthew 25:26).

Once again, remembering that this parable was given as part of Christ's answer on how to prepare for his second coming, what do we learn from the parable of the talents? Statements from two of our modern prophets help us see what the Savior was trying to teach us with this parable.

President Joseph Fielding Smith linked the parable to the obligations of priesthood holders: "Each man holding the priesthood should learn his duty from the Parable of the Talents. . . . We are under obligation as men holding the priesthood to put to service the authority which we have received. If we do this, then we shall have other responsibilities and glory added, and we shall receive an abundance, that is, the fullness of the Father's kingdom; but if we bury our priesthood, then we are not entitled to receive any reward—we cannot be exalted."[20]

And President Spencer W. Kimball talked about the meaning of the parable for all Church members: "The Church member who has the attitude of leaving it to others will have much to answer for. There are many who say: 'My wife does the Church work!' Others say, 'I'm just not the religious kind,' as though it does not take effort for most people to serve and do their duty. But God has endowed us with talents and time, with latent abilities and with opportunities to use and develop them in his service. He therefore expects much of us, his privileged children. The parable of the talents is a brilliant summary of the many scriptural passages outlining promises for the diligent and penalties for the slothful."[21]

What is the lesson of this parable for those who wish to better prepare themselves spiritually? We are to use those things the Lord has bestowed upon us—gifts, talents, abilities, goods, services—in furthering his work. That is what is meant by the principle of consecration. It is a principle often taught in the scriptures. For example, in the Sermon on the Mount, the Savior said: "Seek not the things of this world but seek ye first to build up the kingdom of God, and to establish his righteousness" (JST Matthew 6:33). And an oft-repeated charge given to early leaders of the Church was to "seek to bring forth and establish the cause of Zion" (D&C 6:6; see also 12:6; 14:6).

And here is an interesting point. When we take this second charge—to strive to use whatever we have been given to further God's work—then we also fulfill the lesson of the first parable and add oil to our supply. Note how Nephi directly connected the effort to build Zion to having greater power through the Spirit: "And blessed are they who shall seek to bring forth my Zion at that day, for they shall have the gift and the power of the Holy Ghost" (1 Nephi 13:37).

If we are diligent in consecrating to his service whatever the Lord has blessed us with, not only shall we be greatly blessed spiritually now but when the Lord comes he shall say to us, as he said to the first two servants in the parable, "Well done, thou good and faithful servant."

THE PARABLE OF THE SHEEP AND THE GOATS (MATTHEW 25:31–46)

The parable of the sheep and the goats, the last parable given by the Savior on the Mount of Olives, is another well-known and often-cited parable that is not often directly related to preparing for the Second Coming, although that is the context in which it was given. It compares the final judgment to a shepherd's separating his flock. In the Near East, shepherds commonly allow sheep and goats to graze together, but when it comes time for sale, shearing, or other purposes, the sheep and the goats are separated. So shall it be at the Judgment.

In the parable, those compared to the sheep are asked to sit at the right hand of God. To them, the king says, "Come, ye blessed of my Father, inherit the kingdom prepared for you from the foundation of the world: for I was an hungred, and ye gave me meat: I was thirsty, and ye gave me drink: I was a stranger, and ye took me in: Naked, and ye clothed me: I was sick, and ye visited me: I was in prison, and ye came unto me" (Matthew 25:34–36).

Surprised at the Savior's comments, those on his right hand asked, "Lord, when saw we thee an hungred, and fed thee? or thirsty, and gave thee drink? When saw we thee a stranger, and took thee in? or naked, and clothed thee? or when saw we thee sick, or in prison, and came unto thee?" (Matthew 25:37–39). The Lord's answer summarizes a most important gospel principle: "Verily I say unto you, Inasmuch as ye have done it unto one of the least of these my brethren, ye have done it unto me" (Matthew 25:40).

Those who are put on the left hand of God (those compared to the goats) are dismayed, and they demand to know why they are so placed. Again the Lord explains, this time saying that they did not do any of those things for him.

This parable teaches a third area of spiritual preparation, which is that we must serve our fellowmen as though we were serving Christ. Like the doctrine of consecration, the doctrine of service to our fellowman is taught in numerous other places in the scriptures. For example, in the Lord's preface to the Doctrine and Covenants, the Lord specifically linked how we will be judged to how we have treated our fellowmen (see D&C 1:10). King Benjamin taught that when we serve our fellowman, we are serving God (see Mosiah 2:17).

Modern prophets have taught the same principle. Christian service was often stressed by President Spencer W. Kimball:

"None of us should become so busy in our formal Church assignments that there is no room left for quiet Christian service to our neighbors."[22]

"Recently [the Church] established the new consolidated schedule which is aimed at enriching family life even further, together with greater opportunity for individual and family gospel scholarship *and for more Christian service.* We are trying to provide more time and emphasis on Christian service, so that our example can be more powerful in the world and so that those who are so worthy of attention might get more attention than they sometimes have in the past."[23]

"How much easier it is to understand and accept [the gospel] if the seeker after truth can also see the principles of the gospel at work in the lives of other believers. No greater service can be given to the missionary calling of this Church than to be exemplary in positive Christian virtues in our lives."[24]

These three wonderful parables show us how to prepare ourselves spiritually for the Second Coming. First, we live so that we will have the influence of the Holy Ghost to give us testimony and guide us (the lesson of the five wise virgins). Second, we render service to the Church and kingdom of God, doing all we can to further the cause of Zion and aid the Lord in doing his work (the lesson of the talents). Third, we show we love God by loving and compassionately serving our fellowman (the lesson of the sheep and the goats).

CONCLUSION

We prepare ourselves for Christ's second coming by gaining greater knowledge and understanding; by becoming temporally self-reliant in education, health, employment, home storage, ırce management, and social, emotional, and spiritual strength; and by increasing our spirituality so that we have the Spirit, consecrating the things with which the Lord has blessed us to build his kingdom, and serving our fellowman. When we have made such preparation, then surely we will better understand the Lord's promise: "If ye are prepared ye shall not fear" (D&C 38:30).

President Brigham Young gave some marvelous advice about what our focus should be as we strive to be better prepared for Christ's coming: "Are you prepared for the day of vengeance to come, when the Lord will consume the wicked by the brightness of his coming? No. Then do not be too anxious for the Lord to hasten his work. *Let our anxiety be centred upon this one thing, the sanctification of our own hearts,* the purifying of our own affections, the preparing of ourselves for the approach of the events that are hastening upon us. *This should be our concern, this should be our study, this should be our daily prayer,* and not to be in a hurry to see the overthrow of the wicked. . . . Seek not to hasten it, but be satisfied to let the Lord have his own time and way, and be patient. *Seek to have the Spirit of Christ,* that we may wait patiently the time of the Lord, and prepare ourselves for the times that are coming. This is our duty."[25]

NOTES

1. Jedediah M. Grant, "The Hand of God in Events on Earth," *Improvement Era,* Feb. 1915, 286; italics added.

2. Marion G. Romney, in Conference Report, Oct. 1966, 51–52; italics added.

3. Joseph Fielding Smith, *The Signs of the Times* (Salt Lake City: Deseret Book, 1964), 154–55; italics added.

4. First Presidency [Brigham Young, Heber C. Kimball, and Willard Richards] of The Church of Jesus Christ of Latter-day Saints, Fifth General Epistle, 7 Apr. 1851; in *Millennial Star* 13 (15 July 1851): 210.

5. Melvin J. Ballard, in Conference Report, Apr. 1930, 157; italics added.

6. Thomas S. Monson, *Ensign,* Nov. 1990, 67.

7. Ezra Taft Benson, *Ensign,* Nov. 1987, 49.

8. Spencer W. Kimball, in Conference Report, Oct. 1977, 124.

9. Harold B. Lee, address delivered at LDS Church employees Christmas devotional in Salt Lake City, Utah, 13 Dec. 1973, 6; italics added.

10. Marion G. Romney, in Conference Report, Apr. 1975, 165; italics added.

11. Spencer W. Kimball, in Conference Report, Apr. 1974, 184–85; italics added.

12. Heber C. Kimball, in *Journal of Discourses,* 26 vols. (London: Latter-day Saints' Book Depot, 1854–86), 4:106; 5:10; italics added.

13. Orson Pratt, in *Journal of Discourses,* 2:60–61; italics added.

14. Ibid., 3:16–17.

15. Victor L. Brown, *Ensign,* May 1976, 111–12; italics in original.

16. Ezra Taft Benson, *The Teachings of Ezra Taft Benson* (Salt Lake City: Bookcraft, 1988), 106; italics added.

17. George Mackie, *Bible Manners and Customs* (New York: Fleming H. Revell, 1898), 123–26.

18. Spencer W. Kimball, *Faith Precedes the Miracle* (Salt Lake City: Deseret Book, 1972), 253–56; italics added.

19. Orson F. Whitney, *Life of Heber C. Kimball* (Salt Lake City: Bookcraft, 1945), 446, 449–450; cited in Harold B. Lee, in Conference Report, Oct. 1965, 128.

20. Joseph Fielding Smith, in Conference Report, Apr. 1966, 102.

21. Spencer W. Kimball, *The Teachings of Spencer W. Kimball,* ed. Edward L. Kimball (Salt Lake City: Bookcraft, 1992), 149.

22. Ibid., 256.

23. Ibid., 493.

24. Ibid., 555.

25. Brigham Young, in *Journal of Discourses,* 9:3; italics added.

CHAPTER NINE

ENDURING TO THE END

STEPHEN E. ROBINSON

Few promises made in scripture have the credentials and the guarantees of the promise made to those who "endure to the end": "Look unto me, and endure to the end, and ye shall live; for unto him that endureth to the end will I give eternal life" (3 Nephi 15:9). Nearly thirty other passages from all four standard works similarly affirm that those who endure to the end shall be saved in the kingdom of God. Such overwhelming scriptural attestation and affirmation is truly extraordinary. Besides the many prophets who have repeated this promise in the name of God, scripture quotes both the Father (2 Nephi 31:15, 20) and the Son (3 Nephi 27:16) as making this promise directly in the first person. There can simply be no doubt that those who endure to the end will be saved.

Yet exactly what does it mean to endure to the end? Endure what, and how? And when is the end? For most people the word *endure* first calls up images of torture on the rack or tar and feathers. But few Saints are actually faced with such persecutions today. Are we therefore less tested than the Saints of former times? Is it easier for us, with fewer physical trials, to endure to the end? I think not. In fact, enduring affliction is only a small part of what "enduring to the end" really means.

Most frequently the scriptures use the term *endure* to mean "to last," "to continue," or "to remain" rather than "to suffer." For example, Alma expresses hope that his son Shiblon "will *continue* in keeping [God's] commandments; for blessed is he that *endureth* to the end." Here enduring to the end is clearly equated with remaining

---

Stephen E. Robinson is chair of the department of ancient scripture at Brigham Young University.

steadfast while in mortality. Nephi had already made that clea
reconciled unto Christ, and enter into the narrow gate, and w
the strait path which leads to life, and *continue* in the path *un... ...*
end of the day of probation" (2 Nephi 33:9; italics added).

Thus, to "endure" is to continue in the path we adopted at baptism by keeping our commitments to Christ. "The end" is the end
of our mortal probation (2 Nephi 33:9). To endure to the end means
we don't quit or lose our testimony because of life's difficulties or
temptations. Conversely, failing to endure means backing away
from what we've started—first promising loyalty to God and then
withholding what we promised, thus proving unreliable and
unfaithful. Endurance is not so much a matter of stamina as it is a
matter of integrity, of keeping our promises to God.

Just as a spouse who can be trusted to keep the marriage
covenant is called faithful, so those who can be trusted to keep their
gospel covenants are called faithful. In the Old Testament, the
words for *faith, faithful,* and *faithfulness* all come from the Hebrew
'aman ("to be firm or reliable"), which implies primarily qualities
of loyalty and determination rather than qualities of belief. The
words for *security, certainty,* and *guarantee* all come from the same
Hebrew root. Thus being faithful does not have as much to do with
one's belief or even one's activity in the Church as it does with
whether one can be trusted to do one's duty in the kingdom. The
covenants of baptism and of the temple are solemn promises we
make to God about how we will conduct our lives. Enduring to the
end is keeping those promises throughout our lives—no matter
what.

Usually the scriptures link "enduring to the end" specifically
with remaining faithful to one's Christian covenants and to the
covenant community that is the Church. For example, Doctrine and
Covenants 20:29 states, "And we know that all men must repent
and believe on the name of Jesus Christ, and worship the Father in
his name, and endure in faith on his name to the end, or they cannot be saved in the kingdom of God" (see also 2 Nephi 9:24).

The Savior reinforces this covenant dimension of enduring to the end in his teaching of the Nephites, specifically, the covenant obligations of repentance and baptism: "And it shall come to pass, that whoso repenteth and is baptized in my name shall be filled; and if he endureth to the end, behold, him will I hold guiltless before my Father at that day when I shall stand to judge the world" (3 Nephi 27:16).

So, enduring to the end means entering into the gospel covenant (through faith in Christ, repentance, baptism, and receiving the Holy Ghost) and then remaining faithful. Doctrine and Covenants 20:37 even makes "determination to serve [Christ] to the end" a condition of baptism into the Church.

Besides remaining faithful to our baptismal covenants, the components of enduring faithful to the end include the following:

1. Looking unto Christ (3 Nephi 15:9)
2. Taking upon us the name of Christ (3 Nephi 27:6)
3. Feasting upon the words of Christ in steadfastness, hope, and love (2 Nephi 31:20; Moroni 8:26)
4. Offering our whole souls to Christ in fasting and prayer (Omni 1:26)
5. Following the example of Christ (2 Nephi 31:16)
6. Worshipping the Father in the name of Christ (D&C 20:29)
7. Keeping the commandments (1 Nephi 22:31; Alma 38:2; D&C 14:7)
8. Seeking to bring forth Zion with patience and humility (1 Nephi 13:37; Alma 32:15; D&C 24:8)

Notice that the focus of all of these exhortations to endure to the end is not suffering but loyalty to Christ. Consequently, enduring to the end is more than just "being active" in the Church. Enduring to the end requires a personal awareness of covenant obligations and a personal determination to keep them faithfully. Whereas the phrase "being active" describes visible behavior, "enduring faithful to the end" describes an inner commitment to the gospel and church of Jesus Christ. Of course, it's better to be active than to be inactive, but a conscious awareness of one's covenant obligations and a determination to keep them is better than either.

I knew a man once who had to decide whether to pay his tithing every time his check came, whether to go to his meetings every time they were held, whether to take a drink every time he was offered one. Finally I asked him, "Why can't you just decide once and for all which side you're on? Why do you have to check your loyalty first every time a decision is called for? You are spiritually reinventing the wheel over and over again, and you will never make any progress until you can build on what you already know."

A few weeks later he called and asked for a ride to our stake meetings. I was pleased he was going, and when I told him so, he responded, "You know, I wouldn't like it if my wife told me she had to decide every morning whether she still loved me or not, or if she told me she only stayed with me because she hadn't found a reason to leave . . . yet. I guess the Lord is entitled to more of a commitment than that from me. I'm ready to stop reinventing the wheel and move on. I'm a Mormon now."

Some people are saying, essentially, "Well, *today* I think the Church is true but ask me again tomorrow." There must come a point at which our commitment to the gospel and our conviction of its truth settles such questions in advance and determines our response to whatever commandments we may receive or whatever sacrifice we are called upon to make. A testimony isn't like a hypothesis in science, which may be supported by the evidence one day and destroyed by it the next. It is a conviction beyond experience that some things are eternally true. The "provisionally converted" are those who just haven't found a reason to leave . . . yet.

Just as such an attitude is unsatisfactory in a marriage, so is it unsatisfactory in the spiritual marriage of the gospel. Such individuals need to become converted, to receive the witness of the Spirit and the conviction beyond experience. Just as the partners in a celestial marriage say, "We are sealed—no matter what," so a truly converted member says, "I am a member of this Church; my lot is cast with the apostles and prophets—no matter what. Above all other issues, loyalties, agendas, and commitments, *this* is where I stand."

Without such a prior commitment, some new commandment or sacrifice or some imagined (or real) offense on the part of Church leaders might challenge our endurance. It may be possible to be an active member of the Church without such a conviction, but it may not be possible to endure to the end. The Lord spoke of such in one of his parables as those who had no depth of earth and who, when faced with trials or afflictions, were offended (Matthew 13:5, 21; Mark 4:16–17). We must not fear to send our roots deep—deep into the gospel and deep into the Church.

Often those who do not keep their commitments seek to justify themselves by separating loyalty to Christ from loyalty to his Church, but that is impossible. Our covenants in the restored gospel of Christ are covenants that specifically include our relationship with his Church and are administered through his Church—The Church of Jesus Christ of Latter-day Saints. We cannot endure to the end in those covenants without enduring to the end in that Church. That truth is made clear by the Savior himself: "And now, behold, whosoever is *of my church,* and endureth *of my church* to the end, him will I establish upon my rock, and the gates of hell shall not prevail against them" (D&C 10:69; italics added).

There are no side bets or private arrangements. Enduring in one's covenants means enduring in the Church. God will not excuse those who leave the Church thinking that they have good reasons or that they can keep covenants made in and through the Church while rejecting the Church. No matter what their intentions, they are deceived. By definition, if they have not lasted, they have failed to endure to the end.

In Matthew 24:9–13 the Savior's promise to those who endure includes a warning against three specific hazards to individual endurance: affliction, deception, and iniquity. The Lord said

concerning affliction: "Then shall they deliver you up to be afflicted, and shall kill you: and ye shall be hated of all nations for my
name's sake. And then shall many be offended, and shall betray one
an-other, and shall hate one another" (vv. 9–10).

Church history, both ancient and modern, provides us with
many examples of those who couldn't take the heat and broke their
covenants rather than face persecution. They couldn't bear the
malice of the world. When Satan threatened them with pain or loss,
they waffled and gave up the kingdom.

On the other hand, Church history provides no better examples
of enduring afflictions than those of the early pioneers. Consider
someone such as Hosea Stout, who buried his wife and five of his
six children on the journey west. After arriving in the Valley, he
wrote simply in his journal: "A year ago we were eight. Now we
are two." In the resurrection how will we face those who lost their
lives, who lost their homes and fortunes, who buried their loved
ones in shallow graves—all for the gospel's sake—if we wither in
the face of lesser trials?

The Savior warned of a second hazard to our endurance, perhaps even more relevant to today's Saints than affliction. That is the
hazard of deception. "And many false prophets shall rise, and shall
deceive many" (Matthew 24:11). "For in those days there shall also
arise false Christs, and false prophets, and shall show great signs
and wonders, insomuch, that, if possible, they shall deceive the
very elect, who are the elect according to the covenant" (Joseph
Smith–Matthew 1:22). If Satan can't intimidate us with physical
trials, he'll often try to fool us with substitute programs. He would
like us to invest our time, talent, or energy into causes that are not
the cause of Zion, in the hope they may ultimately replace our commitment to the gospel. Often these other concerns are valid and
worthwhile. The deception comes in giving them a higher priority
than we give our covenants. Those who are fooled in this way usually feel the Church is not doing enough in the area of their pet concerns. They may become disenchanted with the program of the

Church and begin to follow "alternate voices." Those members do not lack zeal—indeed, they are often strong enough to endure tremendous trials—but Satan has diverted their zeal to the wrong causes, and they don't perceive their shifting loyalties as unfaithfulness. The deceived do not generally reject Christ; they just decide to interpret his will differently or to serve him in different ways according to new standards and values, and their original commitments take a back seat to their new agenda. But the bottom line is still that they couldn't be trusted to hold their original course and keep their original commitments. They didn't endure.

Again and again the Lord has warned the Church about following other voices: "And this shall be a law unto you, that ye receive not the teachings of any that shall come before you as revelations or commandments; and this I give unto you that you may not be deceived, that you may know they are not of me" (D&C 43:5–6). In our premortal life all of us rejected Satan's alternate plan. Now we must do it again. If we are to endure, we must avoid religious "special interest" groups. Right now there are many alternate voices vying for the attention of the Saints. There are social voices, intellectual voices, political voices, and yet other voices. I have a friend who is going through a difficult time. He is politically very intense, and he can't understand why the Church doesn't seem as concerned as he is about these threats. He spends a great deal of time trying to rouse other members of the Church, whom he believes to be asleep, and he privately wonders if the Church leaders aren't also asleep.

Essentially, his thinking runs like this, "My Church and my politics are telling me two different things, and I *know* that my politics are true . . . so there must be something wrong with the Church." He does not consider the other logical possibility, nor does he recognize his incipient apostasy, the reversal of loyalty evident in this thinking. There is often truth in what he says, but that is not the point. The point is that he is listening to other voices and has transferred his highest loyalty to programs other than the

Lord's. Tragically, his politics have become the idol to which all else in his life must bow—even his commitment to the Church.

This shouldn't be a difficult concept for most of us—the Church is true. It's as simple as that. All may not be well in Zion, but the Church is still true. It's not anemic; it doesn't need supplements. It's not true *if,* and it's not true *but,* and it's not true *except.* It's just *true!* Moreover, the Church is not off course, it's not going too slow, and it's not going too fast. Its leaders are not asleep, and they don't need any help from the passengers to steer the boat. *The Church is true!* And those who maintain otherwise are the deceivers or the deceived, who have lost their faith and changed their loyalty—who have not endured to the end.

Some protection from the hazard of deception may be found in the principle of "more or less": "And truth is knowledge of things as they are, and as they were, and as they are to come; And whatsoever is more or less than this is the spirit of that wicked one who was a liar from the beginning" (D&C 93:24–25; see also 3 Nephi 11:40; 18:13; D&C 10:68; 98:7).

In the context of the gospel, truth is what God has *actually* said, what he *actually* directs, what he *actually* requires—no more and no less. On a strait and narrow path, it doesn't matter whether we fall off to the right or to the left—we are in trouble either way. It doesn't matter whether we are liberals or conservatives, whether we believe too little or too much. If Satan can't get us to abandon the principles of the gospel, he is content that we should live them obsessively or fanatically. One is less than the will of the Lord; the other is more. Either puts us in the territory of the wicked one.

We have in the Church today those who are embarrassed that God has said so much and who go about trying to discredit the Brethren and neutralize the revelations and commandments. We have others who are embarrassed that God has not said more and who go about preaching programs and principles the Lord has never revealed. One takes words out of God's mouth; the other puts them in. Each preaches a "new, improved" gospel inspired by that wicked one who was a liar from the beginning, the very first alternate voice.

It requires discipline to embrace as gospel and to teach as gospel exactly what the Lord has revealed, no more and no less, and to avoid revising the gospel to suit ourselves. But those who can do it will know things as they really are (Jacob 4:13) and will avoid deception.

The third hazard Jesus warned about is iniquity: "And because iniquity shall abound, the love of many shall wax cold" (Matthew 24:12). If Satan can't shake us with affliction or trick us with other plans, sometimes he'll just try to buy us. In the latter days many will take the money and run—will take the cash, the flesh, or the fame, and run from their covenant obligations. A final test of our endurance is to refrain from falling in love with this world's pleasures. The faithful can't be bought with these things. On Sundays they're in church; they willingly pay tithes and offerings. They keep their physical appetites and desires within bounds; they are honest in their dealings. Their loyalty is not weakened by the possessions and powers God has placed in their care.

Still, failing to endure is not a sin one commits once and for all time. While we remain in mortality, we always have the option of repenting of our failures and trying again. Not long ago, a former student came to see me who had lost his membership as a result of repeated, willful iniquity. He said he wanted to straighten out his life. I asked him if he had a testimony, and he said no, he didn't. Surprised, I asked him why he wanted to repent and regain his membership if he didn't have a testimony. I will never forget his answer: "I don't know right now that the Church is true, but I know that I once knew, and I know God knows I once knew. The Church didn't change between then and now—I did. And now I want to know again what I knew before, and I am willing to repent to do it." Even where one's endurance has failed before the end, repentance can always bring about a new beginning.

Trials, deception, and iniquity—these are the enemies of

endurance. Those who can bear the pain of trials, who can ignore alternate voices, whose loyalty can't be bought with sinful pleasures—these will not betray their Master's trust. They will faithfully maintain the charted course. They will endure.

INDEX

Aaron, 95
Abomination of desolation, 136–38
Abrahamic covenant, 65–67
Accountability, 56
Adam, 79, 159
Adam-ondi-Ahman, 115, 159–60
Adoption, doctrine of, 75, 84
Adoptionists, 42
Affliction, 225
Alternate voices, 226
American Revolution, 64
Apologists, 44–45
Apostates, 11
Apostles, 4, 97, 147
Arius, 45
Armageddon, battle of, 196
Athanasius, 46

Ballard, Melvin J., 197
Ballard, M. Russell, 12
Baptism by fire, of earth, 169
Benson, Ezra Taft: on last days, 9,
   161; decries expansion of
   wickedness, 16; on nature of test to
   come, 18; on cleansing of Church,
   20; on chosen generation, 23; on
   Saints' preparedness to meet
   Savior, 26; enjoins priesthood
   leaders to read scriptures, 35; on
   Book of Mormon and Second
   Coming, 36; on daily reading of
   Book of Mormon, 37; on becoming
   Zion people, 126; on holy places,
   154–55, 207; on resurrection, 171;
   on temporal preparedness, 199; on
   spiritual preparation, 207
Berlin Wall, 198
Bible: figurative language in, 9;
   deficiencies in, 10; modern
   revelation and, 11

Blake, William, 48
Book of Mormon: as instrument of
   personal revelation, 17, 31; as
   instrument of preparation for
   Second Coming, 26–27, 36; other
   uses of, 27–28; daily reading of,
   enjoined by Ezra Taft Benson, 37;
   sealed portion of, 183
Brass plates, 183
Bridegroom, 164, 209–13
Brown, Victor L., 205–7
Burnings of earth, 167–69

Cannon, George Q., 178, 186
Catholic Counter-Reformation, 64
Christ: appearance of, at Bountiful, 36;
   rejection of, by Jews, 40–42;
   lineage of, 43, 98; misconceptions
   about, 47–49, 60; love of, 56;
   statements of, evaluated, 58;
   atonement of, 67; earthly ministry
   of, 71–72; appearance of, in
   Kirtland Temple, 80; current works
   of, 80–81; on Second Coming,
   134–36; appearance of, on Mount
   of Olives, 144, 161; latter-day
   appearances of, 158; as
   Bridegroom, 164, 209–13; return
   of, 192; prophesies destruction of
   Herod's temple, 193–94; parables
   of, 164, 195–96, 209–17; loyalty
   to, required to endure to end, 222
Christianity, 49–50
Christology, 44
Church of Firstborn, 187
Churches, during Millennium, 175
City of Zion. See Zion
Clergy, corrupt, 49
Commitment, 24–25, 223
Constantine, 45

231

Constitution of United States, 64
Converts (LDS), demographics of, by
    lineage, 90
Cornelius, 74, 143
Cowdery, Oliver, 80
Crime, 51
Czechoslovakia, 198

Deception, 145–46, 228
Depression (economic), 199
Desolation of abomination, 136–38
Devil, 64
Diaspora, 39
Dispensation of fulness of times, 77,
    79, 183
Docetism, 43
Dostoyevsky, 49
Doxey, Graham W., 125
Durrant, Will, 46

Earth, to be made celestial, 187
Earthquakes, 135, 136, 199
East Berlin, 198
Eastern Europe, 198
Ebionites, 42–43
Economic turmoil, 199
Egyptian religion, 46
Elect, deception of, 144–46, 228
Elias, appears to Joseph Smith, 80
Enduring to end, 220–23
Enoch, 172
Ephraim: significance of, 89–91; and
    Joseph Smith's lineage, 91; and
    relationship to modern prophets
    and apostles, 97
Exaltation, 57

Faith: Bruce R. McConkie on, 25;
    healing power of, 71; blessings
    resulting from, 72; gathering
    promotes, 120; Brigham Young on,
    145; as spritual gift, 149; provides
    protection, 153; "eyes of," 167,
    197; achieving unity of, 179; of
    brother of Jared, 183; as means of
    escape, 196; loss of, 196;
    accumulation of, 212; enduring in,
    to the end, 221

Faithfulness, 7, 145, 215, 221–22
False doctrines, 11
False Christs: as sign of times, 39;
    Lord warns against, 41; in false
    systems of salvation, 48, 56–57;
    creation of, 48–49; inordinate faith
    in knowledge and, 51–52; and
    inordinate belief in law, 52; and
    "easy grace," 54; and fun, 56; and
    out-of-body experiences, 56; and
    gospel imbalance, 57; and
    erroneous historical studies, 57–58;
    in modern world, 58; futility of
    worshipping, 59; traditional
    doctrines of Holy Trinity as
    example of, 60; detection of,
    60–61; to attempt to deceive elect,
    144–45
Family home evening, 208
Fear, 156
Fig tree, parable of, 195
Fire, baptism of, 167–69, 211
First Vision, 74
First Presidency, keys held by, 5, 80
Floods, 199–200
Food storage and shortages, 199–200
Fulness of Gentiles, 140–41
Fun, fallacy of teaching gospel
    through, 55

Garden of Eden, 112
Gathering of Israel: 76, 94, 96; likened
    to resurrection, 78; of Jews, 81, 98;
    places of, named, 105; First
    Presidency statements on (1907,
    1921), 122–23; Harold B. Lee on,
    123; Bruce R. McConkie on, 124;
    as means of protection, 153–54;
    during Millennium, 181–82
General Authorities: on last days, 5, 7;
    on obedience, 12
Gentiles: defined, 68, 141; in LDS
    hymns, 82; fulness of, defined,
    140–42
Gnostics, 41
Gog and Magog, 187
"Gospel hobbyism," 14
Grace, 16, 54

Grant, Jedediah M., 193
Great and dreadful day of Lord, 192–93, 195–96
Greece, 198
Greek culture, Christianity and, 39, 41, 46

Heaven, materiality of life in, 187–88
Herod's temple, 40, 194
Holy places, 154–55, 207
Holy Ghost: protects against deception, 2, 12–13, 16, 60; obtaining, 11, 28, 34, 37, 222; gifts of, 28–30, 149–50, 203; manifestations of, 32–33, 211; symbolized by olive oil, 211; power of, 28, 75, 213, 215, 223; testifies of Christ, 30–31, 99, 175; guidance by, 23, 24, 31, 217; and establishing Zion, 37, 129–30
Holy Trinity, 60
Hungary, 198
Hurricanes, 199
Hyde, Orson, 97–98
Hymns, 81–84

Immorality, 168
Independence, Missouri, 182
Iniquity, 228
Intelligence, 52
Israel: defined, 65; favored status of, 74; scattering of, 76; gathering of, likened to resurrection, 78; present-day nation of, 81; in Latter-day Saint hymns, 81–84; characteristics of tribes of, 95

Jackson County, Missouri: designation of, as Zion, 111; historical events in, 114–15; myths about, 125
Jared, brother of, 183
Jews: dispersal of, 39; gathering of, 81, 98; adoption of, when converted, 95; some, to be believing, 143; conversion of, as a people, 144; Lord's appearance to, 161
Joseph of Egypt, 85–88

Keys of kingdom, 5, 80
Kimball, Heber C.: on "test" to come, 17–18, 212–13; on individual enlightenment, 26; on Zion as city of refuge, 203; on parable of ten virgins, 212
Kimball, Spencer W.: on blood of Israel and Latter-day Saints, 89; describes Zion, 125–56; on immorality in public life, 152; on self-reliance, 200; on welfare program, 201–2; on parable of ten virgins, 211–12; on parable of talents, 214; on Christian service, 217
Kirtland, Ohio, 110, 116
Knowledge, as criterion for salvation, 51

Last days, defined, 63
Law, inordinate faith in, 52–53
Law of chastity, 49, 155
Lee, Harold B.: warns about those who sensationalize last days, 3; on those attracted to "loose writings," 7; on gathering to Zion, 123–14; on sources of personal revelation, 150; on welfare program, 201
Leningrad Branch, 198
Lewis, C. S., 59
Liahona, 31–32
Lineage: declaration of, by patriarchs, 85–88, 90, 92–94; Joseph Smith's, 86–87, 89; of Latter-day Saints, 87, 89; Jesus Christ's, 89
"Loose writings," 2
Lost tribes of Israel, 73, 183, 192

Manasseh, 89, 90–93
Marriage customs in Holy Land, 209–13
Materiality of heavenly life, 187–88
Maxwell, Neal A., 183
McConkie, Bruce R.: on commitment, 24–25; on faith, 25; on obtaining Spirit, 28; defines seed of Abraham, 85; on non-Israelite descendants of Abraham, 96; on

gathering to Zion, 124; on sign
of Son of Man, 157–58; on
chronology of Second Coming,
158; on millennial living
conditions, 172–73; on missionary
work during Millennium, 181; on
Second Comforter, 185
Michael, 79, 159, 187
Millennium: defined, 134; to be
ushered in by power, 169–70; types
of beings on earth during, 172–73;
conditions on earth during, 174–75;
daily life during, 176–77; temple
work during, 178–80; missionary
work during, 181
Missionary work, 128, 175, 181
Monson, Thomas S., 198
Moses: appears to Joseph Smith, 80;
not descendant of Joseph of Egypt,
89
Mount of Olives: Lord's appearance
on, 144, 161; discourse on, 194

Natural disasters, 199–200
Nauvoo, Illinois, 117
Neo-Platonism, 44
New Jerusalem: to be built in America,
107, 126; location of, 111–12; to be
one of two world centers, 129; as
place of peace, 202
Nicaea, council of, 45–46
Nietzsche, 48
Noah, 151

Oaks, Dallin H., on power of
scriptures, 28–29
Obedience, 56
Olive oil, 210–12
Out-of-body experiences, 56
Overzealousness: futility of, 2;
warnings against, 13

Packer, Boyd K.: on deceivers, 6; on
spiritual nourishment, 29; on
hearing voice of Lord, 33
Pagan religions, influence of, on
Christianity, 46
Page, John E., 97–98

Page, Hiram, 4
Parables: of the ten virgins, 164,
209–13; of fig tree, 195–96; of
talents, 213–15; of sheep and goats,
215–17
Partridge, Edward, 106
Patriarchal blessings, lineage declared
in, 92–94
Peace, 154
Penrose, Charles W., 160
Philo, 45
Pioneers, and endurance, 225
Plainness of scriptures, 8
Plato, 41, 45
Poland, 198
Pratt, Orson: on gathering of Israel,
105–6; on building city of Zion,
120; on earth's baptism by fire,
169; on materiality of heavenly life,
187–88; on those who will flock to
Zion for help, 203–4
Pratt, Parley P., 116
Prayer, family, 208
Premortal existence, 98
Preparation: temporal 12, 199;
spiritual, 207
Pride, 186
Priesthood: and Abraham's seed,
65–67; and lineage, 97
Prophecies, relative importance of
ancient, 9
Prophecy, spirit of, 29
Prophets, importance of, 4; prerogative
of, to interpret scriptures, 8; lineage
of, 97; false, 144; following
counsel of, 147
Protestant Reformation, 63

Quickened persons, 172
Quorum of Twelve Apostles, 5, 80

Real estate, Church acquires, in eastern
and midwestern United States, 123
Recession, 199
Renaissance, 63
Repentance: mistaken notion of, 54,
56; example of, 222

Restoration of Israel: 76; differentiated
    from gathering, 81
Resurrection, 66–67, 170–71
Revelation: latter-day, 9; helps avoid
    deception, 19
Romney, Marion G.: on relevance of
    latter-day revelations, 10; on events
    of last days, 194; on welfare
    program, 201
Russia, 197

Sacrifice, necessary for salvation, 22
Salvation, 52
Satan, 64, 185–86
Scholarly pursuits, 57
School of the Prophets, 197
Schweitzer, Albert, 48, 57–58
Scott, Richard G., on importance of
    Book of Mormon, 31
Scripture study, personal, 208
Scriptures: importance of, 4; plainness
    of, 8; hearing voice of Lord
    through, 29–30; as personal
    Liahona or Urim and Thummim,
    31; priesthood leaders enjoined to
    read, 35; as stay against deception,
    146;
Second Coming: events of, 134–36;
    described, 161–62; timing of, 162
Second Comforter, 75, 185
Sects, proliferation of, during
    Millennium, 175
Self-reliance, 200, 202, 207
Sensationalism: futility of, 2;
    attractiveness of, 7; warnings
    against, 13;
Sexually transmitted diseases, 155
Shaw, George Bernard, 48
Sheep and goats, parable of, 215–17
Shepherds, 216
Sign of Son of Man, 157–58
Slavery, 49
Smith, Hyrum, 116
Smith, Hyrum G., 90–91
Smith, Joseph: on biblical deficiencies,
    10; as revelator to this generation,
    10; promise to, of his fame, 47;
    vision of, in grove, 74; on adoption
into house of Israel, 75; on
    dispensation of fulness of times,
    79; in Latter-day Saint hymns,
    83–84; as descendant of Abraham,
    85; as descendant of Joseph of
    Egypt, 85–86; lineage of, 86; on
    temple building, 94; and right of,
    to the priesthood, 99; on
    establishment of Zion, 105;
    commanded to build up Zion, 109;
    on location of Zion, 118; warns of
    deception of "chosen ones," 145;
    on "adversary's traps," 146; on
    Saints' not escaping latter-day
    judgments, 153; on peace in Zion,
    154; on sign of Son of Man, 157;
    on signs of times, 157; on timing
    of Second Coming, 162–63; on
    millennial conditions, 176; on
    limited powers of Satan, 185
Smith, Joseph F.: warns against
    disobedience and overzealousness,
    13; on proliferation of temples,
    128; on deception of elect, 145; on
    millennial temple work, 178
Smith, Joseph Fielding: on wickedness
    of world, 152; on missionary work
    during Millennium, 175; on events
    of last days, 196; on parable of
    talents, 214
Solomon's temple, 40
Soviet Union, 197
Speculation, 2
Stakes of Zion, metaphor of, 112
Stoicism, 44
Stout, Hosea, 225
Suffering, 22, 225
Swinburne, A. C., 49

Talents, parable of, 213–15
Tares, 16, 18, 20, 143
Taylor, John, 21, 23
Teachers (instructors), evaluation of,
    148–49
Temples: as holy places, 12, 154, 207;
    gathering at, in Bountiful, 36;
    marriages in, 36; Christ's
    appearance in, 36, 80, 160, 169;

ancient grandeur of, 40; destruction
of, 40, 134–36; blessings of,
reserved for righteous, 61; Joseph
Smith on, 94; building of, 100;
location of, in Independence, 111;
in city of Zion, 113, 119–20; at
Nauvoo, 118; in Utah, 120;
proliferation of, 127–28, 179; work
in, during Millennium, 178–80; of
Herod, 193; attendance in, 208;
covenants in, 221;
Temporal preparation, 12, 199
Tests, 17–18
Three Nephites, 172
Times of Gentiles, 140–41
Tolstoy, 48
Transgression, 55
Translated beings, 172
Trials, to be endured by Saints, 17–18,
21, 228
Tribulation, latter-day, 156
Truth, 227

United States of America, as Gentile
nation, 85, 142
Urim and Thummim: scriptures as, 31;
use of, by Joseph Smith, 32;
millennial uses of, 178

Virgins, parable of ten, 209–13
Wars, 64, 199
Welfare program, 201, 204–5
Wentworth Letter, 118
West Berlin, 198
Wheat and tares, 18, 143
Wheat storage, 208

Whitmer, David, 34–35
Whitney, Newel K., 115
Wickedness: before Second Coming,
150–52; during Millennium, 176
Wolves, 20
Word of Wisdom, 155
Woodruff, Wilford, 86, 178

Year's supply, 199
Young, Brigham: on government of
kingdom of God, 25–26; on Joseph
Smith's lineage, 86; on lineage of
Latter-day Saints, 87; on Church's
return to Jackson County, 121–22;
on proliferation of temples, 127; on
faith, 145; on deception of elect,
145; on millennial conditions,
174–75; on millennial temple work,
178; on preparation for Second
Coming, 218
Youth, 55

Zeal, warnings against inordinate, 13
Zenos, 76, 168
Zion: requires Zion people, 26;
definition and location of, 108;
construction of, 109; layout of, 112;
Saints fail to establish, in Missouri,
114; in North and South America,
118; city of, 120; Spencer W.
Kimball describes, 125; to be
established in hearts of Latter-day
Saints, 129; not to be established
in haste, 130; as refuge for
nonmembers, 203